A WISH
CAN CHANGE
YOUR LIFE

How to Use the Ancient Wisdom of Kabbalah
to Make Your Dreams Come True

GAHL SASSON AND STEVE WEINSTEIN

A Fireside Book
Published by Simon & Schuster
New York London Toronto Sydney

FIRESIDE
Rockefeller Center
1230 Avenue of the Americas
New York, NY 10020

For information regarding special discounts for bulk purchases,
please contact Simon & Schuster Special Sales at 1-800-456-6798
or business@simonandschuster.com

Designed by Jaime Putorti

Manufactured in the United States of America

10   9   8   7   6   5   4

Library of Congress Cataloging-in-Publication Data

Sasson, Gahl.
    A wish can change your life : how to use the ancient wisdom of Kabbalah
to make your dreams come true / Gahl Sasson and Steve Weinstein.
        p.   cm.
    Includes bibliographical references.
        1. Cabala. 2. Tree of life. 3. Self-actualization (Psychology)
    I. Weinstein, Steve II. Title.
    BF1623.C2S27 2003
    135'47—dc21   2003045438

ISBN 0-7432-4505-9

For every Tree that was, is, or will be . . .
and for their spirit that lives inside us all.

I believe that the key to lasting happiness and peace
in the world is inner peace. In that state of mind you
can face difficulties with calm and reason, while your
inner happiness is unaffected. The virtues of love,
kindness and tolerance and the conduct of non-
violence are a source of that inner peace. I believe
readers who are interested in these themes may
find much in this book to encourage them.

—His Holiness the fourteenth Dalai Lama

ACKNOWLEDGMENTS

The proof that wishes come true lies between your fingers. Our own journeys on the Tree of Life gave birth to the writing and publication of this book. While we owe everything to this magical Tree, we also were blessed with inestimable assistance of the human kind.

Thank you to the astute Caroline Sutton and everyone else at Simon & Schuster for delivering our book to the world and changing our lives. Thank you to our agent, Betsy Amster, for believing in our wish. And thank you, thank you to our parents, Naomi and Moshe Sasson and Clare and Charles Weinstein, and to our brothers and sisters as well. Who knows when or why, but something at sometime that you said or did planted the seeds of our happy affinity with the Tree of Light and of all our wishes come true.

An extra special thanks to Gurmukh Kaur Khalsa, Julian Neil, Belinda Casas, Rachel Berkowitz, Sabrina Diaz, and His Holiness the fourteenth Dalai Lama for their enduring support and inspiration. More thanks to Jorge Najera for his irreplaceable teachings on the Kabbalah, and to Alejandra Mora and everyone at the Circulo Dorado in Guadalajara, Mexico. We are tremendously grateful to the master, Joseph Campbell, for paving the way. And to the writing angels—Elizabeth Miles, D'Jamila Salem Fitzgerald, and her peewee lama Ronan Fitzgerald—we only wish that every author could find sweet souls like you, who crack corny jokes when the sentences read like gobbledygook and then lovingly urge again and again, "Keep going."

Finally, we send our infinite gratitude to all the marvelous and courageous warriors of Light who attended the workshops week after week and shared the stories, wisdom, and experiences gleaned from their travels on the Tree. This book does not exist without you.

—G.S. and S.W.

CONTENTS

A WISH
CAN CHANGE
YOUR LIFE

INTRODUCTION

The Tree of Life at the Center of the Cosmos;
How to Use God's Blueprint to Fulfill Your Every Wish

If you are planting a tree and someone arrives and
tells you that the Messiah has come, you should first
finish planting your tree and only when you are done
go out and see if the Messiah is in fact there.

—The Talmud

We travel the Milky Way together, trees and man.

—John Muir

*Bridging heaven and Earth, I stand, as always, awaiting your embrace. Hug
me, climb me, use me; and I will make your wish come true. A tree is all you
need. I am the Wish-Fulfilling Tree. The Tree of Life. The Tree of Light.*

Trees endure as the ultimate symbols of egalitarianism. They
provide the same amount of oxygen, shelter, and shade indis-
criminately to rich and poor, sinners and saints, caterpillars and
humans. Virtually every culture on every continent has treasured
the tree as the centerpiece of its mythology—from the Tree of
Life in the Garden of Eden to the Bodhi Tree of the Buddha; the
Dreaming Tree of the Aborigines to the Native American Sioux's
belief that the first man on Earth was a tree that learned to walk.
Such universal reverence among peoples so diverse and disparate
indicates that trees brandish immense power. All these cultures
cherished different gods and rituals; they devoted themselves to

clashing diets and socioeconomic systems. And yet all these traditions exalted the Tree because each intuitively understood that
trees stand for more than shade from the hot Sun. Deep down,
every human being recognizes that the Tree is in fact the ultimate
tool of creation. The Tree creates oxygen. The Tree creates life.

Kabbalah is a mystical, universal interpretation of the meaning and mechanics of life that has been preserved for thousands
of years chiefly through the teachings of Judaic seekers and
scholars. This ancient theosophy instructs that God uses the Tree
as the everlasting blueprint for the construction of the universe.
Everything—you, your dog, Julia Roberts, the Taj Mahal, and the
constellation Gemini—emerged from the ten life-giving energy
forces vibrating through this magnificent cosmic tree.

What few of us realize is that these primal forces didn't just
assemble the universe and then vanish, abandoning us to cope as
best we can. They live still and always, available this minute to
every human being. In one of most famous lines of the Bible, God
said, "Let us make man in our image" (Genesis 1:25). This sentence promises that humans are nothing less than reflections of
God, imbued with a godlike gift and desire to create. In other
words, each of us owns the ability to fashion all kinds of stuff
seemingly from thin air. All it takes is to retrace the same steps
that God took to create the universe. Dust off the master
builder's template, and you can breathe life into your fondest
dream right here and now.

You start by making a wish—any wish, from earning more
money to finding your true love, from renewed intimacy with your
spouse to a bigger house or a smaller waistline. Then you simply follow God's recipe, surfing the Tree of Life from one archetypal energy
to the next. Each chapter of this book will immerse you in one of the
ten spheres that make up this Tree of Light, the ten archetypal energies inherent in everything and every person. Kabbalists have given
each of these ten spheres an official name—translated here from

Hebrew—which corresponds to the multilayered energy it generates: Crown (will), Wisdom (intuition), Understanding (discipline), Mercy (compassion), Severity (strength or action), Beauty (love), Eternity (relationships), Splendor (communication), Foundation (sexuality and death), and Kingdom (practicality). By devoting one week to each of these singular cosmic forces, you will transform your wish from a dream to a reality.

A journey through the chapters of this book will make you a partner in the Tree's resplendent mystery. We too possess a marvelous talent akin to photosynthesis—which is the miraculous ability literally to manufacture life through Light. This inspired impulse is our chief reason for being, and the Tree offers a plan that will enhance personal creativity in every area of your life. It will also spur you to internalize the central Kabbalistic mandate to balance giving and receiving. A key side effect of wish fulfillment is learning to be a better giver, and the Tree's program will endow you with a new capacity to balance and repair your personal relationships.

But this book does more than supply a ticket to the procurement of your worldly desires. Working with these archetypal energies simultaneously fulfills the higher calling of the human soul. It will transform you into a warrior of Light, a spiritual torchbearer who, by absorbing and applying the timeless axioms of the Tree, will have helped to heal the universe.

A Spiritual Icon for All

Though the characteristics of the Tree of Life have been documented and debated over the centuries primarily by rabbis and Kabbalists, you will fast discover that the Tree's lessons embrace every denomination imaginable. Every chapter blends myths and theologies from all over the globe to illustrate the Tree's universal reach. The truths embodied in the Tree of Life are not only Jewish but central to every religion. Though all of these distinct traditions employ different names, stories, and metaphors to portray archetypal precepts, at heart each describes and venerates the same essential truths.

This book trusts in myths from assorted cultures not just to inspire and entertain, but because God planted stories at the core of human existence. The first line of the *Sefer Yitzerah* (Book of Formation), the oldest and most fundamental Kabbalistic text, states that God created the universe with story. In other words, God did not construct the universe in a single stroke but is instead continually narrating the cosmos into existence. Every person harbors his or her own myth. Sometimes we call them diaries. Sometimes we relate the story of our day over coffee. We greet our friends with "What's your story?" as a way of asking how they are. Ageless myths are merely personal tales blown up large. Recounting the exaggerated antics of gods and heroes enables us to scrutinize minute human behaviors with heightened precision. Myths function like microscopes, enlarging invisible molecules so that we might understand their structure. If, for example, we magnify a routine tryst between Venus and Mars into mythic melodrama, we are then able to more keenly dissect and decipher the intricate mysteries of love and romance.

In the same spirit, this book assembles myths from civilizations across the globe to illuminate the secrets of Creation. It draws from the ancient scriptures of Judaism, Christianity, Islam, Buddhism, Hinduism, Paganism, and tribal lore as well as from personal stories of today; it explores the enduring mythologies of ancient Greece, Egypt, Europe, and Native America, as well as documented historical events. Heroes and traditions as varied as Hermes, the Buddha of Compassion, the Passover Exodus, Christ, the Ramayana, Celtic Oak worshipers, The Egyptian Book of the Dead, ancient Phrygia, the Yoruba of West

Africa and the Caribbean, Lao-tzu, Charles Darwin, Mother Goose, and Indiana Jones all find a home in the Tree of Life.

The Tree welcomes everyone in its quest to propagate creativity, healing, and fulfillment.

How to Use the Tree to Fulfill Your Wish

This book invites you to read it at your own pace as an innovative guide to world mythologies, Kabbalah, and ageless spiritual tenets. But if you also want to make use of its life-tested blueprint for wish fulfillment, all you have to do is spend one week basking in the radiance of each of the Tree's ten archetypal energy spheres, one after another from the top of the Tree to the bottom.

Ten spheres. Ten chapters. Ten weeks. One wish.

Based on workshops conducted by Gahl Sasson in the United States, Mexico, and Israel, the teachings and techniques outlined here have helped thousands of people to manifest their dreams. They constitute a spiritual thrill ride designed to activate dormant but powerful facets of your essential nature that will foster achievement, growth, and a magnified sense of both peace and purpose.

Start your journey of transformation by reading all the way through the introduction. Then select a specific hour on a specific day—Wednesday at 7 P.M., for example—that you will devote to each new energy. Treat this day and time as a vital appointment that you will not miss for anything. Sit down at that hour and read Chapter 1, which details the fundaments, mechanics, and myths of the sphere called Crown. For the next seven days, you will marinate your life in this one archetypal force. Spend time every day tackling the chapter's Wish Maker exercises. These tasks will amplify the resonance of the weekly vibration and bring your wish to life. It is most critical to set aside several minutes every day to meditate as instructed, chanting the appropriate secret name of God as your mantra to arouse the magic of that sphere in your daily existence.

When Wednesday 7 P.M.—or whatever day and time you set as your weekly changeover—rolls around again, proceed to the next chapter. Read it through. Then dedicate that subsequent week to the new sphere, the new exercises, and the new meditation. When your changeover day arrives again the following week, advance into the energetic realm of the succeeding sphere. You might be tempted to skip ahead—to dig for information or stories that suit your beliefs and disposition more snugly. Simply remember that in Kabbalah, the accomplishment of any goal and life itself are processes. Everything you want, everything you do, requires all ten cosmic energies. Try not to shortchange any of these majestic forces. Each is a gift from the Light. And this journey works best when we pay the requisite respect to each and every one.

As you progress through the ten weeks, you will discover that the Tree operates within the enchanted world of synchronicity. Over the ages, Kabbalists have discerned that every sphere corresponds to a color, a planet, a number, a part of the body, and various real-world talismans. Mythic personalities and folklore from myriad cultures spring from each cosmic force as well. For example, Beauty, the sixth stop on your voyage through the Tree, represents the heart, Christ consciousness, the folktale of the Beauty and the Beast, the colors gold and yellow, roses, the number six, and the Sun at the center of our solar system.

Hunt for the ambassadors of each archetypal energy as you conduct your business in the world that week and recall your dreams each morning. Synchronous brushes with these emissaries of the spheres are likely to relay messages critical to the realization of your wish. In Chapter 1, you will be urged to initiate a journal to help you to track and make sense of these signs, symbols, and the ten-week journey as a whole. This ongoing record of your triumphs, fears, insights, and coincidental encounters—this snapshot of the interconnectedness of your every step and triviality—will spur you to view your life through a vibrant new prism. It will rouse you to think and feel in a brand new way.

The Tree of Life recounts the Hero's Journey of the Light as It transfigured the infinite possibilities of heaven into every material thing that we know and imagine. Making a wish casts you as the hero of that same miraculous journey. You possess the power to emulate God. You are a Creator. Climb aboard the Tree and create your wish come true.

PREPARING THE SOIL

The Ten Archetypal Energies That Animate Everything in the Universe; the Mechanics of Creation According to Kabbalah

Know this: Nothing is certain.

—Lao-tzu

All Is One and One Is All

Before a gardener decides what type of tree to plant in his field, it behooves him to understand the general characteristics of the soil and climate at his disposal in order to optimize the success of his endeavor. Haphazardly seeding his backyard with citrus trees would be foolhardy if he lives in a cold northern latitude. Likewise, we are obliged to pay some respect and attention to the basic history and mechanics of the Tree of Life if we aspire to suffuse our own efforts with the best chance to bear fruit. It's akin to reading the sowing instructions on the back of the seed packet.

The story of the Tree begins in emptiness. Every religious cosmology shares the idea that everything issued from nothing. In the Bible, it's called Tohu Vavohu—"Now the Earth was unformed and void" (Genesis 1:2). The Babylonian myth *Enuma Elish* states that in the beginning "the gods were nameless, natureless, futureless." The Tongva, the original inhabitants of Los Angeles, honor Quaoar, the formless force that sang Sky Father, Earth Mother, and Grandfather Sun into existence. The Greek writer Hesiod explained in the eighth century B.C. that the world evolved from a shapeless darkness he dubbed chaos or "a yawning void." Norse mythology names it Ginnungagap, "the yawning emptiness," while Buddhism labels it Sunyata.

"Brahman is the void, joy verily, that is the same as the void. The void, verily, that is the same as joy," the Hindu Upanishads agree. Buddhists greet every sunrise with the hypnotic "Prajnaparamita Hridaya: Heart of Perfect Wisdom" to instill this crucial truth: "Form is emptiness, emptiness is form. No eye, ear, nose, tongue, body, mind. No me, no you. All things are impermanent." The Taoist master Kuan-tzu writes, "the Tao of heaven is empty and formless." And the brilliant Chinese sage Lao-tzu, that wisest of tricksters, who spoke God's formulas in riddles, reminds us in the quote above that Nothing is the only fact that is certain, the only thing we can count on for sure.

Even science plays along. In a December 2000 article chronicling the ongoing search for the Higgs field—the hypothesized underlying structure of the universe—the *Los Angeles Times* reported that without this field "the universe would still be as it was in the beginning of time, a featureless mist of particles and forces— everything the same, no gravity, no electricity, no quarks or atoms or stars." In other words, the article continued, the entire cosmos, everything imaginable, was once an "undifferentiated chaos." Physicists further testify that the Big Bang that sired this universe originated in an infinitesimally small, infinitely dense single point that exploded and formed everything we know.

That's not religion or esoteric spirituality. That's hardcore Harvard science. Before that Big Bang, we were all stuck together in this dimensionless point. All of us. Everything—the Virgin Mary, daffodils, mosquitoes, atomic bombs, supermodels, chainsaws and redwood trees, anarchists and prime ministers, micro-scopic germs, you and Attila the Hun, too. We perceive distinc-tions now only because the individual particles that materialized from the explosion cooled at different rates. Some traveled east and some flew south. But in the beginning, at heart, everything is One and the same. "There is neither Jew nor Greek, there is nei-ther bond nor free, there is neither male nor female," the New Testament instructs. "For you are all One" (Galatians 3:28).

So how did we get here?

Imagine the Creator as a painter, fashioning the cosmos in his image, constructing his self-portrait. First, God requires a canvas on which to design a celestial masterpiece. This canvas signifies the emptiness—the blank first stage of any creation. Next, God needs Light. Have you ever tried to paint in the dark? You can't tell one color from the next. And so God says, "Let there be Light," and the light switches on. Astrophysicists call this "switching on" of the Light the Big Bang. Then God applies the paint—the cosmic primary colors. God's paints are none other than the ten archetypal energy forces, the ten spheres of the Tree of Life, each vibrating with its own tone and frequency as it mixes with the other spheres on the blank canvas.

WISH MAKER: In Chapter 1, you will find detailed instruc-tions on how to choose a wish. For now, simply contemplate this metaphor as you prepare yourself for the journey through the ten spheres. Start with a blank slate—a place of emptiness, free of desire, want, and expectation. It is here that you will discover your authentic wish. Then "switch on the Light." You add Light to any project by making sure that it will contribute to the greater good of all sentient beings. And finally you will lay in one color after another as you progress from one sphere to the next until your painting—your wish—is complete.

As Above, So Below

The tree marks the ultimate bridge between the divinity above and the material Earth below. Its roots spread out beneath the surface unseen, just as the branches splay up toward the Sun. If the roots falter, the leaves won't thrive. If the tree is beheaded, the roots rot and die, too. Horticulture proves it. Japanese gardeners craft their impossibly small bonsai trees by repeatedly cutting the roots short. Aborting the growth of the roots below similarly stunts the advance of tree and branches above.

The Zohar, one of the primary texts of the Kabbalah, compiled in thirteenth-century Spain, declares that all the planets and constellations of the skies serve as messengers and officers to the world; every single blade of grass is assigned a heavenly entity to guide its progress. The angels that attend to the throne of God above do so by nursing the plants, weeds, worms, and people here on Earth. "As above, so below" reminds us that if God and the angels wield a magic wand in heaven, then that magic stick— that magic Tree—must exist for us down here too.

Why the Tree?

Think about life, actual survival. What do you absolutely need to stay alive this very second? Nothing, really. Nothing except breath.

Air, more than food, water, clothes, sex, or money, equals life. In the Bible, when God animated man for the first time, He didn't douse him with a bucket of water, roast him over a flame, or force-feed him a banana. The Light brought humanity to life by breathing into our nostrils. When a baby first enters the world, the only thing that matters in that instant is that she sucks in a tiny lung full of air. The Hindus call it Prana, the breath of God, our most direct connection to the One. Christianity named it the Holy Ghost. The ancient Greek philosopher Anaximander taught that "pneuma," or the cosmic breath, represented the most essential force in the cosmos, greater than all the gods and demigods in the pantheon combined.

Here on the blue planet, distinguished from all neighbors by the nontoxic atmosphere that surrounds it, breath is life. The air in our blue sky makes us possible. But the Earth didn't arrive fully assembled with that blessed atmosphere intact. Trees created it. Trees—inhaling carbon dioxide and exhaling oxygen for millions of years—are the reason we're here. As the *Encyclopædia Britannica* bluntly states: "Without photosynthesis, not only would replenishment of the fundamental food supply halt, but the Earth would eventually become devoid of oxygen." Some three thousand years earlier, the author of the Bible apprehended that too. In Genesis, trees took root on the third day of creation to prepare the planet for life. Human beings didn't arrive until Day Six.

Trees, Trees, Everywhere a Tree

Nothing crosses cultures and continents like the tree. It has flourished as the central symbol of life, immortality, and transcendence for virtually every tribe and religion that ever was. And when we see the same symbol repeated over and over in spectacularly incongruous traditions among peoples from far-flung regions of the globe, we realize that these repetitions herald something bigger than dogma or Bible or folktales. They reveal universal truths. Not just Jewish truths, Christian truths, Cherokee or Greenpeace truths. But the authentic keys to life.

Moses, the star of the Old Testament, attained his enlightenment from a burning bush. (Tree, bush—in the desert, even God must improvise.) The Koran, the holy book of Islam, extols the centrality of the Tree of Blessing, the symbol of divine gifts and spiritual illumination. Ishmael, the patriarch of the Arabs, was saved from death as a baby when a tree heard his thirsty wailing. The Buddha attained his enlightenment in the sixth century B.C. under the Bodhi tree, the Tree of Wisdom. For five hundred years, this personification of Light, this original Buddha, was depicted not as a smiling man but as a tree. The Hindu *Taittiriya Brahmana* similarly portrays the god Brahma as a "tree from which they shaped heaven and Earth." As in Genesis, Hindu scripture memorializes a Tree of Life called *Aditi* and a Tree of Knowledge named *Diti*, or separation, which symbolizes the concept of *samsara*, or this mortal coil. The Taoists revere the peach as the Tree of Immortality, its intertwining branches evoking the balance of yin and yang.

Christ, a carpenter—he who refines the wood of a tree—was also crucified on one. His death on the wooden cross led to his resurrection and enlightenment. Saemund's *Prose Edda* recounts that the chief Norse god, Odin, pursued transcendence by hanging himself upside down on the Yggdrasil, the great ash tree that binds heaven, the underworld, and the Earth in between. In the mythology of Phrygia, an ancient culture of Asia Minor, the Sun god Attis emasculated himself under a pine tree, killing himself but bestowing (evergreen) immortality on the tree and symbolically to all human souls.

Countless traditions portray the tree as the original human being. Norse mythology reports that Odin assembled the first man and woman from two trees, imbuing them with ten qualities—spirit, life, wit, feeling, form, speech, hearing, sight, clothing, and names—that correspond rather precisely to the specific energies of the ten spheres of the Kabbalistic Tree. The Great Spirit of the Native American Sioux fashioned the first man, whose feet then rooted into the ground like a tree. He stood immobile for thousands of years until a female tree shot up beside him. A snake then gnawed at their roots and the couple wandered off and spawned every human that has ever lived. Zoroastrianism, the religion of ancient Iran, recounts that Ormazd, the eternal source of all that is good, created Gayomart, the primordial man. When he died, a plant that supported a male and a female shoot emerged from a drop of his sperm. It matured into an immense tree that bore as its fruit the ten races of mankind.

According to official materials supplied by the New York Stock Exchange, even the supreme engine of modern capitalism was manufactured with the aid of a tree. On May 17, 1792, twenty-four stockbrokers resolved their liquidity crisis by consenting to trade only among themselves. They christened their two-sentence document—which gave birth to the world's largest stock market—the Buttonwood Agreement in honor of their informal meeting place under a buttonwood tree at 68 Wall Street, New York City.

Other cultures that exalted the sanctity of the tree include:

- The Aborigines, whose Yaraando or Dreaming Tree of Life symbolizes "dreamtime," the metaphysical state of bliss and creativity that flourished long before man arrived on Earth. In ritual ceremonies, the Aborigines plant an inverted tree with its roots pointing to the skies to commemorate the axiom that all life originates in the heavens.

- The cult of the forest goddess Diana in pre-Roman Italy, which celebrated a hero called the Wood King, who stood guard before the Golden Bough (the cluster of seeds that spawn new growth). According to Sir James G. Fraser, the author of the nineteenth-century anthropological classic *The Golden Bough*, virile young rivals continually dueled against the reigning king in an effort to usurp his throne, ensuring that this personification of the *élan vital* of the trees would never grow old or feeble.

 The Celts of northwestern Europe, whose priests called themselves Druids, literally "Men of the Oaks." This sect worshiped trees so fanatically that they refused to build any temples. Every man-made church paled in majesty to the actual forest, and so they let the tree stand as their sanctuary, the forest their holy ground. Merlin, the marvelous magician of the Arthurian legend, ultimately was frozen inside a tree. Once charged with unifying all of the United Kingdom, Merlin's next mission, according to the myth, will be to unite all of humanity. He will emerge from the tree to do so. Or perhaps he will simply continue on as a spirit inside and allow trees to teach us how to do it ourselves.

And, if only to certify that trees endure still as a potent icon of awe, a young American named Julia Butterfly Hill scaled a towering California redwood in 1997 and lived 180 feet above the ground for more than two years to protect it from a lumber company's ax. Clinging for her life one black night in hundred-mile-per-hour gales, she claimed that the tree she called Luna spoke to her, advising not to fight the forces of nature, but to let go and sway with them.

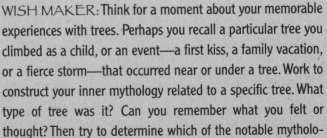

WISH MAKER: Think for a moment about your memorable experiences with trees. Perhaps you recall a particular tree you climbed as a child, or an event—a first kiss, a family vacation, or a fierce storm—that occurred near or under a tree. Work to construct your inner mythology related to a specific tree. What type of tree was it? Can you remember what you felt or thought? Then try to determine which of the notable mythologies listed above most closely resembles your own. As you will see, Kabbalah, like Eastern religions, espouses the doctrine of reincarnation. And if you work at this exercise sincerely, it might provide you with a glimpse of one of your previous lifetimes or of the culture to which your mystical roots belong.

The Structure of the Tree of Life

On the threshold of the wish-fulfilling journey, we prepare ourselves with a glance at the road map of the terrain we are about to traverse. The Kabbalistic Tree of Life, our unerring guide, is comprised of ten spheres arrayed in three columns (see diagram on next page). These spheres operate as cosmic-energy generators, each responsible for producing a singular archetypal force. The Tree itself functions like a fiberoptic cable that shares data, audio, and pictures among various computers—or in this case among these ten spheres of energy. It endures as the channel that enables the Light of the Creator to vibrate in this universe. It's no surprise that the English term *cable* resembles the word *Kabbalah*.

The ten spheres of the Tree hang from three pillars. The right column—containing the spheres Wisdom, Mercy, and Eternity—represents the positive or yang forces of expansion and growth. The left column of form and structure—comprised of the spheres Understanding, Severity, and Splendor—embodies the negative or yin forces of limitation, pressure, and restriction. The remaining four spheres flicker in between as the middle pillar of consciousness. This central column—composed of the spheres Crown, Beauty, Foundation, and Kingdom—evokes the energy of synthesis, unity, and balance.

Take care not to confuse the negative pillar with evil or the positive with good. We need the restrictive energies to balance

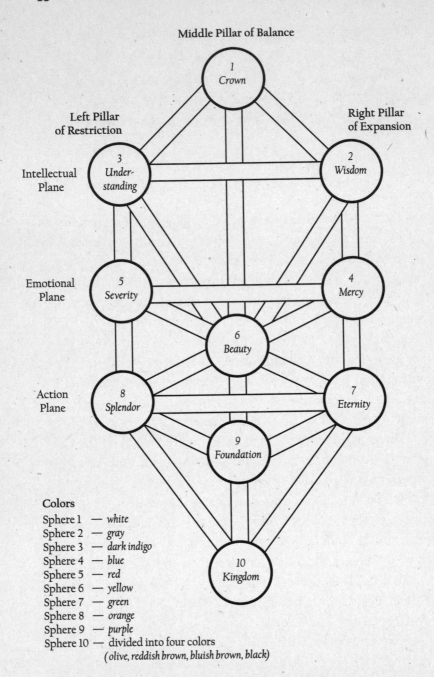

Middle Pillar of Balance

Left Pillar of Restriction

Right Pillar of Expansion

1 Crown

3 Under-standing

2 Wisdom

Intellectual Plane

Emotional Plane

5 Severity

4 Mercy

6 Beauty

Action Plane

8 Splendor

7 Eternity

9 Foundation

10 Kingdom

Colors

Sphere 1 — *white*
Sphere 2 — *gray*
Sphere 3 — *dark indigo*
Sphere 4 — *blue*
Sphere 5 — *red*
Sphere 6 — *yellow*
Sphere 7 — *green*
Sphere 8 — *orange*
Sphere 9 — *purple*
Sphere 10 — divided into four colors
  (*olive, reddish brown, bluish brown, black*)

The Kabbalistic Tree of Life

the expansive just as we need to inhale and exhale both. If, for example, you undertake a physical fitness program, you will probably profit from a connection to the restrictive pillar of discipline and martial strength. A wish to foster more honesty and feeling with your partner will, conversely, necessitate a more intimate rapport with the expansive pillar. Neither is good or bad. They simply represent two distinct forces that are equally vital to us all.

The Power of the Spheres

As you proceed down the Tree, transporting your wish from nothingness to material reality, you will enjoy a weeklong sojourn in each of the ten spheres, ping-ponging back and forth among all three columns, adding another layer of energy atop all those that came before. Trees have leaves to convert light, water, earth, and air in the form of carbon dioxide into oxygen, into life. We have the ten spheres.

The Hebrew word for spheres is *Sephirot*. In this ancient language, many words share the same three-letter root, and Kabbalah posits that these phonetic similarities also signal an important energetic connection. The root of the word *sphere* (SPhR) also creates SePheR, meaning "book" or "text," SePhaR, meaning "number," and SiPpuR, which translates to "story" or "communication." In other words, each sphere is a book written in the language of numbers and story, mathematics and myth. Each sphere operates as a manual crammed with information, formulas, and recipes that everyone can access to fulfill his or her wish.

The spheres' intimate relationship with language, numbers, and communication suggests that they essentially function as cell phones to the divine. God pushes the buttons of the ten spheres to communicate with the creation, and we must activate the spheres' Power button to talk back. Without this device, the Light would be utterly unreachable. But, via the Tree, your prayers, wishes, gratitude, and tears have the chance to find their way to the ear of God.

Finally, the Hebrew word for *sphere* also connects energetically to SaPHiR, which means "sapphire." This sparkling jewel possesses the ability to refract light, to break it into observable pieces just as a prism splinters white light into seven visible colors. The filtering mechanism of the ten spheres allows us to perceive the Light of the Creator. In the Torah, God cautions that "no one can see me and live." No human, no matter how righteous, can gaze upon the absolute Light and survive its awesome vibration. In *Raiders of the Lost Ark*, Indiana Jones witnesses the opening of the Holy Ark and warns his partner, "Close your eyes!" The wise professor knew his Kabbalah. The cinematic Nazis stared at the Light and perished on the spot. Indiana Jones survived to make more movies. No one can see God. Unless he uses the sapphires. Unless she travels the Tree.

The first stop on the freeway to wish fulfillment is the sphere called **Crown,** which signifies the will of God, the seed of the tree, and the seed of your wish. **Wisdom,** the second sphere, invokes intuition. The third sphere, **Understanding,** serves as the materializing force that gives birth to the concepts of discipline, pressure, and time. The fourth sphere is **Mercy,** the quintessence of compassion and unconditional love. **Severity,** sphere number five, generates the energy of strength, aggression, action, and judgment. The sixth sphere, **Beauty,** symbolizes love, creativity, and sacrifice. Next, you will visit **Eternity,** the seventh sphere, which engenders the energy of relationship, Mother Nature, and repetition. **Splendor,** the eighth sphere, introduces communication and magic. **Foundation,** sphere number nine, is the seat of sexuality, death, and transformation. And finally you will settle in **Kingdom,** the tenth and final sphere, which demarcates the here and now, the entire universe as we know it, and the land where your wish comes true.

The Balance of Give and Take

Success on this hero's journey requires that you honor the Tree as more than a natural wonder beautifying your yard and more than an expedient device to realize your dreams. The Tree encapsulates Kabbalah's most crucial lesson. In Hebrew, the word *Kabbalah* means "to receive." The tree illustrates why. The leaves on every tree receive sunlight. But at the same time, these leaves continually give away oxygen.

That is the secret of life: understanding how to receive in order to give. On the surface it sounds simple. But it's as miraculous a phenomenon as photosynthesis. It's as delicate and breathtaking a juggling act as the split second when day turns into night and twilight floods the world in its heavenly glow. Hollywood calls it the "magic hour," the brief enchanted moment when day lays a kiss on the night. For most human beings, straddling the delicate balance between giving and receiving is just as beautiful and just as rare. And that's why for so many thousands of years we have cherished the tree—our finest role model, our matchless teacher.

Rabbi Isaac Luria, a venerated Kabbalist who lived in sixteenth-century Safed, Israel, professed that in the beginning, ten vessels—the Tree's ten energy spheres—filled with Light that emanated from the One. The first three spheres—the high numinous energies called Crown, Wisdom, and Understanding—handled the mighty luminosity of the Light without a snag. But when the infinite Light force cascaded to the fourth sphere, called Mercy, the mechanism faltered. Mercy embodies the energy of compassion—the quality of selfless giving. When roused by the

Light, the sphere awakened to its innate longing to confer compassion. But with the Light surging in, regaling the vessel without recess, Mercy found itself stuck permanently in the mode of receiving. Deprived of the opportunity to give, the sphere was unable to fulfill its sole reason for being. The vessel called Mercy foresaw no other option but to refuse the Light. It attempted to squelch its own receiving so that it could claim the space to share.

It was like trying to close the barn door on a category 5 hurricane. The omnipotent torrent of the endless Light slammed into the shuttered vessel and shattered it into a million pieces. The next five spheres on the Tree disintegrated in a chain reaction as well, scattering sparks of the primordial Light all over the Kingdom, the tenth sphere of the Tree, the realm of all physical matter, the one vessel most suited to seizing, collecting, and retaining. In the wake of this cosmic cataclysm, our purpose, Rabbi Luria postulated, is to retrieve all those broken sparks. We accomplish that task through good deeds and sharing with all the other fractured particles of those original vessels—be they flowers, stones, dogs, or other people. Each spark of Light liberated in this way signifies a rectification or *Tikkun*—the Hebrew word for "fixing"—of the broken spheres, a restoration of the vessels' perfect unity with the Light of God, and a fixing of our own human soul.

It's a lovely allegory. But the splintering of the spheres into all these dissimilar fragments also carries a dark side: the temptation to receive and never give—the continual undertow of greed. All humans evolved from the shards of those ruptured vessels, and so each of us is a vessel first—designed primarily to hold stuff. That desire to acquire and clutch looms as the primal tendency of every human being. To overcome our intrinsic selfishness, we must strive willfully to do what the Tree accomplishes with ease—receive in order to share.

WISH MAKER: As you pursue your wish, make sure that you balance your desire to receive by giving something in return. For example, if you wish for an investment in a business project, you must find a way to reciprocate. It doesn't have to be a one-for-one exchange, but rather a sharing of anything that you deem commensurate to your desire. Trees take in water, nutrients, and sunlight and discharge something altogether new in the form of oxygen. To harmonize your desire to receive money, perhaps you could allocate some of your time to a charitable organization or to the neglected emotional needs of your family. One businesswoman promised to donate 8 percent of all additional income when she fulfilled her wish to increase her sales commissions. She is still paying that charitable pledge today.

The Trees of Paradise

A word of advice as you embark on the voyage to fulfill your wish. Remember the Tree of Knowledge and the Tree of Life in the Garden of Eden—the trees that so afflicted Adam and Eve? These two arboreal icons are actually the same tree. The Tree of Life thrived on the inside and the Tree of Knowledge of Good and Evil encased it on the outside.

The minute they snacked on the intoxicating fruit from the exterior of the tree, Adam and Eve perceived the disparity of their genders and scurried to the fig tree to conceal their nakedness. That sparked the initial fragmentation between the masculine and the feminine that torments us to this day. Next, the couple veiled themselves from God, and that original game of hide-and-seek aggrieved them and us even more because it marked the fundamental breach between the divine and the mundane, between spirit and matter. Before that bite of the "knowledge of good and evil," before the dawning of duality, all was One. All was Eden.

Like an LSD trip or any other sort of artificial high, Adam and Eve reveled in the euphoria of infinite knowledge the moment they indulged in the fruit. But then the inevitable low ensued— the brutal hangover in the morning, symbolized by the couple's unfortunate fall to Earth. This entire tale, retold faithfully for thousands of years, sounds as a warning to avoid the sickening hangover that we suffer whenever we elect to live in our heads rather than our hearts; whenever we opt for the heady rush of duality over nourishment from the divine truth that lies encased inside us all.

Many of us suckle still on the fruits of the Tree of Knowledge. Overly reliant on our intellects, too intent on the exactitude of our yoga poses, excessively focused on acquiring facts about fashionable spiritual paths, we construct a detachment from those paths and from life itself. We no longer engage in relation- ships because we read books about relationships. We don't even meditate; we instead attend lectures on meditation.

The Kabbalistic Tree of Life advocates the opposite: to live life, to love experience, to conjoin with all the sparks of the divine. Trees live. Each day they transform sunlight into food, reaching their branches skyward to capture more light, stretch- ing their arms to heaven, spreading their roots deep into the earth, unifying the two. "Because man is a tree of the field" (Deuteronomy 20:19), it's our job to live as a tree, to taste from the inside of that One Tree in Eden. Working a wish through the ten energy spheres guides you deep into the heart of the Tree of Life. The wish, the exercises, and the meditations impel you to climb inside the Tree. To live inside the Tree. It's time to take that journey. And like a tree that sheds its withered foliage each win- ter only to embrace life afresh and revivified in the spring, you too have nothing to lose but your old dried-up leaves.

Ten Steps to Wish Fulfillment

🖙 1. Know what you want. Write it down.

🖙 2. Capitalize on intuition. Hunt for synchronicities and coincidences. Allow the universe to proffer insights and information.

🖙 3. Devise a well-defined plan and time frame for achieving your goal. Vow to stick to it.

NO FEAR!

🖙 4. Plunge ahead, embracing all opportunities without judgment. Just do it.

🖙 5. Cut out everything that doesn't serve your aims and fight for everything that does.

🖙 6. Practice creative visualization to imagine your wish fulfilled exactly as you want it. Willingly sacrifice something to make yourself more beautiful (godly) in your own eyes.

🖙 7. Repeat again and again all the behaviors and thoughts that have paid off thus far.

🖙 8. Rewrite your wish and note how it has changed. Identify any snags in the plan and strive to untangle them.

🖙 9. Blend all of your experiences to date into a revisualization of your wish fulfilled. Consciously let go of the world or mindset in which your wish was just a dream. Allow that old you to die and find yourself reborn as a wish-fulfilled human being.

🖙 10. Give thanks to the universe for granting your wish. Enjoy all that you have accomplished. Start all over again with a brand-new ambition.

CHAPTER ONE

CROWN:

The Infinite Will of God and Your Will to Wish

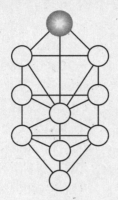

SPHERE 1

KEYWORD: Will of God

WISH IMPERATIVE: Meditate and decide with conviction precisely what you want to wish for. Write it down.

HEBREW NAME OF SPHERE: Keter

MYTH AND PERSONALITIES: No-Thing

PLANET: None (Crown is simply the will to create; nothing yet has been formed)

DARK SIDE: None

COLOR: White bright light

NUMBER: 1

TREE: Seed of the Tree of Life

BODY PART: Crown of the head

HEBREW NAME OF GOD (MANTRA): Eheyeh (I am that I am)

Roots of the Divine

The Crown lies beyond words; it flickers beyond insight. Mere mortals cannot hope to understand the Crown or the second sphere, called Wisdom, because the concept of Understanding itself was not invented until the third sphere. Even the wisest person on the planet cannot fully grasp the Crown because Wisdom—the Tree's second sphere—had not arrived yet either. Some theologians equate the Crown with enlightenment. But Buddha, the twenty-five-hundred-year-old master, apprehended that the Crown could not be taught. He affirmed that he could only coach his followers in "the way" to arrive at this idyllic destination.

With any mystical doctrine, the limitations of our brains saddle us with an insurmountable problem. How can we delineate the infinite mind of God—a transcendent idealization with no beginning and no end—when our all-too-human mind is encumbered by both? Any attempt to explain infinity duplicates the futility of trying to pour the Pacific Ocean into a coffee mug. The cup might succeed in capturing a tiny sampling of the sea for us to inspect, taste, and analyze, but the vast majority of the ocean and its contents are bound to spill unknowable over the borders of the vessel.

Only in the spiritual realm beyond the confines of our physical existence do we discover tools like imagination and faith that endow us with the capacity to experience the nature of God. We fabricate myths that hint at the truth. We anthropomorphize the qualities of the divine to assist us in grasping a least one constructive sliver of infinity. The bottom line is this: The Tree of Life functions to convert the infinite into something concrete. It chronicles the journey of the Light that resulted in the formation of the universe. And it lives still as the same path that you will follow to transform your wish into an actuality. The Crown is the first step on that voyage of creation. It initiates every process.

WISH MAKER: Initiate yours right now. Make a wish. What do you want? Get a blank journal or notebook and, without judgment, without scrutiny, write down your first impulse. Later in this chapter, you will find exercises that will help you to mold and refine it. But for now, here at the Crown of the Tree, spell out the nascent stirrings of your wish.

The Will of God

The luminescent Crown resembles a ray of Light that extends from the nothingness toward the Creation; it is the elementary force that activates everything. In human terms, the Crown is the Will of God.

The will precedes thoughts, actions, and emotions. It galvanizes the primal impulse that initiates change. Take something as basic as feeding yourself. First, you need the will to do that. This spark to life triggers the realization that to enjoy the homemade pasta, you must carry it up to your mouth. Without that activating will, your hand will not move, and you will not eat. When we describe severely depressed people, we often report that they have lost the will to live, the will to get out of bed in the morning. They lack the vital ignition that spurs every action.

Before a person dies he often writes a will, which is essentially a wish for what should be done with his possessions. This wish equals the will or Crown. The actual money and property to be distributed represent the person's Kingdom, the lowest sphere on the Tree. If a person neglects to leave a will, he might bequeath antipathy and lawsuits to loved ones left behind. A will is essential. Otherwise, the Kingdom—the material world we aim to transform with our wish—degenerates into chaos.

Perhaps the most famous sentence in the New Testament evokes the message of the Crown: "Thy Will be done." Whose will? God's will. Immerse yourself in that passage this week. If your will—your wish—matches God's, then it is already done. Basically, your job is to substantiate to God that your wish is the will of the One.

Consider God a venture capitalist and your wish a start-up company. By employing the Tree, you knock on the door of God's office and request an investment. As with any patron, you cannot demand, "Hey, give me the spiritual currency to finance my business plan." Protocol compels you to outline the mission and the advantages that will accrue to the investor and the world. You must persuade the venture capitalist that he will profit from it. You must demonstrate that your business is God's business. If so, then "thy will be done"—like a genie automatically granting your wish.

How do you know whether your will matches the will of the Light? You have to sense it. One man aspired to run a marathon. He had served in the army and had injured his back severely. But with the help of his doctors, he'd managed to recuperate. He yearned to confirm that he had conquered his disability and reverted back to his old self. He'd been training for a month when he made his wish on the Tree. But during the week of Crown, he injured himself again. His doctor diagnosed it as "overtraining syndrome." His body simply refused to continue with the harsh regimen. Was his wish to run a marathon equivalent to the will of the One? Probably not.

The disappointed jogger reacted bitterly. He complained that the Tree didn't work. But in actuality, the Tree performed valiantly. It prevented him from overdoing it and probably saved him from permanent damage. The Crown helped to reveal that his body had rejected the wish. It disclosed that his wish was rooted in a compulsion for self-aggrandizement and not in the will of God. Soon this man overcame his frustration and elected instead to wish for clarity about why he harbored such an obsessive craving to prove himself, to win even at the expense of his own welfare. Tuning in to the frequency of the Crown allowed him to dredge up a more felicitous goal. And after wending his way through the Tree, the soldier realized that his fanatical ambition sprang from the voice of his despotic father, who had threatened and cajoled his sons into expectations of achievements that were beyond the grasp of mortals. The younger man came to see that he had internalized those unreasonable demands at great expense to his happiness and well-being. He never ran a marathon. But his alternate wish spurred him to accept his human limitations and to appreciate his true strengths.

How to Wish

One day the Buddha presented a seed to a group of acolytes. "What do you see?" the Buddha asked. "A seed," they all agreed. "Look harder," said the Buddha. "It is the entire forest." Within one seed lies the potential regeneration of a multitude of trees, mutations, life-forms, and possibilities. In the Kabbalistic scheme, the Crown represents the seed and source of everything. And just as a seed contains the full-grown tree, the Crown holds all of the subsequent spheres inside it. Within your Crown lies your own infinite potential. To tap it, you make a wish.

Start by imagining how you would reply if a genie appeared and said, "I'll grant you anything." Don't be humble. Contemplate what you really want. Money, love, health, a car that won't break down every week? It's okay if it sounds trite or selfish at first.

Choose a wish that is feasible. Don't wish for enlightenment. In ten weeks, it's probably not going to happen. Millions of dollars might be tough too. You may wish for money for a new business. You may wish for additional clients or for more financial abundance in general. You can wish for a love relationship, for the most propitious partner. You might want to wish for better communication with your spouse or your child or for the time and energy to care for your dream flower garden.

The will represents the initial idea—the "hmmm, I want to write a book," or "I wish I had a new car." You don't need to know the title of the book, whether it's fiction or nonfiction, how many pages it will have, what it's about, where you will find the time to write it, or how on earth you will ever get it published. You don't have to determine what type of car you will buy, what color it should be, or how you will acquire the money to pay for it. You will address all of those questions as you proceed down the Tree. For now, you simply summon the spark, the itch to bring something new into your life.

Make Your Wish

1. Start a list with the initial impulse you jotted down. Then brainstorm. Ask yourself what you want and generate as many new options as possible. Answer this question: What am I missing in my life? Write down every single thing that springs to mind—no matter how silly or trivial. Put aside your pen and do something else for a few hours or a couple of days. Then return to your list and ask yourself the same question. Add all of your new ideas to your list.

2. It might take time to sift through the false starts, your polite instincts, and the stuff you think you *should* want. Now read through your list and circle the three wishes that seem most urgent. Read these three possibilities out loud. Close your eyes and speak them again. Try to determine which one makes you *feel* the most, which stirs a sensation of

expansion or relaxation. Pay attention to your body. Do you feel lighter, a pleasant or warm tingling? If so, this is a good wish. Do you find it tough to concentrate when you imagine the wish fulfilled? Do stray thoughts race through your mind? These physical markers probably indicate that the wish might not be so advantageous for you right now.

3. Ask yourself some questions about each wish. Is it worthwhile? Is it something solid and identifiable? Can I picture it vividly? Can I envision this wish coming true? Will it really gratify me? Is it the one thing I need the most in my life? Will it make me a better person?

4. Don't look to the Tree for therapy. "I wish to be happier" or "I wish to be less cruel to myself" are noble goals, but difficult to appraise. Awareness and self-improvement, emotional breakthroughs, and a more joyous and accepting disposition will evolve naturally as you advance through the energetic spheres. But for now, the Tree wants to give you a present, something concrete and quantifiable.

5. Choose now what you want to accomplish in your journey on the Tree. Write down your wish in one or two sentences. This is your will—your mission statement. Short, sweet, and easily understood.

Over the course of the next ten weeks, you likely will mold and refine this wish. Often the voyage on the Tree stirs us to alter the wish entirely. Like the thwarted marathoner, you might realize that you don't want your wish at all. Wishes adapt to the realities of our lives just as a tree bends to fit its environment. If you plant a tree in an overly shady locale, it won't automatically shrivel and die. More often, the tree will adjust, twisting and shooting off branches in new directions to hunt for more light. Your wish is apt to follow the example of that tree. But for now, you merely need to begin.

The Contract

Wishes are fun. Remember when you were a kid: "Starlight, star bright, the first star I see this night. I wish I may, I wish I might, have this wish I wish tonight." The Tree works when you have fun. But it will work only if you agree to the following conditions.

1. Prime directive: You may wish only for yourself. You cannot wish for someone else unless that person specifically requests your help. And even then it is far better for that person to wish on his or her own. Wishes come true as a result of the personal spiritual development gleaned by traveling the Tree. Wishing for another won't foster his transformation unless he too tackles the meditations and the work. Try taking the journey together.

2. Your wish must be one with the One. It must be for good. It cannot provoke harm to any sentient being. You must not wish for anything that promotes ignorance, violence, or disharmony. Misaligned with the will of the One, such wishes will not procure any funding from the Light. If you wish for revenge or for the failure of your rivals, the Tree will ignore you. You may not wish: "I want the other candidates competing for my new job to falter." That wish likely will prompt you to misstep yourself. Instead,

rephrase your goal: "I wish to perform to the top of my ability and find a high-paying job in which I will thrive and excel."

Your signature or initials here on this page or beside your wish written out in your journal seals your agreement with the above conditions.

You gave your word. And in the world of magic, the Word creates. The phrasing of your wish is critical. It casts the spell. If you "spell" out what you want, you arouse the Tree to team with you to make it real. Be specific. Define your wish in precise, unambiguous terms. Try to envision it fulfilled in concrete ways. Say you want to lose twenty pounds. Spend time visualizing how you would look without the excess weight. Imagine shopping for clothes that suit your slimmer physique. Picture details such as what styles you would wear, how they would fit, the size of your new waistline, the reactions of others, etc.

And remember this cautionary tale: A well-intentioned young man used similar spiritual techniques to fulfill his biggest dream. He worked as an accountant, slaving nine to five, but he aspired to be a millionaire. "I wish to have a million dollars in my hands," he declared. A millionaire needs a million dollars, right? Two months later, his employer transferred him to a desk in the vault of a major bank. Every day he counted the money on its way to the safe. Every day he held more than a million dollars in his hands.

WISH MAKER: Once you are pleased with the content and phrasing of your wish, read it aloud several times. Memorize it. Then spend a few moments thanking God for already granting your wish. Since the Crown contains all the other spheres inside its white radiance, your wish in many ways has already come true. The chapters that follow serve simply to help you to recognize it.

The Crown Chakra

As above, so below; the Tree mirrors the human form. Every sphere corresponds to a part of our body, and the Crown logi-cally coincides with the top of the head. Tantric Hinduism dubs it the Crown chakra, the antenna that collects the messages from above. It's the spot on which we receive kisses from the divine.

Acupuncturists regard this chakra as one of the most power-ful points in the body. Religions, too. Jews wear a yarmulke to cover it, while some Christian and Buddhist monks shave it clean. Orthodox Jewish women shave their heads and then swathe them in wigs. Sikhs and Christian nuns conceal the Crown in sacramental cloth. When you enter a church you must remove your hat, but in a synagogue you put on a skullcap. These conflicting customs indicate that no one truly understands the power of the Crown or what to do with it. But they all sense that we ought to do something. Every religion recognizes that the Crown is extraordinarily sacred.

WISH MAKER: The Crown obligates us to try to find something sacred in our wish. Test your wish to make sure that it represents more than some selfish desire. Focus on the top of your head as often as possible and contemplate the keywords of the Crown: absolute unity, sacredness, and pure divine Light. The more we bother to consider these qualities of divinity, the more we will perceive them in ourselves and in the world around us. As you ponder the sacred—as you drive, eat, work, or play with your kids—you are apt to stum-ble upon clues that will supply evidence of the worth of your wish.

For example, a forty-two-year-old mother of a thirteen-year-old boy yearned for a baby girl. Her husband opposed it because he feared the risks inherent in over-forty pregnancies. She mulled it over for days, running through a host of alternate wishes. But each sounded trivial when measured against her longing for a little girl. Still, she fretted. What if it was vanity? A silly girlhood fantasy? How could she justify putting her husband and son through an ordeal they didn't want? These doubts oppressed her, and she nearly abandoned the idea of wishing on the Tree. But during the week of Crown, bizarre coincidences guided her to the truth. First, a friend invited her to a movie. Eager to escape her quandary, she agreed without asking the name the film. It turned out to be *All About My Mother*. The following day, she went to a yoga class and mistakenly found herself in a session geared to pregnant women. Driving home, her favorite talk radio station commenced a discussion of natural childbirth. That night, she dreamed that her late father commanded her to have another baby. She could not ignore the signs. She made her wish. And ten months later, she gave birth to a baby daughter.

The Divine Umbilical

We're born with the antenna at the top of our head wide open. We call it the soft spot, and we vigilantly avoid pressing on any newborn's crown with too much force. Only later does the bone harden, encasing our celestial receiver inside the skull, symbolically cutting off our direct line to God.

A young couple in Mexico had two children—a three-year-old and a newborn. Like many modern parents, they purchased a baby-monitoring system to enable them to hear what was going on in the nursery at all times. One night, while they lay in their bed, the parents listened through the speaker as their eldest entered the baby's room down the hall. He approached the cradle of his tiny brother and shook it to wake him up. "Hey," the three-year-old whispered to the newcomer, unaware that his parents could hear him. "Hey, tell me about God, because I already forgot."

This family was not religious in any way. The parents never spoke about God or church or anything mystical. And yet, without prompting, this young boy instinctively understood where to turn. He realized that the infant couldn't talk, but he knew that the baby—as opposed to his parents—was a reliable informant for news of God because the little one had just arrived from the source. Perhaps he still could discern the thread of white light linking the infant's crown receptors to heaven. The hardening of his own skull had severed the young boy's own umbilical to God. But he remembered it. As we all do. And he yearned for it. As we all do.

This true story reminds us that God does not live in the parsing of complicated religious texts, but rather in every moment of our lives. That's the purpose of this book: to find God in all the incidents large and small that occupy each of us. The boy wished to know God. To fulfill that wish, he sought out an expert—his infant brother. The Crown instructs that the answer to many of our most dear and thorny questions can be found by adopting the attitude of innocence of a three-year-old. As you pursue your wish over the next ten weeks, try as often as possible to view your goals, your setbacks, and the world at large with this same brand of openness and wonder.

All the Colors

Each of the ten spheres vibrates on a different frequency, on a distinct wavelength of the divine. Colors represent one tangible manifestation of these frequencies. They function as envoys direct from that particular sphere. Watch for them. These ambassadors of the spheres frequently convey messages vital to a successful journey on the Tree. If possible, wear clothes that match the color of the energy and listen attentively to the words of people dressed in that color. Search your world for objects, painted walls in your home, and anything else that is of similar hue. By deliberating on the color of the week, you construct an energy field around you and your environment that will amplify the power of the sphere in your life.

The brilliant white light of the divine is the color of the Crown. Prisms break white light into every color we can see. It holds all of the other colors within it just as the Crown carries all of the other spheres yet to come. White is a beginning and yet it is complete. This week, white will point you in the direction you ought to follow, just as the white rabbit guided Alice on her adventure into Wonderland. It represents purity, possibilities, the blank page that can be filled with anything. Observe white wherever you go and imagine what sort of life story—or wish story—you aspire to write.

One

The first sphere in the Tree, the Crown is the place of wholeness, the complete and seamless confluence of all things. It is egoless and genderless, indivisible and perfect.

In playing cards, the ace represents the number one. It is the top dog, more powerful than the king and queen. Its supremacy derives from the fact that it embodies the potential of everything that follows. Many of us exert great energy at the outset of projects, relationships, and life itself. The challenge is to continue with that same vigor long enough to transform the one into two, three, four, and so on. This week, and every week during your journey on the Tree, scan the world for the number of the sphere—in this case, one. Search for these numbers in songs, billboards, newspaper headlines, and conversations. Locate them anywhere and discover signposts sent by the Tree.

The number one connotes initiation, the beginning of a new sequence or a new start. It invites you to commence a new project while simultaneously reminding you to align that new process with the indivisible whole. It impels you to sync up your goal with the will of the One. Does your wish serve unity? Or does it divide you from others? This week the number one will help you to uncover the truth.

The Reason We Wish

Restoring unity is the purpose of this entire process. While pursuing your personal wish, it is instructive to remember the creation myth of Humpty-Dumpty, a story that closely parallels Rabbi Luria's Kabbalistic parable about the breaking of the vessels that created the universe. In this timeless nursery rhyme, the egg—a spherical symbol of undifferentiated totality, of unlimited potential—fell and splintered into a million pieces.

The pessimistic Mother Goose then laments that "all the king's horses and all the king's men couldn't put Humpty-Dumpty together again." Kabbalah disagrees. When we overlay the nursery rhyme with the Tree of Life, we find that the king wears the Crown, the top sphere of the Tree—the one most proximate to God. The king's horses and men—all material beings and part of the king's creation—reside in Kingdom, the lowest sphere in the Tree or the physical plane in the cosmic system. The rhyme suggests that everyone in the physical world has been drafted by the king or the Crown to reunify the fractured egg into one inviolable whole.

Like Humpty-Dumpty's horses and men, we will fail in this commission as long as we rely solely on the tools and limitations of the material world of sight, sound, taste, touch, and smell. But we all have access to more than the five senses. We have the Tree. We have nine other spheres above the material Kingdom. And by making a wish and tapping in to these spheres, each of us begins the process of rectifying the broken vessels. We initiate the healing of Humpty-Dumpty.

Luria labeled the breaking of the vessels "the cosmic accident," and the nursery rhyme intimates that Humpty-Dumpty's "great fall" was an accident too. But couldn't God, with His infinite wisdom and might, engineer and construct spheres durable enough to collect the Light without bursting apart, if that was God's intent? Logic demands the conclusion that God intentionally designed the "accident" to allow humankind the opportunity to participate in the Creation. God was and God is compassionate enough to leave us a place in His grand painting to color in for ourselves. God's masterwork is incomplete. All of us—*all* the King's horses and *all* the King's men—must help God finish this ultimate work of art. We must complete and perfect the Creation.

That, and pretty much only that, is the reason each of us is here on this Earth. Here's the question: Have you been doing your part? Have you picked up the brush? Your commitment to this journey through the spheres of the Tree of Life is the first step.

The Name of God

Kabbalistic theology has assigned each sphere a particular name of God. It functions as a mantra, the Sanskrit word for "mental vibrations," which summons the sphere's power into consciousness. These mantras function as a kind of celestial address and phone number, designed to stimulate a particular energy of the One Divine Light.

You will chant these names of God during your meditations each week to propel your wish to fruition. But you can also use them anytime you find yourself in need of the energy of a particular sphere. For example, if at some point you have a desire for more money or more sensual pleasure, use the mantra for Eternity. If you get sick and require physical healing, recite the mantra for Beauty.

The name of God for the Crown is *Eheyeh* (pronounced Eh-He-Yeh). It derives from the biblical scene in which Moses, confronted with the burning bush, asks God for his credentials. God replies, "Eheyeh," or "I am that I am" (Exodus 3:14). In Hebrew, this name springs from the root *Hay Yod Hay*, which translates to "the present that has no end and is not restricted by time." In other words, the endless, the emptiness, infinity.

"I am that I am" also promises that God is in everything that is. "I am" exists within every situation and every moment. If you are in jail, God is there as the jail, imprisoned with you. Amid the pain of childbirth, God lives in the mother's cries. The presence of God is channeled through the Crown at all times. We don't always remember that. And so we remind ourselves by chanting this gorgeous name again and again.

WISH MAKER: This mantra will help you to focus your will and to harness it to your wish. Whenever you find yourself feeling lethargic or indecisive, chant this mantra to access your own antenna to the divine.

How to Meditate

Every day for the next ten weeks, preferably in the morning or just before you go to sleep, devote a few minutes to connect with the Tree. Sit in a comfortable position on the floor or in a chair with your spine as straight as possible. Breathe deeply, pumping the air in and out with your abdomen. Envision the images as instructed in the guided meditations provided in each chapter. (If you wish, record the meditation in your own voice and then play it as you meditate.) At the appropriate point in the meditation, slowly chant the name of God associated with that sphere. Breathe in deeply and intone the name. Continue chanting for at least five minutes. Feel free to repeat the mantra for as long as you like. Many people report that they obtain much better results when they chant for fifteen or twenty minutes at a time.

The Crown Meditation

Sit in a comfortable position and breathe deeply. Envision yourself perched on a throne overlooking a boundless ocean. You feel secure and comfortable. The view is breathtaking. Now imagine a dimensionless point of absolute light hovering in front of you at eye level. Watch as this point of light slowly expands as you breathe in and out. It grows to the size of a tennis ball, then slowly swells into a great sphere of shining bright light. Imagine that this sphere engulfs you entirely. Find yourself sitting now in the middle of a huge vibrating circle of light. It protects you from all of your problems, from all the hassles of your daily life. Nothing can penetrate this shield of bliss.

Concentrate on your crown. Try to sense it. Try to move it without shifting your head. Focus on the one thing that you would need to see in your life in order to feel this kind of bliss. Whatever fills this need is your will. It is your wish.

Now summon the divine presence of the Crown. Chant in a deep voice the mantra pronounced Eh-He-Yeh. Chant it again and again for a few minutes, taking long breaths in between the chants and drawing out each syllable. *Eheyeh.*

When you finish chanting, inhale deeply and hold the air for as long as you can. Mentally vibrate the mantra inside your head. And breathe out. Breathe in once again and hold the air. Try to envision how each of your cells vibrates to this name of God. Breathe out. Last time, breathe in, hold the air, and imagine your whole body inside and out turning white and transparent.

Picture an angel appearing in front of you. The angel hands you a tiny seed of light. It is the seed of your own Tree of Life. It is the seed of your wish. Dig a hole in the ground and place the seed in the earth. Cover it up and spend a moment imagining yourself watering the seed with light and love. Now look up as the angel places a crown of shining white light on your head. Feel your whole body elevated by this corona of condensed light. Breathe this light and imagine how it travels from the top of your head all the way to the soles of your feet. Meditate a few minutes with this crown of light. When you are ready, retain the crown on your head and allow the giant sphere of light to contract around you. Watch as it shrinks slowly back to its original size, back to the dimensionless point. When it disappears, move your hands and your head and return to the here and now.

The Abralog

Abra translates as "to create." This word in Aramaic—an ancient language similar to Hebrew that was supposedly spoken by Christ—evokes a powerful spell. The magician's word *abra-*

cadabra, for example, means "I create as I speak." Your Abralog is your creation diary, in which you will track your progress on the way to building your wish. Divide a blank journal into ten chapters—one for each sphere in the Tree. During each week of your journey, record your thoughts, feelings, doubts, and achievements. If possible, set aside a few minutes at the end of every day to jot down your experiences.

Pay special attention to your dreams, insights from meditations, any odd coincidences, and any times you encounter the symbols of a particular sphere. Near the end of each chapter, you will find a list of associations for that particular energy. For example, Crown is represented by the color white, the number one, seeds, and the crown worn by a king. Use your Abralog to record any incident in which you see, hear, or interact with these symbols. Use these moments of synchronicity to guide you. If during the week of Crown you receive an invitation embossed with a picture of a crown, go to the event. Something or someone that you meet there will likely invigorate your wish. Recording all of these associations in your journal will help to harness the everyday experiences of your life to your voyage on the Tree. At the end of each week, read through all of your Abralog entries before moving to the next sphere. Circle the symbols, thoughts, or experiences that you deem most significant. Try to decipher the messages encoded in these circles. What were the signs of the sphere trying to tell you? Play with them. Free associate. Let your Abralog musings create your new direction.

AWishCanChangeYourLife.com

This web site has been designed to supplement and augment your work on the Tree of Life. Though the program outlined in the book stands on its own, the content on the web site can help you to connect to others engaged in this spiritual process. And it just might provide additional keys that will facilitate the fulfillment of your wish.

The features available at AWishCanChangeYourLife.com include: a list of wishes that other people have attained via this journey on the Tree of Life; various real-life synchronicities with the symbols of the Tree and how other wish makers interpreted and used them as guideposts along the path to their goals; and a list of frequently asked questions and answers pertaining to Kabbalah and the Tree. This site also contains an interactive mechanism that will allow you to post the comments, doubts, triumphs, and experiences that you accumulate over the course of the next ten weeks. This interactive component will also permit you to ask questions and respond to the thoughts of fellow travelers on the Tree of Life, and perhaps it will encourage you to create your own on-line community of kindred wish seekers. The site also provides free music files of the various chants and names of God that you can use during your meditations each week.

The Tree of Life Grove

Most critically, AWishCanChangeYourLife.com presents a simple method for you to satisfy one of the most vital duties of the Crown: planting your own tree out there in the real world (see exercise 1, below, which also provides information about how to satisfy this imperative by way of phone, check, or regular mail). The authors of this book have teamed up with the respected environmental organization American Forests to plant trees in our own grove within the Tahoe National Forest in California. The saplings purchased as part of this program will be clustered together to create the Tree of Life Grove, a forest of trees—and symbolically of wishes—that will thrive for years, benefiting both the ecological health of the planet as well as the spiritual growth of everyone who plants a tree.

"As above, so below" has endured as a preeminent mystical formula for thousands of years. Alchemists from all traditions have long revered this simple adage as the most potent spell for manifesting anything you want. As you work with your wish through the chapters of this book, you will plant a Tree of Life in the spiritual plane above. To certify your commitment to the process and to activate the magic of the spheres, you must also plant a tree in the below realm here on Earth. Don't short-circuit the enchanted potential that is your birthright. Plant your tree in the Tree of Life Grove and infuse your life with the magic of the ages.

Wish List—Crown

Near the end of each chapter you will find a synopsis of the crucial tasks you must undertake that week to push you closer to the fulfillment of your wish. If you do nothing else, make certain that you attempt to complete these wish-enhancing activities. The Wish Lists will also help you to appraise your progress from week to week.

1. Pick your wish.

2. Revise and rephrase your wish until it is as succinct and precise as possible. Write it on the first page of your journal.

3. Watch for synchronicities related to the color white, the number one, crowns of any kind, seeds, eggs, trees, or the word *will*. Use your Abralog to record your encounters with the symbols of the Crown as well as any interpretations these incidents and associations provoke.

4. Plant a tree (see exercise 1, below).

Exercise Zone

Each chapter also contains several exercises designed to complement the Wish Makers and deepen your relationship with that
particular sphere. All of these exercises will amplify your understanding of your psyche and emotions and/or advance the
process of fulfilling your wish. The more you work at them, the
more intensely the spheres will influence your life.

   1. **Plant your Tree of Life:** In the Crown meditation you sowed the astral or the "above" Tree of
Life. To seal the magical spell that will work to
conjure your wish, it is essential to plant an
actual tree in the "below" realm. After selecting
your wish, this task looms as the single most
important step you can take to ensure a fruitful
journey. The most effective way to fulfill this mission is to participate in the creation of the Tree of
Life Grove—a wilderness renewal program
devised in partnership with American Forests
especially for the readers of *A Wish Can Change
Your Life.* Your tax-deductible contribution will
help to reforest the Onion Valley region of the
Tahoe National Forest in California with a variety
of pine and fir compatible with the topography of
the Sierra Nevada.

     To plant your tree in the Tree of Life Grove, click
on the tree-planting link at AWishCanChangeYour
Life.com, or log on to www.TreeofLife Grove.com. You
may also phone in your contribution to 1-800-545-
TREE. Be sure to specify that you would like your
trees to be included as part of the Tree of Life Grove.
Those who prefer regular mail may send a check
payable to "American Forests—Tree of Life Grove"

to American Forests, P.O. Box 2000, Washington, D.C. 20013. Everyone who enlists in the building of the Tree of Life Grove will receive a certificate acknowledging his or her role in the creation of this magical forest.

You may choose from the following planting options:
- ☞ $10 for ten trees in the Tree of Life Grove (for the ten spheres of the Tree)
- ☞ $18 for eighteen trees (the Hebrew number that signifies *Hai* or "life")
- ☞ $32 for thirty-two trees (for the thirty-two paths of wisdom by which God created the universe)
- ☞ $72 for seventy-two trees (the number of syllables in the ultimate name of God)
- ☞ $108 for one hundred and eight trees (a holy number in traditions across the globe)
- ☞ Or pick any number of trees above ten that is lucky or meaningful to you.

The goal of this project is simple: together with other travelers on the Tree of Life, you will construct a forest of living wishes that will bolster the salubrity of the earth and the air we breathe while at the same time confirming your dedication to the process of creating your energetic wish-fulfilling Tree. Tahoe National Forest has agreed to mark the Onion Valley planting site with a sign that will allow hikers and readers of *A Wish Can Change Your Life* to easily identify their forest. You can obtain highway directions to the Tree of Life Grove from the Internet addresses and phone number listed above. Once you contribute to this communal woodland, you will then be able to visit (or make pilgrimage to) the very tree that symbolizes the fulfillment of your fondest dream.

🖙 2. **Thy will be done:** By this point you should have decided on your wish and written it down in a precise, crisp sentence or two. Now it's time to sell the universe on your dream. Write a personal letter to God, your spiritual investor, explaining with as much passion as possible why your will is God's will. This letter also doubles as an exercise in convincing yourself that your wish is what you really want and that it is truly valuable. If you cannot convince yourself, how can you win over God? If you find that you are unable to formulate a persuasive case for your wish, if you discover that your wish does not reflect your true will, go back to the catalog of wishes you devised earlier in this chapter. Revise your wish or select another that more closely matches your will and God's will and then tackle this exercise again.

🖙 3. **Your anchoring tree:** Spend time outside—in your favorite park or in your garden—and seek out a tree that symbolizes the energies of the Tree of Life. It can be tall or short, leafy or relatively bare. Keep searching until you locate a tree that you especially like. Once you find your tree, strive to make a connection with it. Run your hands along its trunk. Memorize the texture of the bark. Wrap your arms around the base and hug it like a good friend. If you can, climb into its branches. Smell it. Draw it. Photograph it. Talk to it. Familiarize yourself with the characteristics of this tree as thoroughly as possible so that you can summon its image during your meditations. This tree belongs to you. Call on it any time you feel the need to bond more intimately with the power of the Tree of Life.

CHAPTER TWO

WISDOM:

The Energy of Intuition, Synchronicity, and Life Beyond Space/Time

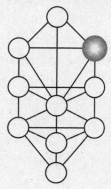

SPHERE 2

KEYWORD: Intuition

WISH IMPERATIVE: Pay attention to intuition and synchronicities. Allow the universe to proffer insights and information that will push your wish toward fruition.

HEBREW NAME OF SPHERE: Hochma

MYTH AND PERSONALITIES: Gandalf the Grey, the Baal Shem Tov

PLANET: Wisdom is beyond planets, but it is associated with the entire wheel of the zodiac

DARK SIDE: Gullibility and confusion

COLOR: Gray or silver

NUMBER: 2

TREE: Redwood

BODY PART: Right brain

HEBREW NAME OF GOD (MANTRA): Yod Hey Vav Hey (Is, was, will be)

Flashes of Light

Moving down the Tree in the quest to translate infinite potential into material stuff, we next encounter the enigmatic gray/silver sphere called Wisdom. It sits at the top of the right pillar of expansion. Whatever you place on this side of the Tree grows and inflates; the left pillar always cuts and restricts. Wisdom expands through involuntary flashes of insight. It works like a lightning bolt, illuminating the entire horizon and then vanishing fast.

This kind of wisdom can best be described as intuition—flashes of inspiration that flicker like electricity. We all experience this energy, even if we can't control when it strikes. Like the Crown, this ethereal sphere precedes the invention of most of the qualities—reason, language, clocks, and calendars—that make us human. Wisdom lies beyond time and space, which were born in the third sphere, called Understanding. No one, not even a master of meditation, can sit down, scrunch up his face, and will the arrival of an intuition by lunchtime. The undifferentiated seat of divine wisdom operates on its own mysterious schedule. "Insights tend to come suddenly and, characteristically, not when sitting at a desk working out the equations," wrote Fritjof Capra in *The Tao of Physics*, "but when relaxing, in the bath, during a walk in the woods or on the beach."

Mirror, Mirror

The color of Wisdom is gray or silver. We often associate old age and gray hair with the state of being wise. Grandmothers and long gray beards evoke the qualities of wisdom. In *The Lord of the Rings*, J.R.R. Tolkein called his marvelous wizard Gandalf the Grey. More important, silver transforms a transparent pane of glass into a mirror. Coat the glass with silver, and suddenly we are able to shave, comb our hair, and glimpse what we really look like.

When God created the universe, the infinite Light began streaming down the Tree. The Crown functions as a clear window, permitting the Light to flow through it virtually unimpeded. But in order for the Light to transform into substantive material like rocks or machines, it must begin a process of consolidation.

The first stage in the transition from unlimited Light to finite objects requires a sense of separating one thing from the next. Wisdom, sphere number two, marks the first differentiation. It provides the concept of identity—the idea that I am I and different from you. The mirror allows us to perceive that distinction.

As you explore your identity in the exercises this week, your wish will assume a denser, more substantive identity as well. The identity provides direction and the activation of a more concrete path. For example, if you wish to start your own business, the identity initiated in Wisdom confers more specificity to your will. What kind of businessperson do you aspire to be? A real estate agent? An antiques-store owner? A jewelry designer? Each of these possibilities defines your identity more explicitly. By urging us to reflect on our identity, Wisdom also ensures that the fulfillment of our wish augments our sense of self. A man with three children who wishes to find a new career, for example, can use Wisdom's mirror to recognize that one of his most important identities is that of provider for his family. The new career and higher income potential will surely buttress this vital facet of his persona.

 WISH MAKER: This week the Tree teaches us to examine the many sides of our individual identities and demands that we mold our wishes so that they will enhance as many of these personal roles as possible. Be sure to work with the identity chart provided in the Exercise Zone at the end of this chapter.

The Wisdom of the Self

Wisdom resides on the right side of the Tree and in the right hemisphere of the brain—the lobe responsible for creativity, music, and spirituality. Epilepsy—a condition that reportedly afflicted Proust, Dostoyevsky, and the Catholic nun St. Teresa of Avila, who recorded all sorts of mystical visions—is precipitated by abnormal activity in certain precincts of the brain. A recent study of epilepsy patients at the Harvard Medical School exposed an amazing fact about human identity. In this experiment, scientists wired test subjects to equipment that measured the electrical activity in their temporal lobes. Then they showed each patient a photograph of himself and another of then President Bill Clinton. When only the left hemisphere functioned, without much activity on the right, these subjects could not distinguish photographs of themselves from that of the President. Their response to each photo: "Oh, I've seen that face a lot. That person is very famous." But when the right hemisphere fired normally, they immediately recognized their faces. This experiment divulged that our identity, our sense of self as distinct from all else, derives from the right hemisphere of the brain—from the seat of Wisdom.

Old Kabbalistic literature presaged this verification that the right brain governs our identity by nicknaming the sphere *Abba*, the Hebrew word for "father." We obtain our surnames from our fathers, our family identity. But our fathers also impart our gender identity. If the sperm contains a Y chromosome we are male; if it contains an X, we are born female. Our father—aka Abba, aka the sphere of Wisdom—encodes our identity in the core of our DNA.

Knowing who we are, then, is an act of Wisdom. And even as it works to forge distinct identities for each person and each wish,

Wisdom paradoxically assures us that deep down our true identity is the mirrored reflection of the pure light emanating from the
Crown. We are the mechanism that the Light—or God—uses to
see itself. The Tree of Life attests that God isn't up there, out
there, separate and distinct from us. The silver-lined mirror of
Wisdom guarantees that God lives in the essence of everything.
Attaining wisdom isn't so hard after all. The wise person appre-
hends merely this one simple thing: God is within us all.

In No Time

The Talmud, the oceanic canon of rabbinical debates and com-
mentaries on the Bible, avows that a wise person is someone who
knows the future. This testimony was not intended to glorify
prophets and crystal-ball gazers. Instead, it impresses upon us
the idea that a wise person—a person from the sphere of
Wisdom—recognizes no difference between the future, the present, and the past. She "knows the future" because the future is
the same as right now. Time does not exist in Wisdom. Everything is happening now. Everything. This concept is incredibly
difficult to grasp because our rational mind functions within the
limited world of time and space, two relentless phenomena that
were not invented until the next sphere on the Tree.

Still, the language we employ for certain human conditions
confirms the illusion of past and future. When someone appears
to glow with happiness, somehow lit by the awe of God, many
religious texts describe it with the phrase "the presence is upon
him." This description suggests that the energy of God—what
they called the Force in *Star Wars*—is with him or her. The phrase
the presence shares its root with "the present," the now. When the
Force is with us, we flow with the now. Albert Einstein's revolutionary theories suggested the same thing. Time is relative. Time

can change, warp, and even run backward. "The distinction between past, present and future is only an illusion, however persistent," the gray-haired scientist stated in 1955.

Carrying the logic of the illusion of time still further, there are no past lives and no next life. It doesn't matter that some amazing psychic declared that you were Ben Franklin or Marie Antoinette in a past life. Though Kabbalistic and Eastern religious doctrines affirm the idea of reincarnation, that psychic's contention is just not true. If you were Ben or Marie, then you *are* Ben or Marie right now. In the realm of Wisdom, all our various incarnations are ongoing at this very moment. The energy of Wisdom triggers glimpses of these other lifetimes in our creative right brain. Mystics and those skilled at meditation tap in to these parallel worlds for their remarkable insights. Some foresee the future because the future they prophesize is occurring as they speak it.

Every person retains the capacity to "grab" these messages. It is virtually impossible for anyone to go through her entire life—no matter how faithless or skeptical she might be—without experiencing intuition, déjà vu, or some potent dream. All of us store a higher, truly wise self stashed away inside—the self that in some incarnation is experiencing enlightenment this very second. In flashes and in dreams, our higher self transmits tips about who we are and what we should do. Wisdom rarely represents the kind of knowledge that we can find in libraries. Wisdom relies on intuition. In-tuition. Tuition means learning; in means in. Intuition: learning from within.

Synchronicities

Most vital this week, open yourself to intuition. Hunt for an insight that shines more Light on your wish. It's tricky. We cannot will the undifferentiated mind to provide on cue. We cannot stomp our foot and declare, "I need intuition now." But you can search for a wise person. Intuition might appear in the form of an old man or woman who happens to cross your path. It might arrive in a throwaway comment from your father. It might come from a line in a book. It could lie hidden in a shard of conversation overheard in line at the bank. It might strike during your meditation or hit you like a lightbulb in a comic strip while cleaning the oven. Many amazing discoveries burst forth in dreams. The Russian chemist Dmitri Mendeleyev received the Periodic Table of Elements complete in a dream in 1872. All he had to do was get up and write it down.

Mystics view synchronicities as junctions or crossroads in our lives. They claim that the more numerous the synchronicities, the nearer we move to a major transformation. Synchronicities function as signposts or clues that point us in the most auspicious direction. If, for example, the song "Just the Two of Us" plays on your car radio, and later that day a friend uses the phrase "it takes two to tango," and then someone else walks up and asks you out for "a couple of beers," pay attention. Life is probably attempting to direct you toward some kind of relationship.

Some Native Americans entrust the names of their children to synchronicity. If a deer runs through camp at the moment of birth, that infant is dubbed Running Deer. They contend that the same cosmic force that occasioned the mother to deliver at that moment also induced the deer to sprint past her tent. Astrology operates on the same principle. Each person's zodiacal configuration represents a serendipitous snapshot of the constellations at the instant of his or her birth. Since Wisdom marks the initial generator of synchronicities in the universe, Kabbalists have assigned not just one planet but all twelve signs of the zodiac to this sphere.

Synchronicities pop up to remind us that all things are interconnected. When we enter into the natural flow of universal energy, we experience happiness and find it easier to manifest our wishes and goals. For example, imagine that you are on the phone and you cannot decide whether the other person is sincere or seeking to exploit you. Try to examine the peripheral sounds that you register alongside that person's voice. If you can hear wind blowing through chimes or some pleasing music, then most likely that person possesses good intentions. If you hear angry shouting or the siren of a police car in the background, these extraneous noises might be warning you to be careful.

One Man's Wisdom

After twelve years of working with his left brain, studying by memory all the organs of the body and the diseases that preyed on them, an oncologist wished to develop a creative outlet. He always had loved music, but with his arduous schedule, he had little time to pursue this hobby, much less to shop for a piano. During the week of Wisdom, a gray-haired man arrived for a checkup, and the doctor announced that the man's skin cancer had disappeared. The grateful patient insisted that the doctor let him do something to repay him. The doctor demurred, saying that he was just doing his job. As the man was about to depart, the physician suddenly asked, "Hey, how's business?" At that moment, he didn't even know what kind of work his patient did. The elderly man answered that he had just finished composing the score for a film and he invited the doctor to drop by for a tour of his recording studio. The would-be musician was startled, but he doubted that he would ever have time to take advantage of this coincidence. Two days later, a couple of patients canceled their appointments, leaving him with a free afternoon. He jumped in his car and drove to visit the composer. And the older man, this fatherly messenger of Wisdom, offered the physician free music lessons and unlimited use of his piano.

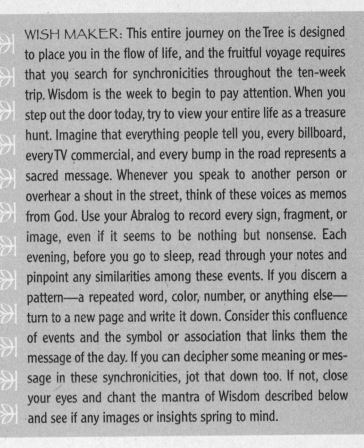

WISH MAKER: This entire journey on the Tree is designed to place you in the flow of life, and the fruitful voyage requires that you search for synchronicities throughout the ten-week trip. Wisdom is the week to begin to pay attention. When you step out the door today, try to view your entire life as a treasure hunt. Imagine that everything people tell you, every billboard, every TV commercial, and every bump in the road represents a sacred message. Whenever you speak to another person or overhear a shout in the street, think of these voices as memos from God. Use your Abralog to record every sign, fragment, or image, even if it seems to be nothing but nonsense. Each evening, before you go to sleep, read through your notes and pinpoint any similarities among these events. If you discern a pattern—a repeated word, color, number, or anything else— turn to a new page and write it down. Consider this confluence of events and the symbol or association that links them the message of the day. If you can decipher some meaning or message in these synchronicities, jot that down too. If not, close your eyes and chant the mantra of Wisdom described below and see if any images or insights spring to mind.

Word from the Wise

The Baal Shem Tov, the splendid Kabbalist and founder of the Hasidic movement, fingered his gray beard and leaped to his feet. "Let's go to Romania," he cried.

"Romania?" one of his students complained. "But, Rabbi, Romania is six days away."

"Oh, never mind that," said the Baal Shem Tov as he hustled them out the door. They hitched an old horse to the carriage and climbed inside. The hooves of the horse pounded out a steady rhythm on the dusty country road. The students dozed. Two hours later, they found themselves in Romania.

Green fields and orchards bloomed to the horizon. They gazed at a farmer's paradise, the air redolent of the Earth's illimitable fertility.

"The Garden of Eden," one student said.

"God is surely here," another agreed.

But the Baal Shem Tov wasn't smiling. He pointed to a lone brown patch marring the verdant vista. "Let's go to that field," the great teacher said.

In the middle of this wretched plot, they discovered a diligent farmer toiling away on his soil. Despite his backbreaking exertion, nothing grew. Not a plant. Not a tree. Not a weed. Laziness, the visitors concluded, was not the problem. The man slaved over his land like the righteous over their holy texts.

One by one, row by row, the farmer buried his seeds in the ground. After two days without a break, he'd finished his entire field. Then, stopping only for a sip of water, the farmer returned to the first row and dug out the first seed. The Baal Shem Tov watched as the man picked out each seed and meticulously cleaned it off before replanting it in the earth. Terrified that a little worm, invisible bacteria, or a bird might come along and damage the seed, the farmer sweated to ensure that every kernel remained unblemished.

The Baal Shem Tov was not much of a farmer, but he was a farmer of men. He approached the man bent over in the dirt. "You know, you've been working so hard and you look so tired. Let me care for your field, and you go inside and sleep for a while."

"Well, I could use a nap," the farmer said, removing his hat and rubbing an itch on the right side of his head. "But I have to attend to the seeds."

"Don't worry. I'll do it," said the Baal Shem Tov.

"But each seed has to be cleaned and . . ."

"Yes, yes," interrupted the rabbi. "I see. I promise."

He ushered the farmer to his shack and tucked him into bed. "Sleep well," said the Baal Shem Tov, but the exhausted man was already snoring. "Hey! Are you asleep?" the Baal Shem Tov screamed.

The farmer jumped up, startled. "What? Is everything okay with the seeds?"

"Yes, yes. Everything is fine. I was just checking to see if you were asleep."

"I'm asleep. I'm asleep," the farmer said. "Leave me alone and go to the field like you promised. Hurry."

The farmer deposited his head on the pillow. The Baal Shem Tov walked to the door. "Are you asleep now?" he yelled again. The farmer awoke again.

"Yes. Can't you see that I'm sleeping?"

"Okay," the Baal Shem Tov said. "I was just making sure that you were really asleep." The two men repeated this odd duet a few times more. Then the Baal Shem Tov climbed into his carriage and headed home, leaving both the farmer and the field alone and in peace.

Seven days later, the man awoke from his nap. He rushed outside in a panic to check on his seeds, but what he saw paralyzed him on the doorstep. His field was green. In every corner, wherever he turned, he found nothing but growth.

The Baal Shem Tov exemplifies the energy of Wisdom. He didn't bother to explicate the folly of the farmer's technique. He didn't bother to persuade with language or logic. Those abilities don't arrive until the third sphere, Understanding. Instead, the master sage employed pure wisdom. He addressed only the right, intuitive side of the farmer's brain. He didn't judge. He never criticized. He simply offered assistance through story, through example, through an insight the farmer had never expected.

The Baal Shem Tov

In Frank Herbert's science fiction classic *Dune*, he writes of a Messiah called Kwisatz Haderach, a name derived from a Hebrew phrase that means "the leap of the way." He was a person "whose organic mental powers would bridge space and time," Herbert wrote. The role of the Messiah, the very name of the Messiah, as Herbert told it, was to bring us true wisdom and shepherd us into a leap of consciousness beyond the illusion of space/time. The Baal Shem Tov is not the Messiah as we generally define it, but he is a messenger of this gravity-defying consciousness who thrives to this day.

He lived in Eastern Europe between 1698 and 1760—just at the cusp of the Age of Reason, the Democratic revolutions in the United States and France, and the nascent glimmer of the Age of Aquarius. And he created one of the most profound revolutions in Jewish history. His name translates to "the holder of the good name"—an honorarium similar to that of saint, which has been bestowed on just one or two others in the annals of Judaism. He was learned, but he was not the sort of rabbi who quoted scripture or what one astute rabbi said and how another, shrewder rabbi argued something else. That kind of left-brain scholarship emanates from the next sphere. The Baal Shem Tov instead cultivated the right hemisphere of the brain. He taught from Wisdom. He encouraged his followers—most of whom led difficult lives scraping out a meager subsistence with little time left over for book study—to conjoin with God through music, dance, and laughter. He urged them to find God not only in the words of the Bible or the rulings of the judges, but through the right hemisphere, through ecstasy, through the silver lining of Wisdom.

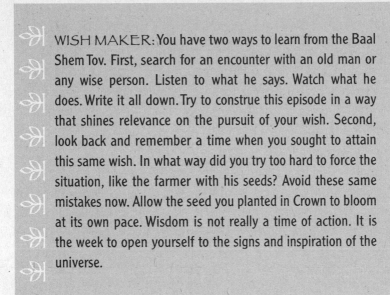

WISH MAKER: You have two ways to learn from the Baal Shem Tov. First, search for an encounter with an old man or any wise person. Listen to what he says. Watch what he does. Write it all down. Try to construe this episode in a way that shines relevance on the pursuit of your wish. Second, look back and remember a time when you sought to attain this same wish. In what way did you try too hard to force the situation, like the farmer with his seeds? Avoid these same mistakes now. Allow the seed you planted in Crown to bloom at its own pace. Wisdom is not really a time of action. It is the week to open yourself to the signs and inspiration of the universe.

The Redwood Tree

All the spheres from this point forward correspond to a particular type of tree. (The previous, translucent sphere known as Crown relates to the unseen seed of every tree.) If possible, locate and visit the tree of the week. Meditate near this tree to amplify the vibration of the sphere. If that particular species is not native to your area, it might be useful to search for a picture of the tree in books or on the Internet. Store this image in your brain. Try to envision it during your meditations. Buttress the power of this process by honoring the tangible icons that endow us all with the breath of life.

Wisdom lives in the redwood. The largest living creatures on the planet, these awesome beings stand taller than the Statue of Liberty. California's coastal redwoods have attained heights of 360 feet, while some giant sequoias measure nearly 40 feet in circumference. Highly resistant to fire, flood, insects, disease, and most every ravage of the material world, these arboreal wonders boast a life-span of more than three thousand years. Many of the same trees flourishing today were alive the day Buddha attained enlightenment. A few were around when Moses delivered the Ten Commandments from Sinai. Massive and virtually immortal, these trees, like Wisdom itself, seem to defy the conventional laws of time and space.

Native Americans called them the Ancient Ones and prayed to these giants to impart the timeless wisdom of the universe to young and old alike. The creation myth of the Talawa nation recounts that in the beginning there was nothing, and the Creator thought (a flash of Wisdom) the first redwood tree into existence. Beneath this tree at the center of the brand-new world, the Creator then placed all of the other plants and animals that have ever lived. "The Big Tree is nature's finest masterpiece, the greatest of all living things," wrote John Muir, the venerated California naturalist. "It belongs to an ancient stock and has a strange air of another day about it, a thoroughbred look inherited from a place [beyond our comprehension]."

The roots of each redwood often intertwine with those of its neighbors. Such fusing enables these trees to collectively withstand the fiercest storms and symbolically illustrates Wisdom's central axiom. The redwoods reveal that separation is an illusion—deep down everything is One. In addition, the cones of the redwood require the enormous heat of a fire—most often ignited by lightning—to crack open and release the seeds inside, echoing the precept that the lightninglike insights of Wisdom open up our paths to new growth and opportunities.

Name of God

Yod Hey Vav Hey, the mantra of Wisdom, is not an actual name of God, but the names of the Hebrew letters that spell the holiest of God's appellations. It's as if you were to chant Gee-Oh-Dee rather than the word *God* itself. This mantra acts as a spell. When you spell out any particular energy—in this case, a holy name—you connect to its underlying power.

The letters of this sacred moniker form three Hebrew words: *Haya*, or the past; *Hoveh*, the present; and *Yehiyeh*, what will be. All that was, is, and will be is condensed within this mantra, just as Wisdom embodies all of the past, present, and future.

In Gematria, a mystical science that assigns particular numbers to each of the twenty-two letters of the Hebrew alphabet, these four glyphs add up to 26, which in numerology reduces to 2 + 6, or 8, the symbol of infinity. (The word *God* in English also adds up to 26. G is the seventh letter in the English alphabet, O is the fifteenth, and D the fourth. 7 + 15 + 4 = 26.) In addition, the four letters of God's holy name represent the four elements of the material world—fire, water, air, and earth—and the four-letter chemical sequence—adenine (A), thymine (T), guanine (G), and cytosine (C)—that constitutes the fundamental building blocks of our DNA. Again we find God encoded in our core.

WISH MAKER: Chant this mantra any time you wish to invoke intuition or are faced with indecision.

Meditation

Sit down and relax. Breathe deeply and slowly and let the sounds of the outside world dissolve into your breath. Try to find a zoneless zone within which you are the only thing that exists. Now imagine a dimensionless point hovering just a few feet in front of you. Watch as it begins to expand. Inflate that point with each breath. Notice how it becomes gray and grows to the size of a balloon; and very quickly it enlarges and swells until it engulfs you completely.

Now find yourself sitting in the middle of this giant gray sphere filled with gray fog. Now and then, you might see flashes of lightning crackling within the sphere. You feel completely at home and comfortable here. Breathe this gray foggy substance into your lungs. Imagine how your cells absorb it; how each round cell in your body has been transformed into a gray sphere with you meditating in the nucleus, within the sacred place of the DNA. Now focus on the right hemisphere of your brain. Imagine yourself massaging and soothing the neurons of your intuitive mind.

When you are totally relaxed, try to envision a huge mirror settling itself in front of you. That mirror reflects your image. You can almost see a bright halo hovering above your head. In this moment you are a saint; in this place you are a sage. Now watch as the face in the mirror shifts and transfigures. Watch it mature until your image transforms into the visage of what you consider a wise person. Your facial features remain your own. But the person you see is very wise. It is the image of your higher self. Stare at this reflection and commune with this wise person inside you. Look the image straight in the eyes—these old wise eyes that have seen all that you have seen in your life as well as all that your soul has witnessed in other incarnations. Relish this picture of how you will look just before you attain enlightenment and unimaginable bliss.

Now it is time to begin a conversation with the wise one. Use telepathy. Listen for a message emanating from your right hemisphere, echoing like music in your brain. Tell the wise soul your wish. Ask for guidance in the fulfillment of that wish.

Register any reply, any flash, any insight, and then chant the name of God for the sphere of Wisdom. Chant slowly—*Yod Hey Vav Hey*. Breathe in and chant the mantra again and again and again. In a duet with the wise reflection before you, chant this mantra as many times as you wish.

When you finish chanting, inhale deeply and hold the air inside for as long as you can. Continue to gaze at the image of the wise soul in the mirror. Notice how the reflection changes as you focus on the mantra echoing inside you. Exhale and then breathe in again and hold it for as long as possible. Exhale and then breathe in and hold the air inside one last time. Now bid goodbye to the wise soul in the mirror. Allow the mirror to disappear as the gray sphere around you begins to shrink back into the original dimensionless point. Remain still for a few seconds more. Then move your hands and head, gently open your eyes, and return to your life.

Wish List—Wisdom

1. Open yourself to intuition and coincidences. Use your journal to record every stray or surprising thought, insight, or feeling. Your will of the previous week symbolizes the idea of where you want to go. The insights of Wisdom function as a chariot that transports you there.

2. Explore your personal identity and make sure that your wish will enhance it. (See exercise 1 below.)

☞ 3. Hunt for synchronicities or encounters with the symbols of Wisdom: gray, silver, father, old men, lightning, wizards, infinity, the number two, and issues of identity.

☞ 4. Wish progress: In Crown you planted the seed of your wish in the astral plane. In the subsequent weeks, you will fertilize, water, and nurture this seed so that it bears fruit in the here and now. In Wisdom you have welcomed the two greatest tools of the spiritual gardener: intuition and synchronicity. If any of your experiences this week cue the need to tweak, adjust, or add specificity to your wish, it would be wise to do so. By the end of this week, your wish should be finalized, defined, and left to germinate peacefully in the soil.

Exercise Zone

☞ 1. **Polishing Your Identity:** This exercise connects your wish (the will of Crown) to the identity imparted by Wisdom. Step one of this process requires you to catalog all of the various roles that you play from day to day. If you held up a mirror to your entire life, what would you see? Mother, friend, accountant, stamp collector, student of karate, gourmet chef, big talker about the latest news, etc. List at least ten distinct identities that describe your life. As an example, let's look at a thirty-eight-year-old married woman and mother of two. She works as a curator in a museum and loves to paint landscapes. She grows her own organic vegetables

and practices yoga three times a week. She wished
to find a larger house. Her identity chart might look
like this:

I am:

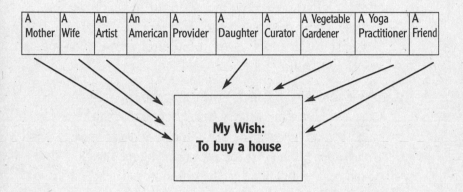

A Mother	A Wife	An Artist	An American	A Provider	A Daughter	A Curator	A Vegetable Gardener	A Yoga Practitioner	A Friend

My Wish:
To buy a house

Draw arrows to connect all the identities that your
wish will enhance. For this woman, a larger and
more harmonious living space would bolster her
identity as a mother and a wife. She would have
more room to paint, to practice yoga and meditation, and to grow vegetables in her garden. She also
would feel more comfortable entertaining and
cooking for her friends and her parents. The majority of her identities would profit from her wish. She
is definitely on the right track.

Your chart should reveal that at least five facets of
your identity would benefit if your wish came true.
If not, you have two options. The first is to reexamine your list of identities. Dig deeper. What are you
neglecting? Meditate and search for alternate identities that describe you. Perhaps these less-obvious

reflections of your character are calling out for recognition. Maybe these identities are driving your need for your wish.

The second option is to change your wish. Study your list of identities. Is this you? Really you? If so, return to the questions in Chapter 1. Ask yourself again: What do I—the me depicted in the boxes above—need most in my life? Test your new answer against the identity chart. Mold and prune your wish until it fits.

☞ 2. **Wisdom on the Page:** Synchronicities and wisdom can come from anywhere. Choose a book that you love and admire. It could be the Bible, a Shakespearean play, a Dr. Seuss story, or any other volume that you hold dear. Think of a specific question—avoid those that can be answered yes or no—and repeat it aloud a few times. Close your eyes and imagine yourself surrounded by the gray energy of Wisdom. With your eyes closed, thumb through the pages of the book. When it feels right, stop and point your finger at the page. Read the sentence under your finger and find the answer to your question. It might require some interpretation, but this technique will, with practice, afford insight to the issue at hand.

CHAPTER THREE

UNDERSTANDING:

The Energy of Time, Space, Discipline, and the Great Mother

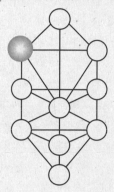

S P H E R E 3

KEYWORDS: Discipline; Time and Space

WISH IMPERATIVE: Here the Tree inculcates the importance of discipline and persistence in achieving any wish. Adopting some sort of personal discipline—swearing off caffeine or pledging to meditate for at least fifteen minutes every day—will invigorate your powers of manifestation.

HEBREW NAME OF SPHERE: Binah

MYTH AND PERSONALITIES: The myth of the Great Mother

PLANET: Saturn

DARK SIDE: Fear

COLOR: Dark indigo

NUMBER: 3

TREE: Beech

BODY PART: Left brain

HEBREW NAME OF GOD (MANTRA): Elohim (the materializing feminine aspect of God)

The Material Plane

With the sphere of Understanding, we travel for the first time to the left or restrictive side of the Tree. While the undifferentiated mind of Wisdom operates without words, separation, or categories, the left hemisphere of Understanding introduces definitions and sharp lines. The inexorable principles that guide the universe as we perceive it originated in Understanding. Time and space were born in this sphere. Pain, vexation, and dread arrived here too. On the heels of the ethereal bliss of Crown and Wisdom, Understanding can seem harsh, even cruel. But it is undeniably blessed. This complex sphere generates the highest force of creative, materializing energy in the cosmos. It gives substance to the Crown's will and Wisdom's flashes of thought. Understanding marks the first tangible step in the Tree's mission to convert the infinite Light into solid material—wishes into reality. Like the dark, constricting birth canal, it is the conduit that engenders all the stuff that we know and desire.

Understanding functions like a consolidation machine. Place anything inside and through time and pressure this sphere will transmute it into new matter. It supplies the force that squeezes a worthless lump of coal into a priceless diamond. Language— one of the magnificent tools of Understanding—also works through restriction. It compresses the plentiful thoughts that race through your mind into the single idea that you write on the page or speak aloud to your friend. Understanding triggers the process of crystallizing the substanceless thoughts of Wisdom by introducing the concrete building blocks of words and sentences.

God did not create the actual universe with a thought. Genesis reports that God *said* "Let there be light." "In the beginning was the word" (John 1:1), the New Testament concurs. The One created with the word, by differentiating one corporeal thing from another in time and space. This separation from others and from God cloaks us in hardships, but it also grants us the room and the raw materials that we need to assemble the creation and to actualize our wishes.

The left hemisphere of the brain edifies through pressure from the outside world. It requires language, teachers, books, logic, learning, and perhaps rote memorization to comprehend that one plus one equals two and that three times three equals nine. It is often a slow and arduous process, one step after another. This type of exertion promises success, but with a few conditions. Understanding demands persistence, practice, and patience. Along the path toward the materialization of your wish, you will inevitably encounter obstructions. It will take effort to surmount them. And it will take time.

WISH MAKER: Tap the material world of time and space for information that will facilitate the pursuit of your wish. Exploit the logical left brain of Understanding by reading books, searching the Internet, and interviewing experts and knowledgeable friends. For example, a pregnant woman wished to experience an easy, natural birth. This week demanded that she learn everything possible from books, pamphlets, videos, and consultations with people experienced in this field.

Time: What Is It Good For?

Tests in school often require students to answer a certain number of questions in a set amount of time. We always call on time to quantify knowledge, to gauge how much we really Understand. We count on time and space to register our progress. I ran five miles today, while last week I could run only three. We scale time by space and space by time. Fifty miles per hour, 186,000 miles per second.

Time illuminates the catalysts of our triumphs and failings. Beset by persistent colds and stomach ailments, a Russian immigrant in Los Angeles resolved to take up yoga. "Since I've been practicing yoga these last two years," she reported, "I haven't been sick." Time presented a yardstick to calibrate her growth. She counterposed her two healthy years against the previous sickly period and found yoga to be the beneficial variable. And so she kept at it.

But time and space also spawn just about every woe we know: missed appointments, traffic jams, lost sleep, gray hair, Alzheimer's, great warriors turned to doddering wrecks. Your best friend lives three thousand miles away in Boston and you're stuck in San Francisco. Telephones, the Internet, and supersonic jets have managed to contract time and space, but you still can't click your heels and see her on a whim. Time is a menace. Space is a nuisance. So why did God need them at all? Why introduce them so high up the Tree, ensuring that they infect everything else that follows below?

The simple answer is that God knew what He was doing. None of the energies we cherish—neither compassion nor love, justice, relationship, communication, success, even sex—can exist without time and space.

Time is not the enemy that youth-obsessed Western culture often makes it out to be. It is not just the pesky irritant making us late for that vital meeting. It is not solely that invincible ogre making us old, achy, and wrinkled. It is in fact the most potent tool in our possession for constructing everything that we treasure most. Without the separation between one piece of matter and another, between one person and another, we could not love, we could not forgive, we could not make art or money, we could not dance, we could not speak, we could not touch, we could not improve. Time and space bequeath the canvas upon which we create our lives.

We depend on time and space to separate one fragment of the original creation from another so that they might interact with each other. And then we require time to heal the pain inherent in that separation. "Time heals" just might be the oldest cliché and the sweetest melody to underscore any plight. Time knits a shattered bone, mends a broken heart, and eventually soothes the sting of death. Without time, even petty disputes among friends would remain forever acrimonious and disruptive, when in truth we all know that these battles often disappear without a trace in just a few days.

Time grants us the chance to understand others even after they have hurt us. It provides the opportunity to grow. You can stick a billion seeds in the soil, but without space for the roots and without the march of time, not a single flower will blossom. We all commenced this lifetime as two microscopic cells that could do nothing on their own, and we ended up here at this moment with countless cells that can accomplish any number of remarkable feats—from brushing our teeth to kissing our beloved to painting the Sistine Chapel. Why? Simply because time passed. And we were persistent.

Man's Best Friend: A Dog Named Discipline

Time pressures us relentlessly. Deadlines provoke stress, but they generally prod us to spectacular achievements. In 1961, President John F. Kennedy announced a seemingly preposterous idea and an even more outlandish deadline. The United States, he promised, would land a man on the moon by the end of the decade. At the time, it sounded impossible—as huge a pipe dream as a woman president. (Perhaps someone ought to set a date for that too.) But the anxiety to outdo the Soviets and the pressure of the deadline propelled NASA to achieve this near miracle on July 20, 1969. Without Kennedy's arbitrary deadline, there's no telling when anyone would have managed to plant a flag on the moon.

Still, deadlines are not enough. Deadlines mean nothing without discipline. Kennedy's moon wish was fulfilled only because thousands of scientists toiled tirelessly to meet it. Discipline is onerous. It requires tackling something you'd prefer to ignore day after day after day. But discipline is the primary gift of Understanding. If you want to make a wish come true, seize discipline by the tail and don't let go.

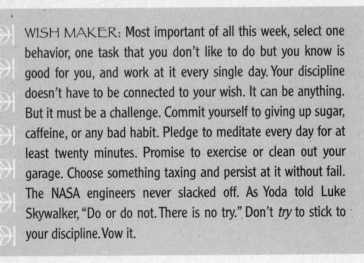

WISH MAKER: Most important of all this week, select one behavior, one task that you don't like to do but you know is good for you, and work at it every single day. Your discipline doesn't have to be connected to your wish. It can be anything. But it must be a challenge. Commit yourself to giving up sugar, caffeine, or any bad habit. Pledge to meditate every day for at least twenty minutes. Promise to exercise or clean out your garage. Choose something taxing and persist at it without fail. The NASA engineers never slacked off. As Yoda told Luke Skywalker, "Do or do not. There is no try." Don't *try* to stick to your discipline. Vow it.

The Great Mother

While Wisdom stands as the father or *Abba* in Hebrew, Kabbalists consider Understanding *Ema*, Hebrew for "mother," because of the sphere's capacity to give birth to matter. Dozens of cultures employ a form of the name *Ema* to summon the mother. In Arabic we say *Ime*, while in Farsi we call *Madar*. The Russians cry *Mat*, and the French, Italians, and Latin Americans all coo *Mama*. In

Egyptian mythology, the goddess *Ma'at* determined whether a dead person should reincarnate on Earth or pass on to a permanent reunion with the One. Ma resounds as the Great Mother energy—the giver of life. In Hebrew, Ma stands for water, and science affirms that life on this planet first incubated in shallow pools. Ye*ma*ya, the Great Mother of the Yoruba religions of Africa and the West Indies, is the goddess of the ocean.

The Gypsies worship Sarah-*ma*, and Sarah, the wife of Abraham, is the grand matriarch in the Old Testament. Hindus often refer to Kali, their supreme goddess, as Kali-*ma*. Kali translates as "the black one"—Kali-ma means "black mother"—again evoking Understanding, the darkest-hued sphere in the Tree of Life. The Sanskrit definition of *Ma* reads "to measure, to form, to construct, to create, and to display." All of these verbs describe the scaling of time and space and the forces of crystallization native to this sphere. *Ma*ya (from the root Ma) is the mother of Buddha. *Ma*ia gave birth to Hermes, the source of all hermetic science. And *Ma*ria is the great mother of Christ. Some Christian writings, including those of Origen (185–254 A.D.), regard *Ma*ry *Ma*gdalene as the great mother or the reincarnation of the great mother. She was the first to observe Christ after the Resurrection, the person who materialized the notion of his godly consciousness.

WISH MAKER: Your mother (or mother figure) represents the ambassador of Understanding in your life. This week, honor the great goddess by phoning to express your gratitude for everything that she has done for you. Perhaps you could share your wish with your mother and make note of her response. If your mother has passed away, build an altar with her picture, candles, flowers, and any meaningful talismans. Then sit before this shrine and reminisce about your happy experiences at her side.

Scary Mama Mia

Her skin speckled with blood, hair crowned with skulls, her face
the menacing mask of a monster, Palden Lhamo is the ugliest creature in the cosmos. Her image, which was plastered on the walls of
homes and temples, accosted early Western visitors to Tibet and
frightened them into christening her "the great She-devil."

It wasn't always this way. Her name means "glorious goddess," and in the beginning she was the most beautiful woman in
the world. Every man and every god begged her to be his queen.
She chose the most esteemed king, who ruled a noble and prosperous land in southern India. And she delivered him two sons.

But nothing comes easy in the restrictive realm of Understanding. Once each year, to ensure the continuance of the wealth
and serenity of his empire, Palden Lhamo's perfect king sacrificed a perfect child. "If it wards off the diseases, wars, and
poverty we observe in so many other lands," the king said, "well,
one child fewer. It's worth it."

One ceremonial afternoon, Palden Lhamo snapped. "You must
cease this shameful ritual," she admonished her husband. "I am a
mother and I know how a mother would feel to lose her baby."

"Don't tell me how to rule my kingdom," the king replied.
"This tradition has served you well."

"It must stop. Now. Or you will lose me forever."

The king waved the sacrificial procession forward. The beau-
teous queen snatched one of her own sons and substituted him
for the unfortunate tot upon the altar.

"Are you crazy?" the king said. "This is my own precious
child." He shouldered his wife aside and slaughtered the
appointed innocent.

"Everyone you kill is someone's precious child," Palden
Lhamo said, her indigo eyes hardening as she spoke. "Beside each
that you murder keens a mother who will weep forever."

A year of prosperity ensued, and the moment of sacrifice arrived once more. Palden Lhamo again placed her own son before the executioner's blade, but the king intervened and dispatched another child to his doom.

A third year dawned and Palden Lhamo again failed to dissuade her king. Desperation steamrollered sanity. She lunged for her firstborn and bit his head clean off. Then she whirled and gutted her second boy from chin to navel and ate his insides.

Flayed by grief, the king proscribed ritual sacrifice forever. But Palden Lhamo could no longer love the man who had sentenced her to kill her babies. She fled the perfect kingdom with the skin of one child as her saddle and the corpse of the other as her shawl.

Her beauty traveled with her, however, and men and gods yet pleaded for her hand. Eventually, the king of the demons whisked her off to his abominable world of cannibalism and cruelty. Palden Lhamo languished for years in this hellish domain, but one night she stole the demon's impregnable sword and his sack of diseases, fought off his sulfurous hordes, and ran screaming back to Earth.

She made her home on a cremation ground, and she resolved that her beauty would never again drive her to ruin. She destroyed it. Her clothes turned to rags, her skin black as the ash that served as her bed. She grew her nails long and sharp as daggers and her hair into a wild monstrous mat. She ate almost nothing, transforming the soft curves of her body into angry sinews. Palden Lhamo settled into this plot of the dead and caressed her fury. But the sickening betrayal of family life crushed her rage to despair. "If there is anyone out there, God or human, who can give me any reason to live," she wailed to the sky, "if anyone can offer me even an ounce of comfort, come now, because I am killing myself."

The Buddha of Compassion, the lord of the next sphere, called Mercy, appeared at her side. "I have a mission for you, beautiful one," the Buddha said. "You have met and vanquished all the demons. You can subdue any menace with your flaming sword and your sack of ills. You know every dirty trick in the book. You have no fear. You will be the shield of all those who follow the path of compassion."

"You trust me to protect these children of the Light? After all I've done?"

"Who else but you?" the Buddha said.

With the Buddha's blessing, in all her grotesquerie, Palden Lhamo finally grew into her given name, "glorious goddess." This long-suffering archetype of motherhood protects us all—her visage so fiendish that even fear is afraid. Doubt, obstruction, and disease flee her in terror. And that is why the Western visitors encountered her alarming image happily on display all over Tibet. And that is why her picture was one of the handful of items the Dalai Lama carried away with him when he escaped the Chinese occupation of his homeland in 1959.

WISH MAKER: Fear is afraid of one thing: not being able to scare. Free-associate on fear in your journal until you hit upon the root terror that has prevented you from fulfilling your wish before now. Most likely, this fear originates in self-doubt. If you wished for a relationship, for example, you probably will find that deep down you're afraid that you are unlovable. One struggling architect wished for greater success in his work, but he was plagued by the trepidation that no one would like his designs. The myth of Palden Lhamo taught him to scare away this dread simply by appreciating his designs himself. His apprehension that others would rebuff his work was a reflection of his own rejection of his talent. Once he decided to love his work no matter what, then at least one person (the architect

himself) would be on the record as believing in his designs, thereby disproving his fear that no one would ever like his work. With this new sense of confidence, he soon found that others responded to his ideas with renewed admiration. This basic technique sounds like a cognitive-therapy mind trick. And in a way it is. But this myth has endured for nearly two thousand years primarily because defanging fears by refusing to give in to · them works.

Saturn

This imposing, dazzling planet of hard lessons and responsibility rules Understanding. Chronos, the Greek version of Saturn, was the god of time. A "chronic" disease, for example, describes an ailment that only heals with time. The planet Saturn takes an especially long time—nearly thirty years—to orbit the Sun, reiterating the lesson of patience inherent in Understanding.

When we contemplate Saturn, we marvel at its rings. These rings symbolize a leash encircling us, constraining us to face up to our mission of hard work and discipline. In astrology, Saturn is often regarded as the malevolent planet, stifling us, tripping us up with setbacks and frustrations.

But anyone who has ever viewed Saturn through a telescope appreciates that these rings are also breathtakingly beautiful. The same is true of Understanding. The pressure of the sphere creates a new structure. Without this crystallizing energy, no thought or dream would ever become substance. Change would never occur. Saturn compels us to confront our problems. It illuminates them like a bright yellow highlighter in the textbook of our life so that we might identify and understand our demons and then conquer them. The Chinese name for this planet reveals

this function quite literally. They call it *Chen Hsing*, which translates as "the exorcist"—in other words, that which helps to expel
our inner demons and our fears.

Out of Darkness Comes the Light

The color of Understanding is dark indigo. This dark shade operates as a metaphor for the fear and aggravation the sphere
unleashes. But the darkness of Understanding is utterly holy.
While Crown and Wisdom transcend the strictures of time and
space, Understanding represents the loftiest source of life energy
available to us in our world of material things, For instance,
Saturday, the Jewish Sabbath, derives from the word *Saturn*. It
ushers in the time when we all can connect most easily to God.
Tradition expounds that we amplify that bond through discipline.
Orthodox Jews adopt all kinds of restrictions—they don't cook,
drive, or use electricity—on the Sabbath. The discipline facilitates
their ascent to this celestial sphere. Other cultures often employ a
vision quest that demands a long fast—yet another restriction
designed to boost us nearer to the One. The Fakirs reclined on a
bed of nails and the Christian monks of the Middle Ages engaged
in self-flagellation to accomplish the same thing.

Native Americans rely on a sweat lodge called Temascal to tap
the power of Understanding. This ritual, which aims to erase constricting memories and patterns (both attributable to time),
occurs in a dark rounded hutch that evokes the womb of the Great
Mother of Understanding. Water is poured over hot rocks—which
symbolize the seeds of the Great Father of Wisdom—suffusing the
room with stifling heat. The participants embrace this oppression
because they believe that the steam washes away the deep-rooted
patterns that block spiritual growth and happiness. Once these
obstacles are released in the darkness, the individuals emerge into

the light cleansed and liberated. At the end of adversity, there follows always, in all these painful rites, a meeting with God. "At the bottom of the abyss comes a voice of salvation," said Joseph Campbell, the scholar of myth. "The black moment is the moment when the real message of transformation [will be found]. In the darkest hour comes the light."

Indigo is also associated with the third-eye chakra—the tantric energy source that blends Wisdom and Understanding. The third eye enables us to visualize images as a way to understand exactly what we want to materialize in the here and now.

 WISH MAKER: It is always darkest before the dawn. Hunt for the color indigo—which is near black or the darkest blue. Whenever you encounter this color, you are also likely to find some understanding about your wish, your fears, or a discipline that you ought to pursue.

The Abyss

This week you will be asked to reject your apprehension and qualms and bound across the Abyss. Understanding and the next sphere, called Mercy, are the only two stations in the journey on the Tree that are not linked by a clearly navigable path. To travel from Understanding to Mercy necessitates a jump over the Abyss, a blind leap of faith across your paramount fear.

Many processes succumb to a premature end in the Abyss. The fear triumphs. One woman, for example, had nearly completed a charming movie script. But the pressure of well-meaning skeptics who warned about the daunting odds of selling a screenplay discouraged her. The mountain ahead began to loom too tall.

Self-doubt seized her. She froze up. She quit writing. And her Hollywood dream died.

But another man deliberately confronted his terror this week. All his adult life he had suffered from acute claustrophobia. He was especially mortified of elevators. He avoided high-rises like he shunned raw meat, and as a result his career in finance suffered. In the past, he had declined interviews for advancement if a company's offices were situated on a high floor. During the week of Understanding, this man decided to jump into the Abyss. He chose the tallest building in town and compelled himself to ride the elevator up and down until he could stand inside without hyperventilating. Elevators still spook him. But verifying that he could survive his biggest phobia opened the door (literally) to loftier job prospects.

Three

The number three is one of the most sacred numbers in spirituality. Earth itself, the sphere of life in our solar system, is of course the third planet from the Sun. And the concept of the trinity symbolizes the hallowed manifestation of divinity in Christianity (Father, Son, and Holy Spirit), ancient Egypt (Osiris, Isis, and Horus), and Buddhism—the Tri-ratna or the three precious jewels called Buddha, Dharma, and Sangha (enlightenment, duty, and the temple). Karl Marx, the father of Communism, who in a sense devised a religion without a god, preached that life flowed among three forces: thesis, antithesis, and synthesis. The three columns of the Tree of Life also echo this eternal ideal.

The material world of time (past, present, and future) and *three*-dimensional space (height, width, and depth) provides the fundamental structure of the universe and every new wish. In nature, farmers live by the cycle of plant, harvest, and dormancy, while animals survive on the instincts of flee, fight, and fortify. Computers operate on the basis of input, output, throughput. Even traffic lights, which bring structure to our transportation system, employ a trio of colors. Authors have paid tribute to the materializing power of three in countless stories: Macbeth's three witches, the three little pigs, the three bears, Charlie's (three) Angels, the Three Musketeers, the three wishes of the genie, and the three magi who journeyed to behold the baby Jesus. Greek mythology reflects Understanding's invention of time in the character of Cerberus, the three-headed hellhound that guards the gates to the Underworld. The monster's three faces invoke the three stages of time: one looks to the past, another to the present, and the third points to the future.

The three Fates of the Romans—the daughters of Necessity, the greatest mother of them all—also personify the principles of Understanding. The first Fate supplies the string of life, the second measures it, and the third cuts it. The realities of space and time supplied by the three Fates demarcate the *matrix*—from the Latin root for "source" and "mother"—of our life; the womb of the great *matri*arch from which all creations emerge. The number three itself epitomizes the fear inherent in a temporal and therefore mortal universe. Both Christ and Buddha surmounted the pressures of three temptations before the dawning of their enlightenment.

Why is three important to you? The classical concept of the trinity tells the story of beginning, middle, and end. In Crown we activated the force of creation by conceptualizing our wish and planting the seed. Wisdom delivered the sustaining energies of synchronicity and intuition—the powers that weave the fabric of life. Here in Understanding we nourish the materializing force that brings solid definition to the original creation. Hindu mythology extols the energy of the triad in the form of the gods Brahma (the creator), Vishnu (the sustainer), and Shiva (commonly referred to as the destroyer). In one sense, the name "Shiva the destroyer" simply implies an end to the creative process as a result of the definitive manifestation of the original will. But the real name of this god appends another nuance to the power of the three. Shiva's full name is "the destroyer of obstacles." In other words, Understanding—the third force of the trinity—materializes any notion or wish by obliterating the obstacles we are bound to bump into on the road to fulfillment. Shiva is considered the god of yoga, which commands us to contort our bodies in disciplined poses that aim to destroy our limitations and give birth to an expanded consciousness.

WISH MAKER: Draft the power of Shiva to vanquish the blocks and snags that have impeded the fulfillment of your wish in the past. Anytime you encounter the number three, examine the occasion for clues that will aid the identification of obstacles or offer keys to surmount them.

The Beech Tree

Often called the Mother of the Woods, the beech's thick canopy of leaves provides abundant shade as well as nuts that can be ingested straight from the branch. In times of famine, humans often ate beechnuts to survive. Beech trees do not begin to produce a full crop of their nutritious fruit until they've lived for fifty years, a nod to time and patience engendered by Understanding.

European cultures revered the beech as an ark of ancient knowledge and truth. The wood from the tree serves as a fabulous writing surface, and slices of the beech were used to fashion the pages of the world's first actual book. (Understanding invented language.) The Anglo-Saxon word for this tree, *boc*, contains the root of the word *book*. The ultrasmooth bark of the tree has long spurred lovers to create a tangible expression of their devotion by carving initials into the living wood. Legends claim that beech wood itself is enchanted. Believers would write a wish on a piece of bark from the tree and bury it in the ground. As the earth reclaimed the wood, the written wish would come true.

WISH MAKER: Resurrect this ancient ritual. Write your wish on a piece of paper that derived from a tree and plant it in the earth.

Name of God

Elohim, the feminine reflection of God, serves as the mantra for Understanding. In the biblical story of creation, it is Elohim who said, "Let there be Light," etc. This name appears thirty-two times in the Creation saga, which corresponds to the Kabbalah's thirty-two paths of wisdom—the ten spheres of the Tree and the twenty-two connections between them. Ancient texts explain that God created Elohim, and Elohim then gave birth to everything else.

Elohim, the equivalent of the Holy Ghost in the Christian trinity, stands for the maternal life-giving energy of God that crystallizes thoughts. A father harbors the capacity to think that he wants a child, but only the mother can actually produce that baby. Elohim transforms thoughts into words. In Genesis, anything Elohim said immediately manifested on Earth.

WISH MAKER: This mantra works like a spell. Chant it any time you want to overcome fear, enhance discipline and focus, or materialize a new project.

Meditation

Sit with your spine as straight as possible. Breathe deeply and relax. Focus on the crown of your head. Imagine a white sphere of transparent light radiating just above you. This is the Crown sphere—your connection to the divine. Allow this ball of absolute light to massage your brain, cool your neurons, and create a sensation of bliss and tranquility. Now imagine that a ray of light shoots from the Crown to your right hemisphere, to the gray sphere of Wisdom. Imagine the gray light covering the right half of your brain, relaxing you further. Now picture another ray of light running from your right hemisphere into your left. There, in your sphere of Understanding, it transforms into a dark indigo ball of light. Wear these three spheres of colored light like a pyramidal hat. This is your holy trinity.

Now place yourself on top of your favorite mountain. Some of the peaks that surround you might be covered with snow. You might see goats scampering off in the distance. Walk and enjoy this beautiful scene. Breathe the crisp, pristine air. Soon you chance upon a cave. Enter the cave and find a path lined with indigo candles. You hear your name spoken from the bosom of the mountain. Head toward the voice—follow the call. As you descend, you feel safe and calm. You seem to be journeying back into a familiar womb—the womb of the Great Mother.

When you reach the bottom of the trail, you find yourself in a gorgeous chamber aglow with the light of many torches. In the middle of the room, you see the Great Mother. Envision the glori-ous goddess appearing before you. She is kind, graceful, adoring, and enchanted. She reaches out with her right hand and touches the left side of your head, charging you with energy and love. Stay a moment to commune and meditate with her. Tell her your wish. Communicate to the Great Mother exactly what you need. If you like, if you feel brave, speak of your doubts too. Give her your biggest fears. Feel her hand on your left hemisphere. Let the Great Mother nourish you. Allow her to chase all your demons away.

Chant the mantra of Understanding: *Elohim* (El-low-heem). Breathe in and intone *Elohim* again. Repeat this mantra for as long as you like.

When you finish chanting, sit quietly and sense how the chamber and its tunnels echo your song. Listen to the chant rever-berating within your body—within your inner caves and tunnels.

Now it's time to return. Say farewell to the Great Mother and start your ascent to the entrance of the cave. As you walk, notice that the walls of the tunnel fill up with drawings and images. These pictures reveal your wish already fulfilled. Gaze at them. Witness your wish come true.

When you exit the cave into the open air of the mountain, gaze down at the valley below and imagine it to be your Promised Land. Down there, your wish is reality. Now take a deep breath and fold the two lower spheres on your right and left hemi-spheres back into the white light of the Crown. Leave this crown of light there with you always. And when you are ready, gently come back to your room and open your eyes.

Wish List—Understanding

☞ 1.   Practice your discipline. Write it in your journal to certify your unwavering commitment to this task.

☞ 2. Use the power of this sphere to understand and scare away your fears (see exercise 2, below).

☞ 3. Stay attuned for synchronicities. Seek clues and messages in your meetings with the symbols of Understanding: three, triangle, Mother, dark indigo, Saturn, obstacles, teachers, clocks and schedules, the past, measurements, pressure, ravines, dark holes, and cliffs. Keep a record of these synchronous encounters in your journal and study them for hidden messages that disclose some sort of understanding of your wish or the steps you should take to fulfill it.

☞ 4. Wish progress: By the end of this week you should have created a rough plan and timeline for achieving your goal. Aim too for a more solid understanding— through reading, research, consultations with experts, etc.—of what will be required to attain your wish (see exercise 1, below).

Exercise Zone

☞ 1. **Crystallize Your Wish:** Write three short paragraphs outlining the details of what your wish and your life will look like when you arrive at your goal. Aim for specifics. Let your mind fly and catalog every happy particular of a perfect, wish-fulfilled existence. List all the benefits—both material and psychological—that you will reap when your dream becomes reality.

Once you see the scope of your wish in concrete terms, try to work up a budget for your wish. How much time will I need to make it happen? What sort of work will I have to do each day? Whom do I need to talk to? Which experts, books, or institutions should I consult? How much money, if any, should I invest in the effort? Will I need to travel to further the evolution of my wish? Writing and language were invented in this sphere. Use these gifts to create a solid plan of action. Then take steps to implement it. If you wish to lose weight, figure out how many pounds per week you plan to shed and how much exercise per day you will devote to the fulfillment of your goal. One man wished to get in shape after a stint in the hospital. He decided that he would drop thirty pounds over the course of four months by dedicating at least a half hour every day to walking, running, or working out at the gym. Don't feel bound by the ten-week time frame of the Tree. Wishes, like individual trees in the forest, often bloom at varying speeds.

2. **Scare Your Fears Away:** Make an inventory of all the obstacles that have prevented you from attaining your wish before today. For example, one woman who wished to create an enduring romantic relationship listed all the barriers that had thwarted her in the past. She was too shy; she jumped at the first man who showed any interest in her; she was attracted to aggressive and sometimes abusive men to compensate for her own fear of asserting herself; she was afraid that she was unlovable. List as many impediments as possible. Then analyze the list and determine which of these hindrances are related to a fear of success—in other words, your self-sabotaging thoughts or behaviors—and which are tied to fear of failure (low self-esteem). Now harvest the

obstacle-crushing energy of Understanding to slay them. The first step requires that you identify the fear and admit that it exists. We dread the unknown most of all, and simply acknowledging and accepting our fears marks a major leap toward stripping their hold on us. Remember that fear is afraid only of not being able to scare, so the second step calls for driving away your apprehensions by ceasing to be afraid of them. It's not easy. It takes discipline to force yourself to stop being shy and to venture out and strike up conversations, not just once, but over and over again. Start by admitting your fear to someone you trust. Then do something harder: Deliberately confront your fear. Step into the elevator. Talk to someone new. Understanding commands discipline (repeatedly practicing the hard thing). This energy, which destroys obstacles to the fulfillment of your wish, demands that you take the leap of faith.

CHAPTER FOUR

MERCY:

The Energy of Compassion, Expansion, and the Dalai Lama

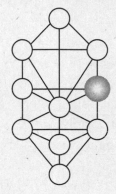

S P H E R E 4

KEYWORDS: Forgiveness; Compassion; Expansion

WISH IMPERATIVE: Open yourself without judgment to each and every meeting, invitation, adventure, or request that presents itself. Trust in the generosity of the sphere and for one week try everything. Emulate the great masters of compassion by offering forgiveness to yourself and to others.

HEBREW NAME OF SPHERE: Hesed

MYTH AND PERSONALITIES: Avalokiteshvara (the Buddha of Compassion); the Dalai Lama

PLANET: Jupiter

DARK SIDE: Attachment and addictions

COLOR: Blue

NUMBER: 4

TREE: Oak

BODY PART: Right shoulder, right arm, right hand

HEBREW NAME OF GOD (MANTRA): El (the high god of the ancient Canaanites)

In the name of Allah, most gracious and Merciful.
—The Koran, Surah 1: Al Fatihah ("The Opening")

Ocean of Bliss

After Understanding's trials of time, patience, and discipline, following the leap of faith across the forbidding Abyss, this ocean of loving-kindness envelops you like a warm bath at the close of a stressful day. Smack in the middle of the right pillar of the Tree, Mercy is the most dramatic and powerful force of expansion any of us will ever know. It amplifies like a variable light switch turned brighter and brighter and brighter, or like a balloon inflating without end.

Intoxicating ecstasy reigns here. The Hasidic movement, the Baal Shem Tov's sect of exultant Judaism, takes its name from *Hesed*, the Hebrew word for this sphere, encouraging its adherents to observe their faith and bind to the Creator through laughter, storytelling, music, and dance. When you first plunge into Mercy, it feels like stepping fretfully into a room where you think you've heard a burglar, only to discover it was the cat. It's the pleasure of diving into a swimming pool on a blistering-hot day.

> WISH MAKER: Sit on the floor. Hold your palms together, elbows straight, high above your head for at least four minutes. In your mind, recite your wish. This yoga pose will be difficult. You will ache and your arms will droop. These challenges are remnants of the previous sphere, Understanding. Push through them. Persevere. Keep your arms up straight. After four minutes, allow your hands to glide slowly to your sides. What you are experiencing now—the relief and the sensation of expansion—is Mercy.

The bliss and benefits of this energy carry a hidden danger: addiction. The euphoria of Mercy is almost like a drug, and it will entrap anyone who becomes too attached to it, puffing him up until he explodes in an ugly hangover. Or worse. The Tree in its sage design infused us with the energy of Understanding and discipline first so that we will have internalized the skills necessary to manage such unbridled expansion. No matter what you put here, Mercy will inflate and inflate it. If you transport positive traits into the sphere, they grow. If you wield the egotistical side of your personality too prominently, Mercy will magnify that too. If you plop down a little flu bug, Mercy will transmute it into a plague. This sphere never referees good from bad. It simply escalates all things toward infinity. And so it is critical to apprehend what the exalted energy of Mercy actually describes. What does it mean to show mercy?

Forgiveness: The Highest Virtue

The true message of this sphere is forgiveness. With Mercy, the Tree imparts the vital Kabbalistic concept of acceptance. If you forgive your enemies or those who have done you wrong, you *accept* them to your bosom regardless of who they are or what pain they might have inflicted. The modern paragon of this energy is the Dalai Lama and Tibet, his Land of Snow. Though Tibet has been invaded and devastated by China, the Dalai Lama resolutely shuns all words of condemnation. As Christ preached in one of the noblest and least-heeded axioms of Western civilization: "If a man strikes you on the right cheek, turn the other cheek towards him as well" (Matthew 5:39). Isn't it then absurd that in European Christian nations, the striking of a glove to an adversary's cheek became the official invitation to a duel? Christ, a carpenter's son, obviously understood the mechanics of the Tree of Life. He specified the right cheek to signify the right pillar of expansion, the home of this sublime force of compassion and forgiveness.

Mercy is more elevated in the Tree than any other tangible human quality. In the canon of Kabbalistic literature, no actual human, no matter how enlightened—not Moses, Abraham, or King Solomon—is ever associated with any of the top three lofty and rather conceptual spheres. Mercy, however, finally hits us with a concrete potential that all of us can shoot for.

On the Tree, the compassion of the fourth sphere stands taller than love, which emanates from the sixth sphere, called Beauty. Compassion prevails as the more exalted virtue because by forgiving your enemy, you behave righteously even in the wake of harm or injustice. You do good after getting back bad. On the other hand, most of us love with the expectation of receiving a palpable blessing, kindness, or tender touch in return. "Love your enemies and pray for those who persecute you," Christ commanded. "For if you love those who love you, what reward will you get? Do not even the tax collectors do as much?" (Matthew 5:46). Love is easy. Compassion is how we earn paradise. The way we create heaven right here on Earth.

WISH MAKER: This week will present you with the chance to exonerate someone. It will happen. When it does, forgive without reservation. Show Mercy and it will propel you toward your wish. Don't wait for some Hollywood scene of extravagant malice and saintly absolution. Any and all tiny incidents that provide the opportunity to forgive will suffice. Also, use this week to pardon yourself—for your shortcomings, for your failings, for any time when you may have faltered.

Back to Compassion

We learn compassion only by transcending our ego-rooted judgments and stepping into the shoes of others. You're driving down a crowded street, late for an appointment, when another car dangerously cuts you off. You slam on the brakes. Infuriated, you curse and blast the horn. Most of us do it automatically. But what if you discovered that this outrageous lunatic is rushing to the hospital because his pregnant wife lies screaming out of view on the backseat, her new baby stuck and struggling to be born without medical help. If you knew that, you wouldn't curse him; if you truly understood his predicament, you'd organize a stampede to get out of his way.

Mercy obliges us to ascertain the backgrounds of others. The preceding sphere instilled the lessons of time and patience. Now we work to implement that training. We can't hope ever to internalize the totality of another person's history, especially that of a stranger, but we can slip on his shoes and imagine his past. Even if he is not confronted with a life-or-death struggle at the moment he behaves badly, somewhere, sometime, that person suffered. While he merits punishment for his transgressions, he too is a product of a past that presses us to recall Shakespeare's transcendent admonition in *The Merchant of Venice:* "The quality of Mercy is not strained; it droppeth as the gentle rain from heaven. . . . [and] blesseth him that gives and him that takes. It is an attribute to God himself, and earthly power doth show like God's when Mercy seasons justice."

In order to probe the background of a stranger, you must mine your imagination, which is ruled by this blue watery sphere. While Wisdom and Understanding represent the intellectual tier of the Tree, Mercy and the next sphere, Severity, generate the emotional plane. Mercy, like all spheres in the right pillar of expansion, generates internal processes—in this case, inner emotions like unconditional empathy that we extend to the world. (Severity, on the other hand, will stimulate outer emotions or reactions to stimuli that come at us from the outside.)

Mercy asks us to dive deep inside, to travel back in time and peer with imagination into the past. Rewind the clock and feel what that other person might have endured back then. That thief, that pitiless thug who just knocked an old man to the ground for a twenty-dollar bill, was once a cheerful baby whose mother, poor and desperate for love herself, latched on to the first man who spattered her with affection. Unfortunately, that man withered under the weight of his financial failures. Like his father before him, he drank to numb his shame and vented his self-loathing by smacking his tiny stepson. The boy eventually found approval in a gang whose leader exacted more and more brutality from his minions as proof of their loyalty. Starving for recognition, this little criminal plunged into the culture of his new family, and he soon learned to equate viciousness with the path to reward and acceptance. He became crueler and crueler. He turned "bad." But what do you discover, what do you feel, when you step into the shoes of that scared, unloved boy?

That old cliché rings snug and cozy: Don't judge a man until you've walked a mile in his shoes. But it's so difficult to do it. To really efface yourself and do it. It's probably the hardest thing of all.

WISH MAKER: Think back first on your life. Step into your old shoes and practice. Remember a time when you stole something. Or, if you never stole, dredge up a moment when you slugged someone or told a hurtful lie. Picture yourself then. Perhaps as a teenager you shoplifted a CD from a music store because you yearned to impress your peers. Or perhaps last year you repeated a nasty rumor about a work colleague simply to entertain others in your crowd. Do you remember what stirred you to do it? Focus on what you feel. Now forgive yourself. And, if possible, atone for it. If you took music, donate to a program that provides musical instruments to schools. If you stole from your mother's purse, send her some flowers or a new handbag.

We Are Merciful to the Core

Mercy arrives to push us toward the impossible. Water—a surface that reflects images—governs this sphere. It helps us to feel. It induces us to imagine, to fill in the blanks. In just about every mythological system, water serves as an esoteric code for feeling, emotion, memory, and the subconscious. The name Dalai Lama itself translates from the Mongolian into "the Ocean of Wisdom." This sphere requires you to put Wisdom (the sphere directly above) in the service of the Ocean, in the service of feeling. The surface of our planet is 71 percent water. Our bodies are comprised of an even higher percentage. We are born into this world when our mothers' waters break. We cry salty tears—the stuff of the ocean—to express our suffering and heightened emotions. We contain the ocean. We emerged from the ocean. We are all creatures of Mercy.

If anyone—philosopher, religious leader, or friend on the street—preaches otherwise, bombards you with that all-too-common mantra that humankind is innately sinful or evil, set that person straight by compassionately replying, "The Tree shows humankind to be Merciful at the core." The Earth is a school of compassion. Souls reincarnate here to master compassion. And they return again and again, lifetime after lifetime, until they accomplish this grueling and magnificent mission.

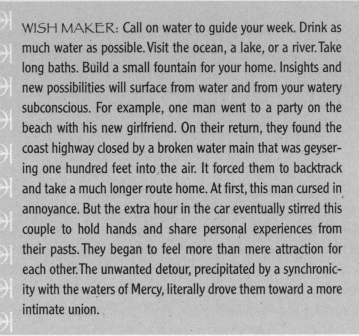

WISH MAKER: Call on water to guide your week. Drink as much water as possible. Visit the ocean, a lake, or a river. Take long baths. Build a small fountain for your home. Insights and new possibilities will surface from water and from your watery subconscious. For example, one man went to a party on the beach with his new girlfriend. On their return, they found the coast highway closed by a broken water main that was geysering one hundred feet into the air. It forced them to backtrack and take a much longer route home. At first, this man cursed in annoyance. But the extra hour in the car eventually stirred this couple to hold hands and share personal experiences from their pasts. They began to feel more than mere attraction for each other. The unwanted detour, precipitated by a synchronicity with the waters of Mercy, literally drove them toward a more intimate union.

The Buddha of Compassion

Avalokiteshvara, the original Buddha of Compassion, took it upon himself to nurse all sentient beings until the lowest of all souls reached eternal nirvana. Obviously, this marvelous Bodhisattva (in Sanskrit, *Bodhi* means "wisdom" or "enlightenment" and *sattva* translates as "essence") is fated to spend quite a bit of time with us. His legend recounts that one thousand princes, including Avalokiteshvara, agreed to attain enlightenment. But simply achieving his own spiritual fulfillment sounded like a selfish and hollow goal to this extraordinary prince. Instead, he promised to transport everyone with him, to emancipate all beings, even the cruelest among us, from the sorrowful cycle of life and death. To prevent any second thoughts, he asked the universe to pulverize his body into one thousand pieces if he ever veered from his task. Avalokiteshvara descended to the lowest hell, and he liberated the fiends he met there one by one. He healed many with the waters of compassion, but new souls gushed in faster than he could repair the old. He lapsed into despair, and in concert with his pact he exploded like a vase dropped from the roof. (The disintegration of the Buddha of Compassion parallels the decimation of Mercy in the Kabbalistic account of the breaking of the vessels, even though the disparate cultures that spawned these twin mythologies were separated by thousands of miles and an equal number of religious rituals).

Just as the breaking of the vessels awarded all of us the chance to rectify God's original Creation, Avalokiteshvara's destruction granted his princely brothers the opportunity to fortify their own compassion and thereby advance their pursuit of enlightenment. Even his demise resonated as a colossal gesture of generosity. The princes rallied to Avalokiteshvara's aid, reconstructing his body and blessing him with Super-Buddha powers. The new and improved Bodhisattva possessed eleven heads and one thousand arms. And on each of his one thousand palms they placed an eye, which symbolized the union of Wisdom (the all-seeing eye) with the skillful hands that carry out acts of loving-kindness.

The magical Avalokiteshvara then chose to reincarnate as a human being in order to teach humility and empathy and to live literally the message of his original pledge. Today he is known as His Holiness the fourteenth Dalai Lama, the temporal and religious leader of Tibet. Born at dawn on July 7, 1936, a Cancer (a water sign that symbolizes mercy and grace) with Cancer rising, he endured the Chinese invasion of Tibet when he was just fourteen. In 1959, after recurring threats to his life, the Dalai Lama escaped on foot to India, and he has lived in exile ever since.

The Chinese government has labored mightily to douse the Light of Tibet through the destruction of thousands of monasteries and the slaughter or imprisonment of religious leaders. But this anguish has not altered the temperament of the Dalai Lama. No matter his own distress, he continues to preach the gospel of compassion all over the world. Not once has he uttered a hateful word against China. "Many times I am asked if I am angry at the Chinese for what has happened," the Dalai Lama has said. (Notice he does not say, "for what they have done"). "Sometimes I lose some temper, but afterwards I get more concern, more compassion towards them. In my daily prayer I take in their suffering, their anger and ignorance and give back compassion."

Compare this attitude to the way other leaders demonize their enemies in an effort to galvanize public support for war and separation. Instead, the Dalai Lama calls the Chinese his greatest teachers. Only when confronted with an antagonist do we discover the opportunity to test and then amplify our compassion. This sphere confirms that sorrow and torment exist simply to spur us to an expanded consciousness, to propel us beyond our limitations, beyond our proclivity to lash back. Mercy empowers us to grow against gravity like a tree thrusting itself higher and higher into the sky. Hardly anyone has lost more than has the Dalai Lama, yet he wrote a book titled *The Art of Happiness*.

Mercy floods us with the thorny challenge of time. We must confront the past as we imagine and feel the backgrounds of others, but we must avoid any expectation of reward in the future as a consequence of our grace. The Dalai Lama proclaims that war and conflict might resolve a problem for now, but such strife fixes nothing down the road. The violent victory of today only shoves the wound festering into another age. According to the doctrine of compassion, the Tibetans, for example, must demonstrate patience and persist in their forgiveness of the Chinese— virtues conveyed by the sphere of Understanding—and trust the future to reimburse them for their mercy at some point in this or perhaps some other lifetime.

In the meanwhile, all is not bleak. The present day hardly

reveals the Tibetans and the Dalai Lama as weak or exploited patsies. Only as a result of the Chinese invasion do we know so much about the glory of compassion. Never before have the Tibetan Empire and the mantra of compassion conquered so many hearts worldwide. In a sense, the physical defeat has elevated Tibetan Buddhism to a throne of superior dominion, distributing the wisdom of the Land of Snow to far-flung places that never see snow.

The trees themselves, living totems of the Kabbalistic path of acceptance, effortlessly mirror the Tibetan creed. Chopped down as you read, they nonetheless forgive and continue to dispense oxygen to us all. You too were made in the image of a tree, imbued with that same compassionate spirit. The Earth spins as the cosmic school of compassion. What kind of grades are you getting?

WISH MAKER: Movies, our modern mythology, often translate the archetypal energies of the Tree into hypnotic, vivid images. *Kundun*, a biography of the Dalai Lama directed by Martin Scorsese, illuminates the message of Mercy. For an extra infusion of the power of compassion, rent and watch this film this week.

Bodhisattvas in Street Clothes—A Contemporary Myth from Actual Events

The woman with the invisible scar collapsed to the floor the moment she heard the news. "No," she gasped. Impossible. The man she'd sent to prison, the man she'd accused with unassailable conviction, hadn't done it. The science of DNA confirmed it was someone else. The woman with the invisible scar unraveled.

She curled up on the linoleum floor and clutched her stomach in an anguish she'd never known.

Mr. Waters emerged from the courtroom the next day draped in his own clothes for the first time in a decade. He smiled at the Sun as TV reporters brandished their red capes of conflict.

"What do you have to say to your accuser?"

"She stole ten years of your life. Do you hate . . ."

Mr. Waters stilled them. "She made a mistake."

"Don't you want revenge? To sue for everything she's . . ."

"I'd like to meet her," Mr. Waters told the camera. "But right now, she's probably suffering far worse than me."

"Unbelievable," Detective Peagram whispered at his TV.

"Oh," howled the woman with two invisible scars.

She was twenty-four when a rapist crawled through her open window. His face loomed inches away. She studied it hard—memorizing the nose, lips, hairline—so that when the time came, she'd be ready. She'd get him then. When the police presented Mr. Waters a few days later, it was done. Him. Emphatically him and again him. She placed her hand on the Bible and testified. The jury believed her. Mr. Waters got life. And she got to move forward again.

Mr. Waters and the woman with the invisible scars are the same age. In the ten years that followed, she did move forward. She finished graduate school, worked her way up, married and had a son. Mr. Waters sat in a cage, moving nowhere. Her mistake squeezed the future right out of him.

Detective Peagram arranged the meeting. Mr. Waters opened his door and walked out on the porch. He reached his hand toward the woman with the invisible scars. She clutched it and tried to speak. Her voice traveled nowhere. She wept and trembled, but kept her gaze glued to his face, commanding her eyes to stick. She'd rehearsed her speech. She would look into this face until she willed the words into the air.

"I'm sorry for what happened to you." It was Mr. Waters who reached across the silent abyss.

Detective Peagram, the big burly seen-it-all with a 9-mm automatic in his jacket, bawled out loud.

The woman with the invisible scars gaped at Mr. Waters, then buckled against him. She keened into his chest as his arms wrapped her close.

They have dinner together now—barbecues, wine tasting, penny-ante poker. The woman with the invisible scar and her husband love the flowers and hummingbirds that thrive in Mr. Waters's garden. Her young son adores him. He signed on to coach the local Little League team and taught the boy to slide into second without skinning his knees. Once in a while, when the little slugger swats at a bad pitch, Mr. Waters will hoot, "Hey Number Four, you see about as well as your mother." Then he laughs loud and hearty like a thunderclap. And everybody in the bleachers—the woman with the invisible scar too—can't help but join him.

Om Sweet Om: The Mantra of Wish Fulfillment

Om Mani Padme Hum, the famous four-word mantra of Avalokiteshvara, gives voice to the message of Mercy, the fourth sphere. Tibetans have long inscribed this mantra of unconditional love on prayer wheels—their version of the Kabbalistic spheres. The Buddhist tradition instructs that the spinning of these spheres and the touching of the sacred words, which translate to "the Jewel is in the Lotus," generate compassion for all. If the world were ever to experience a second in which someone somewhere did not utter this mantra, the Tibetans contend, the entire planet would explode. One moment without Mercy, according to the living masters of this sphere, results in the annihilation of us all.

The Lotus of this prayer flourishes in the water, which connotes Mercy's pure emotional energy. Its roots embed themselves deep in the mud at the bottom of the lake and yet the
flower blooms flawlessly white. It symbolizes the transmuta-
tion of filth and imperfection into an unblemished ideal. The
Jewel signifies the pearl, which also originates underwater,
inside the oyster. When a piece of sand or dirt infiltrates its
shell, the oyster does not expel it like we do with our own trash.
Instead the oyster opts for compassion, kissing and caressing
the irritant with layers of the lustrous nacre that lines its shell.
It offers the intruder pieces of its self, loving and loving until
the alien speck metamorphoses into a gleaming, valuable pearl.
(According to traditional astrology, the pearl is the birthstone
of Cancer, the sign most associated with unconditional love
and compassion.)

We all require a defect, an annoyance, some kind of woe, in
order to test our compassion. In order to create the perfection of
the pearl. The four-word mantra and the fourth sphere, called
Mercy, demand that we dive into the depths of our beings—the
subconscious symbolized by the oyster lying deep under the sea.
We must locate the imperfections there—any deficiency or fear,
any piece of trash that prevents us from attaining our wish. And
then we must look to the oyster as a role model and convert our
flaw into perfection.

It is these imperfections that make us perfect. If we emerged
from the womb without flaw, then we could never hope to be
like God because we would lack the need to create change and
transcend difficulty. Our God-given shortcomings present us
with the opportunity to exercise our godly nature and create perfection ourselves. In the Bible, Jacob famously wrestles with an
angel and limps away wounded in the thigh. But in that moment,
the angel rechristens him Israel to signify his enlightenment. The
esteemed and prosperous Jacob attains his true magnificence

only after he incurs a disability. Jacob, now Israel, names the location of his wrestling match and maiming Peniel, which translates as the "face of God." The place where we struggle, the site of our afflictions, the patriarch proclaims, marks the spot that brings us face to face with God.

A beautiful actress sported a rather inimitable—many said unfortunately large—nose. Though her eyes, hair, lips, skin, and all the rest shimmered like those of a singular goddess, her nose was the first thing people noticed. Most celebrities would have judged it a regrettable blemish and heeded their agent's advice to sprint to the plastic surgeon. But this actress refused to dishonor her uniqueness. She accepted it and admired it and chose instead to emphasize her alleged inadequacy whenever she had the chance. In interviews and public appearances, she often teased herself about her nose until it became her charming trademark and the source of her glory and fame.

We love little children in part because they are so flawed. They wobble and fall down and bungle the pronunciation of common words. They have little bodies and big funny heads. Yet, despite these shortcomings, wouldn't you agree that these tiny people are absolutely perfect? Who wouldn't accept them exactly as they are?

WISH MAKER: Identify your biggest flaw, the physical or psychological trait that displeases you most. This so-called defect probably engendered your wish. Use the reflective energy of Mercy to gaze back in time and excavate its origin. When you find it, become the oyster. Accept this imperfection. And caress it into a pearl.

Our Blue Heaven

The color of the ocean and the sky, blue symbolizes boundless possibilities. "The sky's the limit." If you want miracles, if you crave the endless, "sail into the blue." We live on the "blue planet," which is a metaphor for our true purpose—Mercy. In Hinduism, Indra, the compassionate king of the gods, wore a blue raincoat.

Painters and fashion designers recognize that blue goes with anything. It is a color without ego, devoid of judgment. The most popular piece of clothing in history: blue jeans. Why? Not because denim feels great, but because it is colored blue. Blues music appeals to just about everyone. The vibration of the blue tones seduces us deep inside. But this music, always tinged with melancholy, epitomizes the energy of the sphere— welcoming, comfortable, but also scored by suffering that is designed to teach us compassion. "I've got the blues" means "I'm feeling sad."

Like Mercy itself, blue can be addictive. If we permit the balloon to inflate indefinitely, we invite trouble. Jimi Hendrix and Janis Joplin, both blues musicians at heart, succumbed to their addictions and died young. Blue movies represent another example of something fine—sex—blown out of proportion by the nonjudgmental energy of Mercy into an unsavory addiction. In the embrace of this sphere, we must take care to avoid fixation. The Tree aims to teach us balance. And the red sphere of Severity—Red China versus the Blue Buddha of Compassion—follows next in the journey on the Tree to cut off any of our obsessions with blue before they drown us forever.

WISH MAKER: Cultivate the blue in your life. Do you have a blue room? A blue shirt? A blue car? Use them. If you cannot locate anything blue in your house or closet, venture out in the world in search of it. Place your wish in blue setting. If you wished for money, buy a blue purse. If you asked for a relationship, socialize outdoors beneath the blue sky.

The Planet Jupiter

Jupiter, the giant planet and king of the gods, dwells in Mercy. This massive gas planet appears to be expanding, mimicking precisely the energy of this sphere. Jupiter emits about twice as much energy as it takes in from the Sun. It's the ultimate Kabbalistic planet, giving back more than it receives. In Hebrew, Jupiter is called *Tzedek* ("righteous").

On the surface of the planet swirls a huge never-ending storm. This circular tempest resembles a gigantic blemish on Jupiter's beautiful face—an imperfection akin to the actress's big nose. And, true to the Tree of Life, this blotch appears red—an exact mirror of the trial of compassion that emanates from the red sphere of Severity.

Finally, the easy part: In astrology, Jupiter symbolizes the good father, providing and providing. Jupiter is enormous. If you combined all the other planets of our solar system, they still would not come close to the size of Jupiter. This planet's beneficence is similarly colossal.

WISH MAKER: Profit from the abundance of good fortune and opportunity that Mercy delivers. Pay attention to new prospects and new people no matter how far off the beaten track, no matter how strange. This week, try everything.

Suspend judgment and jump at any chance to enlarge the circle of your life. Because of the reckless expansion endemic to this energy, you likely will experience some false starts. But don't worry about that yet. Go with the flow, like a wave in the ocean.

The Sacred Oak

Sturdy, tall, ancient, the oak is the tree of Jupiter and all gods of thunder. All over Europe, the oak stands as the mystical center of nearly every culture, the most revered of all the trees. Because of their great height and low electrical resistance, oaks serve as prodigious lightning rods. Native to Mercy, which sits below the lightninglike insights of Wisdom, these trees symbolize the bringing down of lightning (of the Light) into a tangible, earthbound form. This sphere represents the practical application of higher, wispy wisdom. No one can do much with a thunderbolt. But all of us can and do use fire.

For the Greeks and Romans, the oaks held the power of prophecy. Jason's ship, the *Argo*, which sailed in search of the Golden Fleece, was built of oracular oaks from the sacred grove of Diana. King Arthur fashioned his Round Table, a symbol that everyone in the group holds equal stature, from a slice of a giant oak. The biblical patriarch Abraham supposedly received his heavenly teachings under an oak, and Augustine preached Christianity to the ancient Britons while standing beneath an oak. Back then, couples got married under the branches of this tree, until the priests decided to relocate these ceremonies to indoor churches.

Oak bark and leaves have long been used to treat wounds and

inflammations, both of which emanate from fiery red Severity. In other words, the oak instructs us to apply the compassion of Mercy to assuage the pain wrought by Severity's war, judgment, and aggression. A footbath containing material from the oak is said not only to soothe weary feet but to facilitate the discovery of the bather's correct path through life. The Druid mystics worshiped the oak as a portal to the higher worlds. And Matt Ryan, a celebrated modern-day rainmaker—who many Montana farmers claim delivered life-saving precipitation to their arid fields—routinely touches and speaks to the oaks whenever he needs to rejuvenate his gift of luring the charitable waters of Mercy from out of the big blue sky.

The Number Four

Four, the number of this sphere, the number of words in the Buddhist mantra of compassion, represents the four directions. Understanding creates time and space, and in Mercy we embrace them. Compassion must be doled out to all four directions of the world—not solely to your family, friends, and nation, but everywhere. It's a big job, underscored by the esoteric fact that the number four symbolizes work in traditional numerology. We must work at mercy and forgiveness. This week, exert yourself to identify your adversaries—both inside and out—and deliberately flood them with compassion. When you chance on the number four this week, examine the moment for information about which areas of your life are crying for more feeling or compassion.

Four also represents the four rivers that streamed from the Garden of Eden. In Norse mythology, four rivers of milk flow in Asgard, the homeland of the gods. According to Pythagoras, four is the number of perfection. The number four intimates that

Mercy and compassion are the pathways (or the rivers) to paradise.

Name of God

Chant *El* as your mantra during your meditations this week. We all know this evocative syllable. Even those who have never spoken a Hebrew word have uttered this name many times. My friend Michael read Sylvia Plath's *Ariel* while on vacation in Carmel. All these nouns end in *el*, which literally means "God." Carmel, for example, translates as "Vines of God"; Ariel as "the Lion of God." El was the high god of the Canaanites, whose ancient nation occupied the lands known as Israel and Palestine today. Allah, the Arabic word for "God," also derives from El.

In Hebrew, El denotes "toward" or "to." The name of God assigned to Mercy elevates us "to" the higher realms. It reiterates the maxim that through our acts of compassion we soar to a more exalted state of existence.

WISH MAKER: Chant this mantra any time you require help in forgiving someone. It is also a wonderful tool for cultivating abundance in your life.

Meditation

Sit in your favorite quiet place. Breathe deeply and relax. Imagine a huge blue sphere. It envelops you. Sit here in the center of this blue energy. Breathe it in. Breathe in the blue of compassion and breathe out forgiveness and kindness. Notice that the blue sphere generates jagged flashes of light that resemble bolts of lightning. Focus these flashes on yourself. Feel this energy and warmth filling your body. Feel yourself expanding, growing, suddenly cognizant of the greatness that is always inside you.

Now picture your wish. Project it on the inside of the blue sphere. Picture it fulfilled. Visualize your wish in as much detail as possible—complete with colors, sounds, and smells. Watch it flicker on the blue sphere.

Now add the soundtrack of your astral journey. Chant aloud the name of God: *El*. Draw it out, long, long, long. Feel the sound creating frequencies that run up and down your spine and reverberate in your chest. Breathe deeply and chant *El* again. And again. Notice how the sound alters the images on your blue screen. Pay attention to the shapes and images that arise. They might hold a message about your wish, about your spiritual path, about compassion. Repeat the chant. Slowly and deeply.

Now imagine the sphere transformed into a wide blue ocean. Dive into it. Soak yourself with compassion. Feel yourself at one with the sea. Notice that you are able to breathe underneath the water as easily as you breathe on land. You are inhaling emotions and exhaling compassion. It's so peaceful. Look around and you will see four dolphins. Let them guide you to the bottom of the sea. There, the dolphins point you toward a little pearl—a beautiful jewel, a gift for you. Pick it up and hold it in your left hand. Accept this present from the ocean—the Ocean of Wisdom. It is yours to keep. It is the wish-fulfilling jewel.

When you're ready, slowly resurface and return to your spot within the blue sphere. Watch as the sphere gradually disappears. Breathe in deeply and hold the air inside. Do this three times. Then slowly open your eyes.

Wish List—Mercy

1. Forgive. Deliberately go out and exonerate others for past wrongs. Unconditionally pardon anyone who aggrieves you this week. Remember to forgive yourself too.

2. Capitalize on the munificence of Jupiter and Mercy. Take advantage of every opportunity that presents itself without judging whether it's apt to be productive. Just go. The week of expansion calls on you to inflate the possibilities of your wish.

3. As always, watch for synchronicities conjured up by Mercy and record any thoughts or conjectures about their significance in your journal. Analyze your dreams (see exercise 1, below) for opportunities to advance your wish. Mercy's symbols include blue, water, ocean, emotions, unexpected opportunities, compassion, grace, Jupiter, pearls, the number four, and the right arm, hand, and shoulder.

4. Wish progress: You ought to enjoy a sensation of expansion this week after the difficulty of the preceding sphere. In addition, the Tree will supply some magic, some unexpected help. Welcome and embrace it. Mercy also adds an emotional dimension to the process following the intellectual emphasis of the previous spheres. You might find yourself prone to tears or sentimentalism. These reactions signal that you have attuned yourself to the mechanics of the Tree, and these moments of emotion are likely to be gilded with clues to direct you toward fulfillment.

Exercise Zone

☞ 1. **Life Is but a Dream:** To fully understand the sphere of inner emotions, we must peer into the inner world of the subconscious, the world of our dreams. Though we dream every night, they often slip from our memories just as water slips through our fingers. We recollect our dreams only when we awaken in the middle of them. This technique to capture your dreams is admittedly harsh, but try it at least once. Before going to sleep, place your journal at your side and set your alarm for 4 A.M. Mercy is the fourth sphere, and in numerous spiritual traditions, 4 A.M. is considered the hour of benevolence, the hour of bountiful Jupiter. In astronomy and astrology, the symbol for Jupiter is ♃, the Arabic glyph for the number four. During this not so "ungodly" hour, we dream or meditate most brilliantly. And this alarm clock technique is the best dream catcher on the market. Wake up and write down your dream in as much detail as possible. Then go back to sleep and review your transcription later that day. If waking up at 4 A.M. proves too difficult, write down your dreams whenever you rise in the morning. If you wake up without any memories of your dreams, don't be discouraged. Simply record any thoughts, insights, feelings, anything off the top of your head. Don't think about it. Write anything— anything except "I feel sleepy."

☞ 2. **Merciful Dollars:** Break a ten-dollar bill into ten singles and stash them in your right pocket or in your purse. Do not spend them. Once you place this money in your pocket, it no longer belongs to you.

Let go, and permit the energy of Mercy to reveal who needs the money. As soon as you encounter a homeless person or anyone asking for help, reach out with your right hand—which is ruled by the sphere of Mercy—and give away one of the bills. Don't discriminate; don't assess whether the recipient truly deserves it. Your mission is to practice generosity. Try to do it with feeling. If possible, stay a minute—smile, make eye contact, strike up a conversation. Donated with this acknowledgment that the other is a fellow human being, that dollar will be blessed with the potential to expand and attract many more. Try to persuade a friend to undertake this exercise as well. Compassion is contagious. Let it start with you. And let it spread.

CHAPTER FIVE

SEVERITY:

The Energy of Action, Judgment, Moses, and Mars

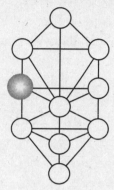

S P H E R E   5

KEYWORDS: Strength; Decisiveness; Energy

WISH IMPERATIVE: Scrutinize all the options you've tried and tested so far and cut out everything that doesn't benefit your wish. Capitalize on the vitalizing power of this sphere to make decisive progress.

HEBREW NAME OF SPHERE: Gevurah

MYTH AND PERSONALITY: Moses

PLANET: Mars

DARK SIDE: Anger and violence

COLOR: Red

NUMBER: 5

TREE: Pine

BODY PART: Left hand, left arm, left shoulder

HEBREW NAME OF GOD (MANTRA): Elohim Gibor (the creative, life-giving force that transforms humans into heroes)

Hitting the Brakes

Moving from the soothing expansion of Mercy to the sharp aggressive sting of Severity might feel like riding a roller coaster that slams to an abrupt stop. If Mercy is the air that fills the balloon, Severity is the needle that pricks it. The red-hot nature of Severity often impels us to shoot first and ask questions later, spurring us to react to maddening stimuli with irrational, even regrettable behavior.

So is this sphere good or bad? It depends. If you suffer from cancer, you might need to embrace the sword of Severity to cut it out. You definitely do not want Mercy to inflate the tumor to infinity. If you eat too much and become perilously heavy, you must curtail your caloric intake and tap the initiating momentum of Severity to exercise and lose weight. Following the dreamy bliss of Mercy, Severity flips on the activating energy that wakes us up and nudges us to go out and live.

Located in the middle of the restrictive pillar, Severity functions to balance the unconditional increase of Mercy. It supplies and applies the brakes, the counterforce that slows the burgeoning Light from blinding the material world. We all need brakes. Imagine yourself in a car atop a mountain covered in white snow (Crown). As you descend toward your hometown (Kingdom), you surely will be required to hit the brakes along the way. Over in Mercy, you stepped hard on the gas. But as you zip downhill and confront a sharp curve or two, brakes will save your life. Without this restrictive force, you'd fly off the cliff and crash.

The sword of Severity offers the ability to cut what we do not need from our lives and fight for what we do. But we must exercise enormous precision whenever we decide to wield its blade. We can employ it to prune the trees so that they produce more fruit. Or we can use it to chop off heads.

This prickly challenge surfaces because Mercy and Severity

comprise the emotional plane of the Tree of Life. And human emotions—fervent passion, anger, vengeance, and jealousy—can be volatile. All the spheres in the left column control external processes. Since Severity governs external emotions, it ignites volatile reactions to whatever flies at it from without. People who irritate you, people who steal your parking place or leave their dirty socks on the floor, all trigger this energy. When outsiders invade your country and you mass with your neighbors to defend your land, that's Severity too. Severity stands as an impartial judge of everything in your life. It urges you to make decisions and stick to them with conviction.

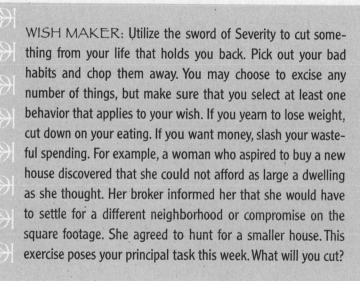

WISH MAKER: Utilize the sword of Severity to cut something from your life that holds you back. Pick out your bad habits and chop them away. You may choose to excise any number of things, but make sure that you select at least one behavior that applies to your wish. If you yearn to lose weight, cut down on your eating. If you want money, slash your wasteful spending. For example, a woman who aspired to buy a new house discovered that she could not afford as large a dwelling as she thought. Her broker informed her that she would have to settle for a different neighborhood or compromise on the square footage. She agreed to hunt for a smaller house. This exercise poses your principal task this week. What will you cut?

Anger Management

In Understanding, the sphere just above in the left column, we learned discipline; in Severity, we execute that discipline. Severity represents the leader. In Hebrew, the sphere is named *Gevurah*, from a root that means "to overcome," "conquer," or "subdue." It also translates as "the hero." Kabbalists sometimes call this sphere *Din*, which is Hebrew for "judgment." Untempered, this energy can turn overly aggressive and judgmental, launching witch hunts and destruction. "Who is strong? He who restrains his urge" (Avot 4:1).

An old samurai story details the journey of a supreme warrior who sought to avenge the death of his master at the hands of a depraved and treacherous killer. He hunted his nemesis for years, finally confronting him in a vicious duel. The samurai gained the advantage and it became clear that he would soon prevail. At that moment, the killer spit in the samurai's face. The samurai reacted by sheathing his sword and walking away. Dumbfounded, his disciples asked, "Why?"

"Because it became personal," the samurai replied. The magnificent warrior refused to permit his rash emotions to cheapen his noble mission into one fueled by anger, impetuousness, or what in *Star Wars* is called "the Dark Side of the Force." Ingest the lesson of the samurai. Severity often attracts disturbances from the world around you. This week, somebody will probably call you to war—at the office, in the bedroom, on the freeway. "Yi yi dai lao," Sun Tzu advised in *The Art of War*. "Pick your battles." Use your sword in service of your goal, not just for the heck of it.

WISH MAKER: Pinpoint the person who irritates you the most. Who pushes your buttons and provokes you to react impulsively? That person is here to teach you the true meaning of Severity. Write down the trait or behavior of that person that rankles you most acutely. Is he hypercritical of you or others? Does she speak only about herself, as if no one else on the planet has any problems? This same disagreeable tendency exists in you. Trade on the energy of Severity to identify it and then work to prune it from your life.

The Color of Blood

While Mercy embodies the element of water, Severity epitomizes fire. It's hot. Red hot. Red lights exploit the restrictive nature of Severity, signaling you to hit the brakes and stop. The red shields you from crashing into cross traffic. If you ignore the red, you might die. Or the police might compel you to stop and pay an annoying fine. When enraged, the human face invokes the energy of Severity by turning red. Inflammation—a word that derives from *flame* (fire)—turns the skin or throat red to signal physiological distress.

Red sticks out more than any other color, attracting the eye and demanding attention. It has attitude, ego, and flair. We can't help but notice red. We are biologically programmed to do so. When red blood spurts from someone's nose, we direct attention to it immediately because we know that red pouring unchecked from the body signals imminent death. Red equals alarm, danger, somebody better do something quick. It's why security teams scream "Red alert!" and not blue or pink alert.

Red lures us whether we like it or not. It explains the widespread fascination with crime stories on the TV news—the ratings-grabbing strategy of "if it bleeds, it leads." Insurance agents report that red cars attract more traffic tickets from the police. But the red soldier energy of Severity also protects. Red cars are stolen less frequently than those of any other color. During the week of Severity, a woman reported that she had lost her red purse, filled with fifteen hundred dollars in cash, in a train station. An hour later it was returned to her with all the money intact. She had misplaced purses of other colors several times before and had never seen them again. Today she carries only red.

Like a scalpel, red, in the hands of a skilled practitioner, can be used therapeutically. Some healers utilize red light therapy to treat a wide array of physical maladies, including shoulder pain (Severity rules the left shoulder), headaches (the astrological sign Aries, most associated with the energy of war, governs the head), skin wounds (casualties of Severity), depression (Severity invigorates), and impotence (again, the rejuvenating properties of Severity have been familiar to prostitutes in *red*-light districts for centuries). Meanwhile, the Red Cross strives to alleviate the aftermath of excess Severity.

Red conjures war, aggression, blood, pain, and fury. But it also conveys propitious attributes like vitality, initiative, and passion. Valentines are red. We send red roses to our lover. The sentiment is dynamic and sharp, transmitting the message "I love you" in an ardent and penetrating way.

WISH MAKER: Single out the areas of your life in which you need help from the soldiers of Severity—the places that could benefit from more vigor or initiative. Now adorn them with the color red. For example, if you desire to be more assertive at work, wear red clothes to the office or buy red file folders. If you crave more passion in your personal life, sprinkle some red around your bedroom. Decide what area of your life could profit from increased attention from others and color it red.

The God of War

The ancient Greeks depicted Ares, the god of war, as a three-hundred-foot hairy brute. Zeus, the king of Olympus, proclaimed that of all the gods, Ares was the most despised. The Athenians reviled the god of war and labored to disgrace him. They invented the unflattering legend of the battle between the Titans and Olympians, in which the bungling and cowardly god of war was emasculated before the fighting had begun.

This civilized society harbored no dreams of conquering

other territories. Devoted instead to pursuits of the mind, the Greeks excised Severity from the Tree of Life of their civilization. They besmirched the god of war and dug a black hole in the Tree. But nature abhors a vacuum, and the absence of red attracted aggression from elsewhere. Incursions by the Persians, Macedonians, and countless others forced the Athenians to abandon the academy and march off to battle. They loathed the disruptions. And they projected their distaste for war onto their god of war. They slandered him. They called him hairy.

And then something horrible happened to this erudite, civilized, and unprotected state. The Romans stormed in and crushed it. They accomplished this triumph by rehabilitating the Greek's own Ares and resurrecting him as Mars. The Romans dubbed themselves the sons of Mars. No longer an oafish incompetent, the god of war metamorphosed into the most eminent deity in the Pantheon. The Romans paid tribute to Mars with huge temples and decorated their armies and flags in the red color of Mars. They constructed new legends that revered Mars as the father of Romulus, the founder of their nation. And as a result of this godly makeover, the Romans conquered more than one-fourth the population of Earth.

But the Tree demands balance. Any creation, person, or society tilted entirely to the restrictive pillar eventually will cut itself to pieces. The ultimate soldier always bathes himself in Mercy first before wielding the sharp tools of Severity. The motto of modern police departments, today's emissaries of Mars, is "to protect and serve"—not to *attack* and serve. And police sirens usually flash red on one side and blue, the color of Mercy, on the other—a compelling reminder that the Tree introduced compassion first so as to afford us a fighting chance to manage the warring nature of Severity.

The Romans lost their balance. They developed a black hole of their own across the Tree in Mercy. Historians theorize that the rapid proliferation of Christianity, which renounced a warrior-god like Mars, hastened the demise of Rome. The citizens of the empire began to worship a victim god who had permitted the red-loving soldiers of Mars to crucify him. But Jesus's merciful "turn the other cheek" proved ineffectual against the ferocious Germanic tribes. About four hundred years after Christ's death, the Roman legions dwindled to nothing because the soldiers preferred to stay home amid the compassion of their families. And the barbarians, meeting little resistance, overran the Empire.

WISH MAKER: Avoid the imbalances of Athens and Rome. Try to redirect energy from one activity that you probably overemphasize into another that might aid the advancement of your wish. For instance, one man sought to enrich his relationship with his wife, who had grown distant. For as long as he could remember, he had spent every morning poring over *The Wall Street Journal*. It was an obsession. During the week of Severity, he decided to relinquish his routine and instead to join his wife on her morning walk. At first they bickered about trivialities as they strolled the neighborhood. The man resented the forfeiture of his productive mornings and took it out on his wife. But even these spats helped to chip at the walls between them. Forced to interact first thing each morning, they found it easier to approach each other the rest of the day as well.

War in Peace . . . and the Holy Grail

Another hazard of unmitigated Severity erupts when the war is finished. What happens to soldiers in times of peace? With no enemy, no outlet for their training, and vast stores of aggression, the defenders of a nation often betray their own people. They become bandits and killers in their own homes.

This ugly phenomenon afflicted even the legendary King
Arthur and his honorable knights. According to legend, this band
of warriors unified all of Britain in the early Middle Ages. They
imposed an unprecedented peace over the immense warring
kingdom. Triumphant, they gathered at their Round Table; but,
bereft of a cause, these tremendous generals grew restless. Lancelot
took a fancy to Arthur's lady Guinevere, and the other knights
squabbled over the size of their fiefdoms.

Fortunately, Merlin, the wise man of magic, interceded. He
defused these incivilities by concocting a new mission for the
macho gang. He dispatched them in search of the Holy Grail—
the chalice that belonged to Christ. Reinvigorated by a noble
undertaking, the knights galloped off, their internal feuds dis-
carded.

The Arthurian saga metaphorically illuminates the best way
to handle the volatile energy of Severity. First, Arthur obtained
his marvelous sword from the lake of Avalon, from the watery
sphere of Mercy. And with that merciful weapon, he brought
amity to Britain. Alchemically, he blended water and fire (Mercy
and Severity) to create peace. The story of the Holy Grail denotes
a similar magic. The chalice contains the holy water (Mercy). The
passion of the knights' quest introduces the fire of Severity. And
who drank from the cup? Christ, who personifies the archetypal
mythology of the golden sphere of Beauty, which follows next in
the Tree. Whenever you balance Severity with Mercy, you generate the gold of the Tree, the perfection of the heart chakra, the
Beauty of life.

Martial arts represent another stratagem in the struggle to convert Severity to Beauty. The word *martial*, from "Mars," reflects the
aggression of Severity, while art emerges from the seventh sphere,
called Eternity. Look at the Tree (see page 18). Wedding these two
energies transports us to the middle sphere of Beauty. And martial
arts can be beautiful to behold. Hollywood has mastered this trick.

Martial arts movies dazzle the senses, and the eye-popping *Crouching Tiger, Hidden Dragon* won four *golden* Oscar statuettes.

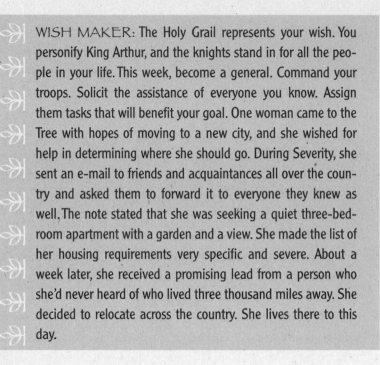

WISH MAKER: The Holy Grail represents your wish. You personify King Arthur, and the knights stand in for all the people in your life. This week, become a general. Command your troops. Solicit the assistance of everyone you know. Assign them tasks that will benefit your goal. One woman came to the Tree with hopes of moving to a new city, and she wished for help in determining where she should go. During Severity, she sent an e-mail to friends and acquaintances all over the country and asked them to forward it to everyone they knew as well. The note stated that she was seeking a quiet three-bedroom apartment with a garden and a view. She made the list of her housing requirements very specific and severe. About a week later, she received a promising lead from a person who she'd never heard of who lived three thousand miles away. She decided to relocate across the country. She lives there to this day.

Move It

Severity wakes us to our true potential. Mercy, the sphere of serenity and sleep, precedes it. Mercy is pleasant and comfortable. But to achieve any goal, in order to progress spiritually, we all need a kick in the rear end every so often. Severity is the force that drives us forward. Alarm clocks, for example, rouse us from our beds in a jarring and severe way. Just as the compassion of Mercy balances Severity's harshness, Severity equilibrates the dreamy lethargy of Mercy.

In the movie *The Matrix*, Morpheus, named after the god of dreams in Greco-Roman mythology, endeavors to wake the hero

Neo (an anagram of One) to his genuine calling. He offers him two pills: one blue (the color of Mercy) and the other red (the color of Severity). The blue pill will put him to sleep, blissfully ignorant of everything that has happened to him. The red pill will jolt him awake and compel him to confront the severe truth of his predicament.

WISH MAKER: This journey on the Tree certifies your decision to swallow the red pill. You have acted. And now there is no turning back. The knowledge and awareness you have amassed thus far will continue to evolve no matter what. You have passed the point of no return on your journey to self-realization and wish fulfillment. The sleeper in you has awakened.

Moses: Severity's Biggest Star

One of the most vital mythologies of all chronicles a hero who was sentenced to death before his birth. The famous saga relates that the ancient Egyptians so feared the mushrooming popula-tion of their Hebrew slaves that Pharaoh ordered the execution of all the infant Israelite boys. Born with Severity upon him, the baby Moses was hidden by his sister and placed in a basket on the river Nile (the waters of Mercy). Throughout his entire life of blood, fire, liberation, and justice—all qualities inaugurated by Severity—Moses never escaped the rescuing and mitigating waters of Mercy.

Found in the river by the daughter of Pharaoh, Moses grew up a prince of Egypt. But as a young man, his innate severity impelled him to murder an Egyptian officer whom he caught beating a slave. It was a rash act that cost him his life of luxury and privilege, but it served to initiate his true mission. The fugitive fled into the blistering desert, the landscape of Severity, his authentic home. Eventually, he stumbled upon a well—a sign of Mercy—and collided with yet another injustice to avenge. He used his fists to rescue seven female shepherds from a gang of bandits. Then he married one of the women and settled in the desert.

The Call

The burning bush interrupted Moses's desert tranquility when it commanded him to return to Egypt to liberate the slaves. God chose to appear in this peculiar guise because He recognized that to persuade a man of Severity, you must appeal to him in the vernacular he understands best: literally with fire and a call to action. At first, the headstrong Moses wasn't impressed. He audaciously demanded God's credentials, as if the burning bush were some meddlesome cop without a badge.

"And God said unto Moses, I am that I am" (Exodus 3:14). With this cryptic sentence, the Light explained that the genuine spiritual drive of us all derives from within. I am—the fundamental identity of Moses, you, and everyone else—is God. The famous cartoon fighter Popeye adapted this phrase to identify himself: "I am what I am and that's all that I am. I'm Popeye the sailor man." Popeye, the champion pugilist and navigator of the oceans (of Mercy), always sports an unlit pipe in his mouth. Dr. Julian Neil, a psychologist and yoga master in Los Angeles, postulates that this prop symbolizes the Native American peace pipe. Though Popeye excels as a fighter, this ever-present totem of comity reiterates the maxim that no matter how fierce the warrior might be, the true purpose of Severity is peace.

Blood, Liberation, Justice

After sparring with God, Moses accepted his mission like a good soldier and returned to Egypt to emancipate the slaves. He inflicted ten plagues on Egypt, including turning the waters of the Nile to blood—Mercy into Severity—and the killing of the firstborn. (The Israelites eluded death because they marked their doors with animal blood. The red symbol of Severity functioned as an antidote and stop sign to the plague.)

Pharaoh surrendered, and the slaves trailed Moses into the desert, where they slammed against the Red Sea—red for Severity and sea as a symbol of Mercy—another metaphor that underscores the imperative to temper aggression and blood with feeling. To escape the pursuing Egyptian army, Moses raised his staff and performed a severe miracle. He sliced the waters of the Red Sea in two, aggressively pushing aside all emotions—fear, despair, anger—long enough for the Hebrews to take action and scramble their way to safety.

The sword of Severity severs the bonds of slavery, and it also doles out justice. It judges good from bad, one option from the next. It instills the mechanism of morality. It demands an eye for an eye. Moses is the world's preeminent lawmaker. After delivering his people from bondage, he trudged up Mt. Sinai to receive the rules: the short version, called the Ten Commandments (for the ten spheres), and the longer list of 613 regulations and good deeds mandated by the Torah. Note 6 + 1 + 3 = 10. The sole reason for Severity's judgment is not punishment but to codify and illuminate the ten spheres of the Tree of Life, the pathway to the One.

Transforming Severity to Illumination

Left on their own, the uprooted Israelites fretted while they awaited the return of Moses and his invisible God, and they decided to construct a more tangible representation of the deity. They built the golden calf. And they threw a big party on the desert floor. Moses descended from the mountaintop in the middle of this orgy toting the Ten Commandments, the only relic in cosmic history actually "written with the finger of God" (Exodus 31:18). He felt the blood swarm to his face, and without a thought he smashed the most precious gift of all into pieces on the ground. Then Moses hurled Severity like a madman. He ordered his soldiers to slaughter those responsible for the idolatry. "And the sons of Levi did according to the word of Moses; and there fell of the people that day about three thousand men" (Exodus 32:27).

But Moses's final act in this drama, though far less trumpeted over the ages, transcended all his other monumental deeds. "He took the [golden] calf which they had made, and burnt it with fire, and ground it to powder, and strewed it upon the water, and made the children of Israel drink of it" (Exodus 32:20). He mixed fire and gold with the compassionate water of Mercy in an effort to heal his recalcitrant tribe. (In India, pills containing flecks of gold are thought to restore the body.) By blending fire, water, and gold—symbolic of the spheres Severity, Mercy, and Beauty— Moses, the homeopath, repaired the internal alchemy of his nation to better prepare the people to receive the Light.

Again he ascended Sinai and there he confronted another severe lesson. God decreed that He would wipe out the insubordinate Hebrew nation and then initiate a new race from Moses's seed alone. Affronted by God's vindictiveness, Moses recognized that his own anger had driven him to a similar brutality. In atonement, he defied God. If you kill any of them, Moses said, then blot my name from your book.

With that remarkable gesture of empathy, Moses attained a revolutionary breakthrough. His glory, his place in history, even the law direct from the mouth of the Lord, lost all relevance. He dived into the compassion of Mercy and lavished unconditional love on his fallible fellow humans in the desert below. He wedded his own fire with water, and eureka!—gold, perfection, enlightenment. At that moment, Moses was allowed to see God. No other figure in the Bible ever merited that privilege. And from then on, Moses's face shone with an awesome golden light. Again, the face that flushed red with rage now radiated Beauty's golden beams of enlightenment.

The Planet of War

From our perspective, the planet Mars flickers more than any other heavenly body. Its vast elliptical orbit carries it anywhere from 35 million to 60 million miles away from Earth. At its nearest, the planet sparkles strikingly bright and red in color. But when farthest away, Mars looks like any other star. The red energy of Severity likewise fluctuates. Aggressiveness, anger, and initiative come and go in everyone.

The T'ang of China regarded Mars as the planet of war, blood, and fire. They called it *Fa Hsing*—the Punishment Star. Channeled correctly, Mars and Severity produce achievement, vitality, life-saving surgery, and liberation. Misused, they can inflict death or cruelty or bring about Armageddon. The Romans exploited the muscle of Mars to kill their foes, but they also considered him to be the god of health and fertility and the protector of crops. The planet's two moons, named Phobus and Deimos, reflect Severity's dual potential. These Greek words, derived from the dogs of Ares, mean Fear and Dread. But the Romans called them Honor and Virtue.

Some astrologers contend that the daring and aggressive energy of Mars drives the personality of the United States. Well versed in the Masonic traditions that included Kabbalah and mysticism, Ben Franklin and the other Founding Fathers chose to deliver their new nation with a signing of the Declaration of Independence in the wee hours of July 4, 1776. They apparently inked the country's birth certificate at such a sleepless moment in order to place Mars, the planet of war and protection, smack on the ascendant of the nation's astrological chart. The Founding Fathers suspected that victory over the most intimidating empire on the planet would require military strength, motivation, and courage, and aligning the nation's fortunes with the god of war infused the fledgling nation with those very traits.

At that time, Mars sat in the sign of Gemini, the twins. And the United States has profited with Gemini as its rising sign, the outward personality of the nation in the world. Gregariousness, intelligence, deftness in business as well as lies and theft (Watergate) all derive from Gemini. It explains why the ideas, products, and culture of the United States—democracy, blue jeans, and MTV—have virtually conquered the world. Even the landmarks of the nation's ultimate city reflect the astrological fiber of the country. New York's Empire State Building evokes the Empire of Rome, aka the sons of Mars. And the Twin Towers of the World Trade Center, which were destroyed in the terrorist attack of Tuesday (the day of Mars), September 11, 2001, symbolized the twins of Gemini and their uncanny aptitude for commerce and communication.

But invoking Severity carries no small risk. In war, it proved invaluable and galvanized the United States to unrivaled power. But Mars in the middle of Gemini inevitably engenders war between the twins. Throughout its history, the United States has been torn by schisms within its borders. The Civil War witnessed brother killing brother. The witch hunts of McCarthyism

destroyed lives. And skirmishes for political and cultural influence have flared repeatedly between Republicans and Democrats,
industry and labor, antiwar protestors and the National Guard,
and the bohemian coasts versus the more conservative heartland.
The civil-rights movement provoked clashes between whites and
blacks. And this internal hostility persists in the recent family
feud between Machiavellian electricity traders in Texas and
energy-hungry California.

WISH MAKER: Capitalize on the invigorating energy of
Mars to enhance your strength, stamina, and productivity.
Initiate an exercise program. Move your body with yoga, mar-
tial arts, jogging—anything that will turn your face red.

Five

Space probes have yet to find life on Mars, but cameras have
captured a provocative land formation that appears to be a pyra-
mid containing five equal sides. Severity is the fifth sphere. The
United States houses its departments of war and defense in a
five-sided fortress named the Pentagon. Energetically, this
design safeguards the country, but it also tends to encourage
aggression, especially in times of peace. The Homeland Security
Advisory System, inaugurated in March 2002 to calibrate the
potential threat of a terrorist attack, features *five* color-coded
levels of risk. In this system, the color red represents what the
government labels "severe risk," the fifth and foremost state of
alert. The Pentagram, the five-pointed star, is an ancient symbol
of protection and magic. But flipped upside-down, it transforms

into the insignia of the devil and arouses terrible fear. North African cultures rely on the *hamsa*, an amulet in the shape of a five-fingered open hand, as a protective charm that supposedly stops negative spirits and thoughts from entering homes, offices, and minds.

Five is the number of humankind—two arms, two legs, and one head, the model of flawless proportion in the celebrated drawing by Leonardo da Vinci. Our physical and metaphorical affinity for five might illuminate humankind's unfortunate predilection for bellicosity and violence. In ancient Egypt, five crocodiles—conspicuously severe animals—were said to inhabit the Nile. Christ bled from five wounds (his points of Severity). And Moses wrote the Pentateuch (the first five books of the Old Testament), the bestseller that invaded and conquered the West. Meanwhile, "give me five" or "high five" serves as an aggressive celebration of triumph on the battlefield of sports.

If four represents the number of work, then five stands outside the four-sided square and serves as the security guard on patrol, protecting the work from outside threats.

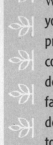

WISH MAKER: Employ this powerful sentry to fortify your wish against attacks from the world. What area of this process requires defending? One woman, who wished to complete the book she'd been contemplating for years, deduced that she needed to protect her time. She loved her family and friends and found it difficult to refuse any of their demands. She tapped the protective power of five this week to put up her hand and say stop. Her loved ones didn't always like it, but she managed to free up some time to sit down and write.

The Pine Tree

The tall straight trunk and sharp needles of the pine recall the form and function of the sword. The pinecone, a phallic symbol of power and fertility, decorated the wand of the fiercely sexual Dionysus. The ancient Greeks awarded crowns of pine in sporting competitions to signify strength and victory. Forest cultures across Europe burned the resin of the pine as incense to ward off evil spirits. And pine branches, stashed in doorways and windowsills, have long been deployed as protection against negativity from the outside.

The Phrygian savior-god Attis crucified himself on a pine tree on the spring equinox—the first day of the Mars-governed sign of Aries. To honor his death and resurrection each year, the Phrygians, an ancient culture of Asia Minor, chopped down a pine tree, carved it into the shape of Attis, and delivered it to the shrine of his mother, Cybele. Then, on March 24, known as "the day of blood," the priests would slice open their own skin and bleed on the pine effigy of Attis.

Name of God

Use Elohim Gibor (pronounced El-low-heem Gi-bore) as the mantra of Severity. Elohim, the feminine name of God, derives from Understanding, the sphere directly above. Gibor translates as "hero" or "brave." This mantra summons the formidable force of the creative, life-giving God that helps to transform humans into heroes.

WISH MAKER: Chant this name of God any time you desire strength, protection, passion, or the determination to overcome setbacks.

Meditation

Breathe deeply and picture yourself sitting around a fire. Feel the flames radiating heat all around you. The fire attracts you. You have the urge to jump in and become one with the flames. To become the light itself. When you're ready, project yourself into the flames. Dance with them. Experience how it feels to be an unpredictable, changing, fluctuating being. Enjoy this new way of expressing yourself.

Now imagine that you have become the light around the flame. As the light, you have the ability to travel at the speed of light. Ascend fast, shooting through a red tunnel to a different realm. You now find yourself in front of a five-sided gate made of iron. Engraved on the metal you read the word *Din*, Hebrew for "judgment." Touch the red letters and watch the door open. You enter a magnificent hall illuminated by red candles. In the middle of the room, you spot a great burning cauldron.

Notice that the light of the fire reveals a silhouette. Walk closer and meet your vision of the ultimate warrior. It could be a man or a woman, superhero or ninja. This soldier might be holding a sword, a laser, or no weapon at all. Your hero climbs onto a gorgeous red stallion and pulls you up behind. The horse begins to gallop at an amazing rate through an opening in the chamber and into a vast field. You fly through the past, present, and future; through the fields of your fears and the meadows of your hopes. Every once in a while, you spot one of your fears costumed as a monster coming at you. And each time your warrior swings and slays the monster with a single blow.

After killing your fears, your conqueror leads you back into the chamber and sits with you beside the fire. Gaze at this mighty figure and tell him or her what you need. Ask for any practical, action-oriented help. Express it to your warrior clearly. Send your superhero off to make it happen for you.

Now chant the name of God, Elohim Gibor, the power of the creative energies of the cosmos. *Elohim Gibor*. Intone it again and again for as long as you like.

When you finish, breathe in deeply. Hold the air inside—feel the energy of red spreading throughout your body. And breathe out. Once again breathe in. Hold the air. Imagine every cell in your body filled with the revitalizing power of red. And breathe out. Breathe in again. Hold it. And let it out. Picture yourself shaking hands with your hero like eternal blood brothers. Then walk toward the fire burning in the cauldron. Jump into it. Join this flame. Now imagine yourself back at your original campfire. Remember to dance with the flames; move and flicker like the light. When you are ready, exit the fire and sit beside the warmth of the embers. Return to your safe spot beside the glowing campfire. And open your eyes.

Wish List—Severity

1. Cut out everything that you and your wish no longer need. Use your journal to list everything that you vow to cut from your life this week.

2. Energize the process by aggressively pursuing activities that will advance your wish. This is not the time to think or feel, but to do. Action, action, action. This week of action presents you with more Wish Maker exercises than most of the others. That is intentional—a strategy to keep you moving.

3. Record all of your synchronous encounters with the emissaries of Severity. They include sharp objects, weapons, red, blood, injuries, hostility,

Mars, fire, the number five, and the left hand, arm, and shoulder. Use them to guide your course of action. For example, a man who wished to find and purchase a rare specialty automobile was on his way to a dealer to buy the car. Halfway there, he spilled hot coffee on his left arm, forcing him to return home to treat the burn. It was a severe and painful moment, but one that saved him much heartache. A few days later, he learned that the car dealer had been implicated in a criminal investigation and his vehicles had been seized as evidence.

☞ 4. Wish progress: You should swing the blade of Severity to sharpen the focus of your wish. No more sitting around and wishing. Severity demands that you venture out to pursue and conquer. Force yourself to take concrete action toward the realization of your goal. Examine all the possibilities that you brought into this week from Mercy and weed out everything that appears superfluous or unproductive.

Exercise Zone

☞ 1. **Purify with Fire:** Prepare a list of everything that you no longer want in your life. Include your habits and tendencies as well as specific people or your reactions to them. Remember that if you don't care for a particular behavior of another person, you can't cut it out for them. You can only amputate your reaction to it. Make the list as exhaustive as you like. Then burn the paper with a red candle. Allow this ritual to inflict a bit of pain. Hold on to the burning page as long as you can before dropping it in the sink. Fire is the strongest form of purification. Esoterically, it induces the most dramatic transformations that we can experience. Let the paper burn to ashes. Allow this list of unnecessary baggage to disappear.

2. **Set Them Free:** The story of Exodus recounts the force of liberation (Moses) separating the personality (the Hebrew slaves) from the ego (Pharaoh and Egypt). We all have the need to "Let my people go." We all need to free our creative force, our divine spark, from the bondage of the I, Me, Mine. Examine your life for signs of slavery. Where are you fettered to your ego, your addictions, to repetitive patterns that drag you down? To what are you a slave? A habit, a relationship, a job, a certain kind of car, to coming off as the smartest person in the room? Use your journal to reconstruct the Exodus story in your own life. Invent an adaptation in which your higher self plays the part of Moses and your restrictive ego stands in for Pharaoh. What must you do to liberate yourself? You might want to devise a list of all the Pharaohs you have met in your life—all the people or things that have kept you enchained. For each person or bad habit (smoking, overeating, isolating yourself in front of the TV when things go badly), write a few sentences to describe this Pharaoh. Then go back and circle the qualities these symbols of bondage share. The commonality among your Pharaohs reveals the mechanisms you use to put yourself down, the methods you utilize to enslave yourself. Once you

recognize what these self-abnegations look like, you will be able to construct your own Moses— your own liberator endowed with the muscle and vigor necessary to overcome the negativity of the insults and doubt that impede you from reaching your true glory.

CHAPTER SIX

BEAUTY:

The Energy of Love, Balance, and Christ Consciousness

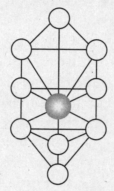

SPHERE 6

KEYWORDS: Love; Balance; Sacrifice

WISH IMPERATIVE: Practice creative visualization and imagine your wish fulfilled exactly as you want it. Sacrifice some part of the old you—a bad habit or a predilection for rash reactions—to make yourself more beautiful (godly) in your own eyes. Avoid emotional extremes and concentrate on balance.

HEBREW NAME: Tiferet

MYTH AND PERSONALITIES: Jesus of Nazareth; Odin; *Beauty and the Beast*

PLANET: Sun

DARK SIDE: Pride; egocentrism

COLOR: Yellow or gold

NUMBER: 6

TREE: Ash

BODY PART: Heart

HEBREW NAME OF GOD (MANTRA): Yod Hey Vav Hey Eloha Vada'at (the intercourse of the energies of Wisdom and Understanding)

The Heart of Things

In the center of the center floats the sixth sphere, called Beauty. It sits on the midpoint of the central column, halfway between the enlightened oneness of the Crown and the dense material realm of the Kingdom; halfway between the divine and the mundane, the soul and the body. Beauty also bisects the right and left pillars of the Tree, balancing the forces of expansion and restriction, giving and receiving. In Beauty, the hands of the right and left columns interlace in union at the heart. It instigates the marriage of the masculine and feminine, the holy matrimony of yin and yang.

Beauty buttresses the entire structure of the Tree just as the Sun, the ruler of the sphere, remains fixed in the center and sustains our solar system. Eight of the nine other spheres connect directly to Beauty. If we remove it from the Tree, all these paths would dangle, loose and aimless, and the entire construct would collapse in on itself like a black hole. Beauty resonates as the most vital sphere of all because the Tree is designed to promulgate equilibrium. One axis connecting heaven and Earth stretches up and down, while a second links the expansive and restrictive forces horizontally. Where these lines cross, the nexus of it all, we find Beauty. We find the center. We find the heart.

And this preeminence illuminates much about the meaning of your heart. It is not simply a muscle that circulates the blood. The heart upholds and nourishes everything. *Tiferet*, the Hebrew name of this sphere, translates as "glory" or "majesty." Beauty, then, is your glory, "your majesty," the king. The Tree decrees that your ruler is not your brain but your heart. According to The Egyptian Book of the Dead, Ma'at, the goddess of justice, adjudicates the fate of all the newly dead by weighing their hearts against the feather of truth. The heart stores all the vital information of who we are and what we have done. The Torah—the five books of Moses in the Old Testament—begins with the letter *Bet* and ends with the letter *Lamed*. When combined, these letters spell the word *Lev*, which means "heart." The whole of Moses's teaching, the entire message of the Torah, is contained within the heart.

So how do we attain Beauty? How do we dwell in the heart of things?

One word: *balance*.

A recent psychological study disclosed that even the subjective perception of physical beauty hinges on balance. People blessed with the most symmetrical features were deemed the most beautiful. True Beauty rarely emerges from the fanatical fringes. It materializes in the midpoint between unbridled sensitivity and rampant judgment; between the zealously spiritual and the markedly materialistic. The Buddha immortalized it as the golden path—gold is the color of Beauty—the middle road between all extremes.

Turning Lead to Gold

The traditional alchemical template for the creation of gold mandated the blending of all four elements—water, fire, earth, and air. The position of the golden sphere of Beauty reflects this recipe. The four energies that introduce each of the four elements of the material world—Mercy (water), Severity (fire), Eternity (earth), and Splendor (air)—closely surround and merge in Beauty. The heart features four chambers—one for each of the four points of the cross, one for each of the four elements. The rose, a classic symbol of Beauty, exemplifies the end product of this alchemical formula for perfection. It appears delicate, emotional, and wet with dew (Mercy), the thorns stab (Severity), it grows in the earth (Eternity), and it communicates through its fragrance that wafts in the air (Splendor).

Alchemy also postulates a shortcut formula that echoes Beauty's essential teaching: the marriage of any two extremes creates an enchanted equilibrium. This abbreviated blueprint dictates a mixture of fire and water, Mercy and Severity. It's a neat trick. Water usually douses fire to create nothing but a mess. But the rainbow—which is spawned when moisture in the air splinters the fiery rays of the Sun into every color the eye can detect—illumines the magic of the wedding done right. And at the end of the rainbow, legend promises, we find a pot of gold. The Navajo's Pollen Path, a Native American version of the Tao or the way to fulfillment, fuses these same opposites to create Beauty. Navajo sand paintings depict a blue line representing the feminine energy of water and the sky (Mercy) coalescing with a jagged red line that symbolizes the masculine qualities of aggression, action, and danger (Severity). Their conjunction inaugurates the yellow Pollen Path, the source of life. "Beauty before me. Beauty behind me," the Navajo chant. "Beauty at my left. Beauty at my right. Beauty above me. Beauty below me. I'm on the Pollen Path."

The King of the Solar System

The lone sphere ruled by a star rather than a planet, Beauty corresponds to the Sun, the most indispensable celestial body. All the planets circumnavigate the Sun just as all the spheres huddle around Beauty. We know that the planets exist and we are able to see them only because they reflect the Sun's light.

Beauty is king—just as gold (or yellow), the color of Beauty and the Sun, is king of the metals. In astrology, the Sun rules the sign of Leo, the king of the jungle. (Lions too sport a golden pelt.) Traditionally, the king functions as God's representative or reflection here in the material world, symbolically uniting God and man within himself. The Chinese character for king mimics the Tree. It features three horizontal lines—signifying God, king, and man (Crown, Beauty, and Kingdom)—and a vertical slash (the connection or the middle pillar of the Tree) running through them.

The most famous advice in cinematic history: "Follow the Yellow Brick Road." Like Dorothy in *The Wizard of Oz*, if we adhere to the Yellow Brick Road—the yellow avenue of Beauty—we arrive in Oz. If you follow your heart, you meet your wizard; you commune with your own divine spark within, which grants you the power to click your heels together and attain your dearest wish. In Hebrew, *Oz* translates as "strength" and "courage." This mythical movie informs us that when we submit to the bidding of our hearts, we become more courageous.

WISH MAKER: In the week of Beauty, strive to perceive a reflection of your wish, of your original will of Crown, beginning to materialize. It is not your wish fulfilled. We yet must mix in several more energies before the creation reveals itself complete in Kingdom. Still, evidence of progress should twinkle a bit now. One woman who wished to double the size of her business negotiated four distribution deals this week. She did not earn any money. For that she would have to wait for Kingdom. But in Beauty she foresaw a glimmer of how her wish would look in the end.

Beauty's Cross

Just as kings throughout history have proven to be some of the biggest drama queens on Earth, immersing yourself in the quintessence of Beauty also requires something dramatic. Beauty demands a sacrifice.

Look at the Tree. We reside at the bottom, in Kingdom. Beauty stands so much taller—halfway to Crown, halfway to enlightenment. It's far. Even more challenging, Kingdom is the only sphere that does not hook up directly to Beauty. We possess no straight path to our heart. We can see the Sun. We can feel it on our skin. We can comprehend how it interacts with green leaves to suffuse the Earth with life. But can we touch it? Even fortified with magical wings, Icarus flew too close to the Sun and crashed. Can any mortal attain such brilliance? And if so, how? Solving the riddle of these enigmas is the raison d'être of virtually every religion humankind has ever devised.

Beauty exists at the nexus of a universal cross, where the line connecting heaven and Earth bisects the axis that joins the expansive and restrictive forces in all creation. And what happens on the cross? A sacrifice. A huge sacrifice. A sacrifice of the ego. A sacrifice of the mundane you, who tends to perceive beauty only through the eyes, to the godly higher self that dwells within your heart.

Beauty represents Christ consciousness. God on Earth. And what do we know about Christ? He willingly sacrificed himself on the cross. He surrendered to God's will and drank the cup (Mercy) of poison (Severity) to achieve Beauty. He crucified himself on the still point between the divine and the mundane, between the masculine and the feminine. The central Christian mythology evokes the cross of Beauty to bridge the chasm between God and man. Christ surrendered himself in Beauty to atone for "original sin." He took upon himself an enormous dose of the collective suffering and pain of the universe, and with that sacrifice purified the dark karma of humanity. Adam and Eve had tasted from the duality of the Tree of Knowledge of Good and Evil and thereby exiled humanity from the One. Humankind was unable to reunify itself with God, this theology professes, until Christ presented us all with the absolution of his sacrifice. Christianity's foremost symbol expounds that Beauty unbolted the door to heaven.

Innumerable works of art have chronicled the unappetizing image of Christ bleeding to death on the cross. A dispassionate description of this gruesome scene would sicken most of us. Yet it has forever remained a blockbuster because any sacrifice under-taken willingly resonates with an intrinsic beauty. Meso-american art portrays Quetzalcoatl, the kingly high priest of that vast Aztec culture, glued to a cross. His name translates as "the feathered serpent," denoting the merger of the high (the soaring eagle) and the low (the snake crawling on the Earth). He ruled over Tollan, the City of the Sun, but then like Christ he opted to renounce his kingdom (the material world) and sacrifice himself for the sake of humankind. His body burned, but from the ashes his heart ascended to become the "morning star," symbolically infusing the universe with more light. In the Far East, scores of drawings have immortalized Hanuman, the Hindu monkey god, exposing his heart to reveal the union of Rama and Sita, the mas-culine and feminine archetypes in the epic *Ramayana*. Similarly, countless portraits lionize Christ opening his chest to display his eternally beating heart, his immortal higher self, his inner king. His body—the Kingdom or the ego self—perished so that his heart would live on. These paintings adorn churches and muse-ums the world over, provoking generation after generation liter-ally to weep at their beauty.

Love, Love, Love

"On the cross, his heart burned like fire and a furnace from which the flames burst forth on all sides," wrote Meister Eckehart, the mystical Christian theologian in thirteenth-century Germany. "So he was inflamed on the cross by his fire of love for the whole world." Christ died for love—his love of God and his love of humanity. It is the heart that generates love—the force of attrac-tion that impels us to merge with others and the impetus that drives us back to God. Love attracts people to other people, to particular lands, to concepts, and to things living and inanimate. Beauty first ignites our love for the sliver of God within our own hearts, and this ultimate form of love geysering up from deep inside imparts the catalyst for our unification with the fragments of God within everything else.

The mergers inspired by love define the act of creation—the amalgamation of two or more separate units to form a new and singular entity. All creativity springs from the magnetic tug of love, from this irresistible impulse to connect. The fire of love— personified by Christ's inflamed heart on the cross—kindles all things beautiful.

Sacrifice—The Universal Symbol

Odin, the chief god of the Norse, sacrificed himself to attain celestial knowledge. He suspended himself upside down over a river from a branch of the exalted ash tree, called *Yggdrasil*. He fabricated a spear from one of the branches and stabbed himself in the liver. After nine days, he discovered the runes engraved on pebbles in the water—the magical letters of divination employed to this day. This Scandinavian myth incorporates all the elements that encircle and conjoin in Beauty. The river is Mercy; the spear symbolizes Severity; the Tree represents Mother Nature or Eternity; and the magic of the runes evokes the communicative energy of Splendor. Odin hung himself upside down for 9 days, which is Beauty's number 6 flipped on end. And the Norse spell the name for the runes, *Futhark*, with the first six letters of their alphabet.

North American nations like the Sioux and Blackfoot commemorated Beauty in a ceremony called the Sun Dance. The braves of these tribes pierced their chests with sharp eagles' claws or wooden spears and then hooked their chests to trees with leather straps. Staring at the Sun, the symbol of Beauty, they danced, swayed, and tugged against the straps until the skin covering their hearts ripped right off their bodies. This ritual facilitated the sacrifice of the initiates' flesh to their higher selves. It afforded them the opportunity to reveal metaphorically and quite literally their beautiful hearts. For the rest of their lives, these men flaunted their ritual scars as badges of distinction. And Native American woman considered them irresistible marks of beauty.

Beauty requires a sacrifice of you this week. You don't have to tear out your flesh, hang upside down, or hammer spears into your liver. We abandon that type of theatricality to myth. But you must willingly climb on the cross to extract your heart from the inside out. You must forfeit something pertaining to your ego. For example, a man who wished to find a fulfilling relationship realized that he invariably filled a couple of hours every day competing in games or conversing with others on the Internet. These activities assuaged some of his loneliness and enabled him to communicate with many entertaining people, but they sucked up a lot of his time. In the week of Beauty, he chose to sacrifice his play on the Internet. Instead, he used those hours to venture out in the world with friends and on his own, trusting in synchronicity to convey him closer to his dream.

WISH MAKER: Sacrifice something that will make you more beautiful in your own eyes. Don't fall back on the concept of discipline you practiced in Understanding. Beauty commands more. Beauty necessitates a permanent destruction for your higher good. Whatever you sacrifice is never coming back. Allow the Tree to guide you to your sacrifice and then accept it. You might want to search your dreams. We passed through Mercy, which granted us access to dreams and the subconscious. Then we traveled to Severity, which infused us with the fire and initiative integral to the accomplishment of the task. In Beauty, you wed these two spheres in sacrifice and uncover your heart.

Beauty and the Beast

A dazzling prince lived alone in a magnificent castle. More beautiful than any movie star and richer than an oil baron, he was no doubt the world's supreme catch. But inside his luminous hardbodied skin, well, let's just say he wasn't so pretty.

One rainy evening, an old hag knocks on his door. "I have here a rose," her ugliness tells him. (In the vernacular of the Tree of Life, "I have here your inner beauty.") "I will give it to you, as long as you provide me shelter from this storm," she says.

"I'd like to help," the prince replies, "but you are so hideous. I just can't deal with people like you. Please go."

"You really don't understand anything, do you?" the woman exclaims. "Take this rose, but know that you must find someone who loves you and wants to marry you before the last petal withers. Find her, or you will die."

The prince chortles. "That's your threat? There isn't a girl alive who can resist me."

"Not quite," says the scary witch. She waves her arthritic hand and switches his insides with his outsides, transfiguring the dreamy prince into a monster.

Meanwhile, far down the road, bad luck visits another rich man. A happy merchant, the father of six boys and six girls, loses everything in a horrible fire. Penniless, the merchant and his children retreat to a shack in the woods to eke out their survival on potatoes and weeds. Then one day the merchant receives news that the last of his ships, crammed full of treasure, has limped into port.

The rich-again merchant gathers his children and asks them their wishes. A car, a DVD, Jimmy Choo shoes, the deprived clan catalog their desires. "I want a rose," the youngest, named Belle, announces at the end over a chorus of snickers from the rest of the brood. Beauty is her name and her heart's desire. She craves nothing but a small slice of alchemy.

Armed with the list, the merchant hits the road, but when he arrives in the city, he discovers that his partners have beaten him to the loot. All has been sold or traded; all of it is gone. On his shameful trip home, a storm wallops him, and he seeks sanctuary in an incomparable palace. "Hello," he calls to the empty house. A sumptuous feast lies untouched on the table. The starving merchant cannot resist the aroma of meats and sauces. He sits and eats until he falls asleep in his plush velvet chair. He wakes the next morning to a plate of buttery croissants and marmalade. "Thank you," he calls out again, then strolls outside into the heart of a resplendent rose garden.

"What a miracle!" he cries. "I have nothing for my children. I failed them all. But at least I can bring my Belle a small taste of beauty."

He plucks a yellow rose. But what happens when you pluck a rose? You bleed.

"You have to die," the noxious Beast snarls as he tosses the merchant to the ground. "You ate my food. I gave you everything, and yet you deign to steal a piece of beauty, though I am such a Beast with so little to spare?"

"But my daughter. I only wanted . . ."

"A daughter!" the Beast interrupts, seizing upon the antidote to the old hag's spell. "You have a choice. Send your daughter to me in your place and I will let you live."

Trembling, the merchant trudges home to make his final goodbyes. "But it's Belle's fault," his children bawl. "That stupid rose. She should go and face the Beast."

Belle wipes a tear and steps forward. The sacrificial lamb. "It is my fault, Father. I asked for the rose. I will go. It is right."

She arrives at sunset, the entire palace aglow in inexplicable color. Inside she finds a table heaped with food that mirrors the hues of the sunset in the sky outside. Scared and repulsed, she dines with the Beast. To break the witch's curse, the Beast understands that he must ask two questions. The first, "Do you love me?," belongs to the expanding pillar of Mercy. The second, "Will you marry me?," epitomizes the restrictive pillar of Severity and the lawful commitments that marriage entails. When commingled like the rainbow, these two pillars fashion the balance of Beauty.

"Do not lie," the Beast begins. "Do you love me? Will you marry me?"

Belle swallows hard. "No. No," she answers. And the Beast skulks sullenly away. That night, Belle dreams of an astonishingly handsome prince. He clutches her hand and declares, "I love you. I am close. Look in your heart. Save me."

The Beast must have imprisoned the prince, Belle concludes. I have to save him. She darts from room to room, flinging open closets and chestnut armoires, unlocking drawers and trapdoors, desperate to unshackle the man of her dreams. In the ballroom, she finds a portrait of the prince. How strange, she thinks. Why would the beast have a picture of his hostage? Day after day she scours the palace. And every evening she sups with the Beast. He's fascinating. He's intelligent. He grows on her. But he's just so unsightly.

And then one afternoon, she peers into a mirror and glimpses her father terribly sick back home. "My father is dying," she pleads to the Beast.

"I love you, my Beauty, but I see that you are suffering." He hands her a magic gold ring. And he dispatches her to the basement to load up four boxes—the four chambers of the heart—with as much treasure for her family as she pleases. He symbolically fills her heart with beauty. "But know this," the Beast declares. "If you don't return in sixty days, I will die."

Belle carts off the gifts—laptops, luscious fabrics, and jewels large and small. She arrives home a hero and nurses her father to health. Sixty days pass before she dreams of her prince again. He sprawls beside a desiccated rose. "You promised to save me," he whispers with his last ounce of vitality. "You are a cruel one."

Belle wakes, panicked. She twists the gold ring and it transports her to the palace. She spots the same withered rose, but it is the Beast that she finds bluish and inert. She's too late. He's gone. She extends her hand to stroke his beastly face.

"Do you love me?" The Beast's eyes blink open a crack.

"Yes."

"Will you marry me?"

"I will."

The spell disintegrates. The Beast reverts to the unspeakably handsome prince. He embraces Belle. And they live happily ever after in the golden idyll of Beauty.

The Moral

See the beauty inside others; don't judge a book (or a beast) by its cover. These core lessons have sustained the life of this old tale for centuries. But the true moral transcends these ageless clichés. This story lays bare much more than the happy communion of two characters named Beauty and Beast. It actually recounts one of the most essential lessons of the Kabbalistic Tree of Life. The prince embodies both the beauty and the beast. Beauty and Beast are One. It's the same for each of us. We all contain Beauty and Beast, Crown and Kingdom, divinity and ego. Our body is the Beast; our soul is the Beauty. Each needs the other. For most of us, it requires tenacity and big sacrifice to surmount the petitions of the body and ego. But this fairy tale urges us to unify Kingdom and Crown, ego and soul, Beast and Beauty. Only when we internalize the fact that they are not isolated do we engender the love, enchantment, and Beauty upon which the entire creation pivots.

We must strive to accept the beastly part of ourselves as well as our beautiful spirit. Only equilibrium builds perfection in our lives. If we tilt too much toward the material world, we end up lonely greedy beasts. If we veer too far toward the spiritual, we might wind up like Belle, locked in dreams, enamored of a fantasy rather than a flesh-and-blood human.

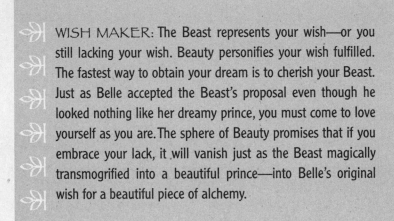

WISH MAKER: The Beast represents your wish—or you still lacking your wish. Beauty personifies your wish fulfilled. The fastest way to obtain your dream is to cherish your Beast. Just as Belle accepted the Beast's proposal even though he looked nothing like her dreamy prince, you must come to love yourself as you are. The sphere of Beauty promises that if you embrace your lack, it will vanish just as the Beast magically transmogrified into a beautiful prince—into Belle's original wish for a beautiful piece of alchemy.

Present's Present

We accomplish the marriage of Beauty and Beast by eloping on a highway named No Regrets. In the story, Belle persistently dodges remorse. She does not rue her request for a rose. She does not lament her captivity with the Beast. Belle avoids the "what if?" She never whines, "If only I hadn't bought those bad stocks or agreed to that divorce." But beyond *accepting* her plight, which is a lesson implanted by Mercy, Belle ascends one step further by mixing in Severity. She takes hardship upon herself. She accedes to a sacrifice. First, she sacrificed herself to the prison of the Beast to rescue her father. And then she consented to marry the revolting creature to save his life. Only then did her wish—for a rose, for magic, for beauty, for love—come true.

Beauty is everywhere. But Beauty always fades. The sunset erupts gorgeously for a few minutes and then dies away fast. The rose withers. Supermodels grow wrinkled. Beauty exists only in the moment. It compels us to live in that moment. Regrets defeat the sovereignty of the present by yanking us back into the past. "If only" cannot be beautiful. Only this moment right now shimmers with beauty. Don't miss it.

WISH MAKER: What do you regret? A decision in the past? An opportunity not taken? Remorse exposes the dark side of your wish, the enemy of your fulfillment. Turn to Mercy and imagine showering yourself with compassion in the moment of those so-called mistakes. You did the best you could. Fortify yourself with the curative power of Beauty. Feel the Sun on your skin. And sacrifice your regret.

The Setting of Beauty

It doesn't matter how many snapshots or video clips of the sunset we have stashed away in our drawers and libraries. This sublime moment when the day kisses the night generates more pictures, more videos, more movie clips, more creativity every single day. We go on vacation and lug home rolls of this same scene. We seek to capture beauty, even though nothing beautiful lasts forever except the concept of beauty itself.

Spiritual masters of the Tree have learned to observe Beauty in every moment and every thing. That is how they make something permanent of Beauty. Artists too strive to ensnare beauty— to freeze it forever on a canvas or symphonic score. In Hebrew, the word for "artist," *Oman*, originates from the same root as the word *Amen*, which means "faith" or "belief." Artists put their faith in beauty; they dedicate their lives to it. Even when no one praises or pays them for their efforts, they continue to believe in their struggle to corral it and to share it with others.

We all can't be artists. Or spiritual masters. But even when we fail to appreciate the beauty of life in every moment—or even in any moment—of our harried days, the sunset arrives each evening to remind us that beauty thrives here on Earth all the time.

The Sphere of Healing

In many traditions, the Sun god also served as the deity of health. In Kabbalistic terms, since the Sun sits in the center of the Tree, rejuvenation results from balance. In Greek mythology, Apollo reigned as both the god of the Sun and the god of healing. His oracle at Delphi resided between two marble posts. One pillar read, KNOW THYSELF, a message from the Tree's right column of expansion. The other pillar warned, NOTHING IN EXCESS, the maxim of the left column of restriction. Beauty's oracle—the representative of the Sun and the energy of remedies and therapeutics—was encamped in the middle.

Beauty rules children—"Oh, your baby is so beautiful." And children are blessed with the facility to recuperate faster than any of us. Scientists postulate that stem cells culled from embryos hold the secrets for vanquishing many diseases of aging. Whenever you crave healing in your body, mind, or soul, invoke the sphere of Beauty—the sphere of the Sun, equilibrium, and childlike playfulness.

 WISH MAKER: Beauty is the sphere of fun, and children know best how to have fun. No mortgage, no insurance premiums, no bosses. More than any of us, they live in the exuberance of the moment. This week, behave like the child you once

> were. Return to the age of nine or ten and recall the activities
> you adored back then. Resurrect those feelings and revisit
> those amusements. For example, one man who wished to
> develop more dependable friendships recalled that as a kid he
> loved to play basketball. He decided to gather some of his
> acquaintances for a weekly game. This long-neglected diver-
> sion not only injected more joy into his life, but it enriched his
> relationships too. It spurred him to realize that he could trea-
> sure his interactions with others even when he found himself
> on the losing end of the score.

The Real Sixth Sense

The most famous mantras in the world contain exactly six words
or syllables to honor the eminence of the heart. The Torah's *Shema
Yisrael Adonai Eloheinu Adonai Ehad* ("Hear O Israel, the Lord is
God, the Lord is One"); the Tibetan *Om Mani Padme Hum*; and the
Hindu *O Nama Shivaya*. It took six days to create the universe, a
signal that everything finds completion in Beauty. Describing
Christ's sacrifice on the cross, the Gospel of Matthew reports:
"From the sixth hour onward there was darkness all over the
Earth." In the New Testament, 666 is the sign of "the Beast"—
another reminder that Beauty and Beast are One.

In numerology, six corresponds to equilibrium and harmony.
One plus two plus three equals six. The sum of Crown, Wisdom,
and Understanding, the highest trinity, is Beauty. Six also embodies the four directions (north, south, east, and west) plus up and
down (the spiritual dimension). The cube, the Kabbalistic symbol
of the universe, has six sides. "The owner of the heart," wrote
Mevlana Jalaluddin Rumi, the great Sufi poet, "becomes a six-

faced mirror; through him God looks out upon all six directions."

The Star of David, the imperial shield that protected the legendary king from negativity, encompasses six points on two interlocking triangles. The triangle that points up (the alchemical symbol for fire) denotes the masculine energy and the divine. The triangle that aims down (the alchemical symbol for water) signifies the feminine energy and humankind. In Beauty, all these opposites (water/fire, male/female, God/human, heaven/earth) conjoin in matchless concord. In Hindu lore, the six-pointed star symbolizes the heart chakra, or *Anahata*. This tradition also celebrates a mini-chakra situated just below the heart called *Kalpataru*, which translates as "the wish-fulfilling tree." The Hindus contend that this energy source aids in the manifestation of wishes just as the sphere of Beauty delivers the first palpable glimmer of your wish fulfilled.

WISH MAKER: An encounter with the number six or the colors yellow or gold—the tangible symbols of Beauty—points toward a sacrifice that you need to make or something beautiful that you ought to acknowledge.

The Ash Tree

Odin's tree of sacrifice, considered the regal god's enchanted steed, flourished as "The World Tree" throughout northern Europe. Imposingly tall and broad, the ash spreads its leaves across several continents. Many cultures proclaimed it the bridge between heaven and Earth. St. Patrick reportedly wielded a staff of ash to banish the snakes from Ireland, metaphorically infusing the land with Christ consciousness. And we make baseball bats, the tools at the heart of what many consider America's most beautiful pastime, out of this hard and sturdy wood.

Ruled by the Sun, the ash attains its regal beauty in the heat of summer. The British burned the tree as the Yule log in winter, recalling the light and warmth of the Sun in the season of darkness. Wood from the ash also bears up heartily in water and endowed Viking ships with speed and maneuverability. This affinity with both fire and water induced ancient empires to envisage the marriage of all opposites in the ash. It symbolized the link between man's inner and outer worlds. Healers used the bark of the tree to alleviate fevers (the fire of Severity). In other words, the sphere of Beauty bestows the antidote for too much Severity.

Name of God

Use Yod Hey Vav Hey Eloha Vada'at (pronounced Yod Hey Vahv Hey El-low-hah Vah-Dah-Aht) as the mantra of Beauty. First it combines the name of God for Wisdom (Yod Hey Vav Hey) and the name of God for Understanding (Eloha, a feminized version of Elohim). Then this mantra adjoins the word *Da'at*, which means "to know" and also "to have intercourse." When Wisdom—the father, the undifferentiated mind, and the power of expansion— makes love to Understanding—the mother, the left hemisphere of language and reason, and the energy of restriction—they beget perfection. The mantra for Beauty marries and mingles logic and intuition as well as time and infinity in the center of your heart.

 WISH MAKER: This mantra operates as a powerful tool to aid creativity. Whenever you require assistance with an artistic project, raising children, or enhancing peace, balance, and beauty in your life, summon this name of God.

Meditation

Sit in a comfortable position and relax. Breathe deeply and imagine yourself in the most beautiful place in the world. Watch as the Sun sets spectacularly before your eyes. Envision yourself sitting inside a golden circle that surrounds you like an aura. Place your hand on your wrist or neck and detect your pulse. Try to decelerate your heartbeat as if you were the conductor of an orchestra, imploring the musicians to play slower and deeper. As the pace drops, listen as the volume of your heartbeat swells. Go deeper into yourself. Slow your breathing. Try to inhale more air with every breath.

Now imagine that you are sitting between two columns within that circle of gold. Picture a white shining sphere of transparent bright light just above the crown of your head. Feel it radiate with power. Project your wish into that sphere—almost as if you are programming a divine computer. Embellish this vision with as many details as possible. Envision your wish exactly as you want it.

Now launch a ray of light toward your heart. Construct the yellow sphere of Beauty. Imagine that the Sun has settled in your heart. You hold the entire solar disk inside your chest, emanating love, beauty, valor, and health all around you. Project an image of your wish already fulfilled into this beautiful sphere of golden light. Picture yourself happy and childlike, delighting in the benefits of your wish like a new toy. Envision yourself offering thanks to God for granting your wish.

Now chant the name of God for Beauty, *Yod Hey Vav Hey Eloha Vada'at*. Repeat it again and again. As you intone this mantra, focus on the brilliant golden sphere pulsing in your heart, illuminating your beautiful soul for all to see. After you have chanted for a few minutes, take a big breath and hold the air inside for as long as you can. Imagine each and every cell in your body transformed into gold, into a tiny sphere of Beauty. Breathe in again and implant the image of your wish fulfilled into each golden cell. Breathe in one last time, hold the air, and listen to the mantra of Beauty vibrating inside you. And then, when you feel ready, gently come back to the here and now.

Wish List—Beauty

1. Sacrifice something to make yourself more beautiful (godly).

2. Avoid all emotional extremes. Seek out the middle path.

3. Visualize your wish fulfilled. (See exercise 1, below.)

4. Find clues of beauty, equilibrium, and sacrifice in your every coincidental meeting with the envoys of the sphere: the Sun, roses, children, gold and yellow, sunset, love, six, stars, celebrities, and the heart. Hunt this week to unveil the beauty in everything.

5. Wish progress: Persist with the course of action you have implemented over the past three weeks. But remember to pause to catch a glimpse of your wish come true. Some progress or manifestation has occurred. Your job is to find it. And enhance it.

Exercise Zone

1. **Visualize the Beauty of Success:** Turn to your Abralog and write six paragraphs describing your wish fulfilled in as many details as possible. Include outcomes and consequences that you have not

allowed yourself to contemplate before. For example, a woman who wished to expand her accounting business imagined her appointment book crammed with meetings from morning until night. She pictured a bigger office and a larger staff, new computers and copy machines too. She saw herself redecorating her new office with antique lamps and her favorite art deco posters. She wrote about finally being able to afford a long-postponed bicycle trip along the Po River in Italy. And of course she imagined her tax forms reporting a tripled income and the requisite increased sum she would have to pay to the IRS. All of this detail enabled her to visualize her wish during her meditations in a more concrete fashion. This exercise will also facilitate your discovery of new and surprising strategies for attaining your wish. Another woman wished to reestablish a loving relationship with her cantankerous father. As she wrote about the outings they would go on together and the appreciative things they would say to each other, she remembered how much her father had loved the homemade honey cakes her deceased mother used to bake for him. She realized that one way to achieve her wish was to bake him some cakes. During the week of Beauty, she brought her father a treat. And as a result she saw a glimmer—at least while he was eating and then graciously thanking her for the cake—of her wish fulfilled.

☞ 2. **Beautiful Them:** Visit a café or other public place. Choose someone—a waitress or another patron—and try to perceive who he or she really is. Invent a history. Is she married? What does he do for fun? What kind of childhood did she have? What will he be like in ten years? Formulate a biography for this person. As she becomes more complete and human in your mind, you will begin to notice the beauty inside her. Beauty in the way he moves. Beauty in the way she blinks her eyes. Don't hunt for beauty only in a young TV star or homecoming queen. Witness the beauty in an average person. Everyone, if we really probe, carries great beauty inside. You will discover that recognizing beauty in others automatically makes you more beautiful. It is the one way we can all become more attractive without makeup.

☞ 3. **The Beauty in You:** Sit naked in front of a full-length mirror for six minutes each day this week and stare at your body—or, in the argot of fairy tales, your Beast. Most of us dislike at least one of our features, one body part that is too big, too small, or too saggy. The only way to heal this discontent is to accept it. This exercise might seem trivial, but it has saved many people a great deal of money in plastic surgery bills. As you gaze at yourself, imagine a society in which you are the supreme symbol of beauty. Your body is the one that everyone desires. You might feel ridiculous the first few times you attempt this exercise. But if you persist in gazing at your Beast throughout this week, your Beauty eventually will, like Belle, fall in love with it. Admiring your body likely will change the way you carry yourself, dress, and even the way you talk. It will free you to expose your inner beauty to the world rather than shroud it behind your self-consciousness. And it will prompt you to see beyond the Beast of others to the Beauty sparkling within them too.

CHAPTER SEVEN

ETERNITY:

The Energy of Relationships, Pleasure, Venus, and the Shaman

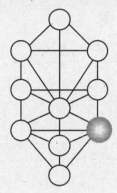

S P H E R E   7

KEYWORDS: Repetition; Relationship; Mother Nature

WISH IMPERATIVE: Replicate again and again all the behaviors and thoughts that have paid dividends thus far.

HEBREW NAME: Netzach

MYTH AND PERSONALITIES: The Seven Orishas of the Yoruba; Bathsheba; all the shamans.

PLANET: Venus

DARK SIDE: Vanity; laziness

COLOR: Green

NUMBER: 7

TREE: Apple or your favorite fruit tree

BODY PART: Right hip, right leg

HEBREW NAME OF GOD (MANTRA): Yod Hey Vav Hey Tzevaot (the armies of the energy of Wisdom)

The Mimeograph Machine

The sphere of Mother Nature, this energy expands through repetition—one cell divides into two identical cells, two into four, four into eight, and so on to infinity. While Wisdom, the sphere at the top of the right pillar of expansion, flashed like a lightning bolt and Mercy inflated like an adjustable switch turned up and up, Eternity, the lowest and most practical energy in the right column, functions like a copy machine. It proliferates through replication, one lit candle after another identical candle until the entire room is filled with Light.

By the time we reach Eternity, we have cascaded down to the forces that breed the dense material stuff of our universe. Eternity and the next sphere, called Splendor, comprise the action plane of the Tree. They prod us toward practical, mechanical measures to compel our creation to bloom. A human being starts out as one cell—the fertilized egg—which splits and duplicates itself billions of times to fabricate the finished product. This process entails no conscious thinking. In nature, it occurs automatically. The sphere of Eternity administers this kind of primal growth. It yields all internal action, including the autonomic physical functions of the human body such as the heartbeat and the digestive system.

While Beauty symbolizes the heart itself, Eternity bestows actual life through the heart's repetitive beat. If you scramble the letters of the word *Netzach* (the Hebrew name of the sphere), it spells the word *Tzanach*, which means "to parachute" or "to drop." This sphere serves to transport all the airy intellectual and fiery emotional axioms of the Tree down to Earth. It grounds us in natural physical processes that maintain our existence.

Evolution

The action plane of Eternity and Splendor prefigured Darwin's theory of evolution. Eternity dispenses the primary force in the evolutionary story—persistent and exact replication. No matter what you deposit in this vessel, Eternity duplicates it again and again. It's like cloning. You start with a white sheep, clone it, and the result is two white sheep comprised of the same DNA. Geraniums multiply in a similar way. Gardeners snip a stem from a living geranium and stick it in the ground. The derivative will be an exact replica of the mother bush. It will present the same look, the same color, and the same diseases, precisely. That's the energy of Mother Nature. Copy-paste, cloning, repetition. No variations anywhere.

Yet every day we confront the astonishing diversity of the natural world. No two people possess the identical hair color or beauty marks. If the creation had terminated in Eternity, then we still would be drifting around as identical amoebas in shallow pools. So what happened? Why are crocodiles different from paramecia? Why are humans more industrious than apes?

The answer is mutation. Millions and millions of "accidents" over a couple of billion years. Across the action plane, in Splendor, the replication of Eternity malfunctions and a mutation springs to life. Most of these abnormalities sputter and die. But every now and then, the anomaly outshines the blueprint. Musicians and artists occasionally blunder their way to glory. The composer clangs an inadvertent chord on the keyboard, and sometimes the mistake elevates the melody in a surprising and brilliant new direction. The accident is a stroke of magic. It inspires a new jazz classic. It begets animals that walk upright. These two complimentary forces on the action plane—repetition and mutation, the relentless internal heartbeat and an external zap of magic—team up perpetually to assemble the variegated biosphere we call home. Eternity epitomizes the jungle, feral and untouched, forever replicating itself and burgeoning out of control. Splendor arrives next to cut through the wilderness, clear roads to connect the villages and towns, and erect civilization as we know it.

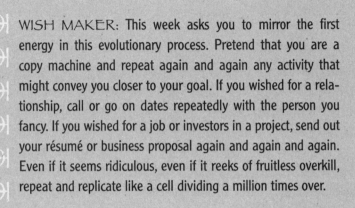

WISH MAKER: This week asks you to mirror the first energy in this evolutionary process. Pretend that you are a copy machine and repeat again and again any activity that might convey you closer to your goal. If you wished for a relationship, call or go on dates repeatedly with the person you fancy. If you wished for a job or investors in a project, send out your résumé or business proposal again and again and again. Even if it seems ridiculous, even if it reeks of fruitless overkill, repeat and replicate like a cell dividing a million times over.

A musician who wished to earn more money from his business opted to fulfill this mission by posting seventy flyers that advertised his private music lessons. He drove from place to place to place, pinning up his flyers again and again. This repetitive act launched him on a wonderful journey that guided him to all sorts of advantageous sites that he never knew existed. He traveled from schools to community centers to bookstores and cafés. At one of the after-school centers he visited, he bumped into the supervisor of activities, who was at that moment looking to hire a music director.

A woman was contemplating a return to school for a master's in psychology. One day the phone rang. She answered and a friend spoke nonstop for an hour about her problems. The woman finally hung up and the phone rang again. A second friend launched into an oration about her troubles. The aspiring psy-

chologist listened compassionately and in the end hung up feeling drained. She went to take a nap, but the phone rang again.
She didn't feel like answering it, but she remembered the energy
of Eternity and figured that her repetition was to answer the
phone. On the other end of the line, another friend whined about
his difficulties. The phone rang again and again that afternoon.
And at the end of the day, the woman realized that she did not
want to be a psychologist.

The Heartbeat of Life

Cells replicate; lungs breathe; hearts beat. Nature's internal
rhythms rumble on. Venus, the goddess of pleasure, relationships,
art, music, dance, sensuality, and money, presides over the green
energy of Eternity. This sphere engenders the instinct of attrac-
tion—the involuntary impulse that drives the sperm toward the
ovum. This reflex resounds in the spring as the internal calling
that impels sentient beings to hunt for mates. Though sexuality is
ruled by Foundation, two spheres below, Eternity instills the
inner voice of desire that incites us to action. This sphere spawns
the nitty-gritty interpersonal love we all cherish, as opposed to
the cosmic unconditional love generated by Mercy or the more
spiritualized, transcendent couplings venerated in Beauty.

Eternity succeeds Beauty and tries desperately to preserve and
prolong it. The sunny resplendence of Beauty exists only in the
moment and then dies in sacrifice to the next beautiful Now. The
repetition of the heartbeat arrives in Eternity like a paramedic with
her CPR, imploring the Beauty of the heart to remain alive. Beauty
sparks the urge to create, while Eternity inaugurates the means to
do it. Artists, for example, find their inspiration to create in
Beauty, but the art itself, which aspires to preserve the ephemeral
flash of Beauty, makes its home in Eternity. A masterpiece like Van

Gogh's *Sunflowers* managed to freeze an instant of perfection on canvas. And, true to the sphere of art, money, and replication, the painting's monetary value doubled and then quadrupled until it evolved into one of the most expensive paintings ever sold. The moment of beauty of those actual sunflowers as Van Gogh perceived them one day in the French countryside evaporated rather quickly. But the energy of Eternity duplicated them on posters and coffee mugs until the beautiful vision in Van Gogh's brain proliferated all over the world.

Trance, Trance, Trance

Music, often driven by an underlying beat, also derives from Eternity. And this drumbeat triggers a kind of trance. Our heart thumps in us involuntarily, unconsciously. Likewise, the beat that transports us into trance—the hypnotist's watch, the reiteration of a mantra, or steady deep breathing—aims to remove us from our controlled thinking self and plug us into the instinctive power of Eternity.

All cultures that celebrate trance rituals—the tradition of the Yoruba in Africa and the West Indies, for example—are embedded in Eternity. Their drum music and cyclical dance moves hypnotize the supplicants into a state in which they cannot control their bodies. They simply become the rhythm. Shamans tap the energy of Eternity to invoke the magic of healing. "The shaman's power rests in his ability to throw himself into a trance at will," Joseph Campbell wrote in *Primitive Mythology*. "The magic of his drum carries him away on the wings of its rhythm, the wings of spirit, and conjures to him his familiars—the beasts and birds, invisible to others, that have supplied him with his power and assist him in his flight. And it is while in his trance of rapture that he performs his miraculous deeds."

All of these shamanistic cultures were and are more attuned to the primal mechanism of the Earth than are most Western societies, and their religious rites originated in the energy of Mother Nature's sphere as well. The Yoruba believe that the One reveals itself through nature, through seven Orishas or angels, which each manifest a specific archetypal energy of God. (Seven is the number of this sphere.) If a Yoruba wishes to connect to the spirit of love and sensuality, for example, he or she conjures Oshun, the goddess of the river, through prescribed drumbeats, rhythms, and movements.

Many of us have experienced driving on the highway and then suddenly snapping to, only to realize that we've traveled a great distance—even missed our off ramp—without recalling how we arrived there. That's not a safe method for seeking the trance, but it is emblematic of the hypnotic state supplied by this sphere. The repetition of a mantra or listening to music often induces a trance state. Staring at a Mark Rothko painting or a Tibetan drawing called *tanka* initiates a similar reverie for some. Dancing uninhibitedly often removes people from their cognitive selves. Running or swimming laps at the Y works too. Even washing the dishes or pulling weeds can elicit a trance.

 WISH MAKER: Explore various methods of hypnotizing yourself. Isolate the activity that delivers your trance. If jogging around a circular track does the job, then whenever you find yourself in trouble or a state of agitation, running and the trance it stirs can serve as your ally. Your trance ritual represents your means of summoning your spirits of potential. When you identify the repetitive behavior that entrances your mind, that stills your thinking, that removes you from the importunate flotsam of your brain, milk it often and observe what sort of messages or feelings the trance consigns to your life.

Mars and Venus on a Date

The goddess of attraction and relationship accumulated bus-loads of lovers. Gods, humans, even Adonis, the most handsome of all, bowed before her seductive charms. But from the moment she emerged resplendent from the sea foam, carnality was not enough. Venus yearned for her true partner. She craved the perfect relationship.

Sometimes even goddesses have trouble fulfilling their wishes. As a solution to some godly intrigue, Venus was compelled to marry Vulcan, the lame and repulsive craftsman, the manufacturer of Zeus's thunderbolts and the wings of Hermes, the gadget guy of Olympus. Venus learned to love Vulcan because he presented her with all sorts of sparkly toys. And he made tons of money. Venus loves money. But her longing for an authentic partnership swelled as the passionless years dragged on. She hungered for someone to adore with her every luscious curve and fiber.

She located him in her polar opposite: the macho, muscular god of war. And once she glanced his way, the duo couldn't keep their hands off each other. Venus and Mars communed in secret late at night, luxuriating in the beguiling succor of their magnetic counterparts.

Nobody's fool, the crafty Vulcan excelled at surveillance too, and he plotted a humiliating revenge. He constructed an invisible net around the bower that Venus and Mars had erected for their trysts. And as the ultimate couple made love on a silky bed of petals, Vulcan sprang his trap, prompting all the gods on Olympus to race to the garden to gawk at the spectacle of a naked Venus and Mars dangling upside down in the invisible snare.

Nine months passed, and Venus gave birth to the most beautiful creature that had ever graced Olympus. The daughter of Venus and Mars personified the marriage of the pure masculine traits of her father and the pristine feminine attributes of her mother. She effloresced as the faultless amalgamation of male and female, right column and left. They called her Harmonia. And to this day, her name, the emblem of the central sphere of Beauty in the Tree of Life, prevails as the most flattering compliment you can pay to just about anything. Harmony in design, in color, in music, in a relationship, in a family, a nation, the world. Harmony (Beauty) certifies that Venus (Eternity) balances Mars (Severity). Green mitigates red. Growth beautifies destruction. Female soothes male and male invigorates female. Earth cradles the burning flame. Neither extinguishes or subdues the other. Instead, they need each other desperately. They marry. They blend. They sire the center of all things—the most beautiful children, the most scrumptious music and food, the enduring prolongation of Beauty.

Neither can do it alone. "It takes two to make a thing go right," "It takes two to tango." Venus and the sphere of Eternity infuse the world with the imperative of relationship—the mandate to find your opposite, to intermingle no matter the hardship, the embarrassment, or the invisible traps that obstruct your path. The heart as defined in Beauty shimmers as a divine, perhaps unattainable ideal. But lower now on the practical plane of the Tree, Eternity delivers the marvel that is our heartbeat, our actual physical life. And with life, like a door prize, comes the gift of relationships—with a spouse, our children, a friend, a dog, with anything—so that we can procreate harmony, balance, and peace in our tangible everyday lives. In a sense, we accentuate our love for God inside of us (Beauty) by practicing in Eternity on others.

These relationships function as our mirrors. "Show me your friends, and I will show you who you are," affirms a famous Muslim proverb. We attract people who reflect both our assets and our Achilles' heels. Like a mirror, our intimates don't conceal a thing, illuminating our coups and talents as well as our shadows, wrinkles, and fears. In Beauty, we mastered the glorious art of sacrifice. Eternity bestows the concept of relationship to allow us the opportunity to build on what we have learned in a more mundane and practical manner—to sacrifice our needs not for the sake of merging with the divine, but for the benefit of a relationship. Relationships always demand compromise. To ensure the survival of any affiliation, each individual must bend. For example, a man who adored classical music was obliged to compromise when he moved in with a younger woman who could not start the day without blasting a raucous rap song. Tolerating her musical proclivities proved to be an enormous concession for this elegant man. But this acquiescence engendered his own Harmonia—a breathtaking aura of beauty around his life that did not exist before. In return for his accommodation to household amity, he received a loving and deliciously happy woman waking up at his side each day, whereas previously he had had nothing but Mozart and his goldfish to keep him company.

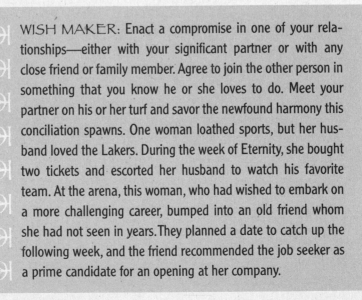

WISH MAKER: Enact a compromise in one of your relationships—either with your significant partner or with any close friend or family member. Agree to join the other person in something that you know he or she loves to do. Meet your partner on his or her turf and savor the newfound harmony this conciliation spawns. One woman loathed sports, but her husband loved the Lakers. During the week of Eternity, she bought two tickets and escorted her husband to watch his favorite team. At the arena, this woman, who had wished to embark on a more challenging career, bumped into an old friend whom she had not seen in years. They planned a date to catch up the following week, and the friend recommended the job seeker as a prime candidate for an opening at her company.

The Color of Money

Green, the clothes of Mother Nature, is the color of Eternity. Experiments have verified that green evokes a sense of peace in the human brain. It makes sense. On the color wheel, green lies in the middle of the spectrum, directly opposite red, the color of blood and war. If red equals war, then green equates to the opposite of war. The root of the Hebrew name of this sphere, *Netzach*, also spells the word *Victory*. Many books on Kabbalah use this alternate translation as the name of the seventh sphere. According to this phonetic interpretation of the Tree, Victory derives not from conquering and ruling over our opponents but from the color green. True Victory is peace. Our real triumph is the compromise and conciliation necessitated by relationship.

In many traditions, green represents immortality (Eternity). It emerges from a mixture of blue (Mercy) and yellow (Beauty). Green therefore embodies the qualities of expansion and creativity. The green lion in the literature of alchemy symbolizes the beginning of a great opus. The Koran (18:59–81) depicts a mysterious character named al-Khidir, which translates as "verdant" or the Green One. This shamanlike spirit, the holy book of Islam reports, served as "the companion" (the relationship energy of Eternity) to Moses and Alexander the Great, both of whom were warriors of the red sphere, Severity. This immortal Green One functioned as the emissary of nature and a source of supernatural wisdom.

In other traditions, green typifies envy. Jealousy and possessiveness originate in the darker qualities of Venus, who, when overindulged, often becomes excessively attached to material things and to other people. Green suggests the power of nature untamed. Bridgit, the Earth goddess of Celtic lore, always wore green. Nitrogen, the primary component of the Earth's atmosphere, is tinted green too. In a sense, we live encased in a gigantic green sphere. It can endow us with peace and pleasure, or it can

provoke jealousy and greed. Money—appropriately tinted green
in the United States—is never about having it. It's all about how
we disburse the currency; how we spend the green energy. The
rich and evocative power of green accounts for the passion of
environmentalists. When we clear-cut the green forest, we simultaneously sever the energy of Eternity and all it stands for.

In color therapy, green is used to calm and soothe. It
decreases blood pressure and quiets the sympathetic nervous
system. A simple walk in nature will dispel the most acute anxiety. A recent study by Francis Kuo and William Sullivan of the
Human Environment Research Laboratory at the University of
Illinois demonstrated that the mere presence of urban parks and
vegetation strengthened community ties, reduced levels of aggression and violence, lowered crime rates, and alleviated everyday
stress. (Eternity supplies the cure for too much Severity.) Their
research also revealed that Attention Deficit Disorder—which
often manifests in hyperactivity (a Severity overdose)—declined
when children paid regular visits to open green spaces. The
twentieth century witnessed the most prolific slaughter of both
human beings and green spaces in recorded history. Using the
energetic logic of the Tree of Life, it is no great leap to the conclusion that the systematic elimination of the world's green canopy
helped to precipitate the unprecedented spasms of genocide that
have scarred the last hundred years.

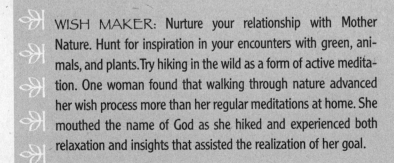

WISH MAKER: Nurture your relationship with Mother
Nature. Hunt for inspiration in your encounters with green, animals, and plants. Try hiking in the wild as a form of active meditation. One woman found that walking through nature advanced
her wish process more than her regular meditations at home. She
mouthed the name of God as she hiked and experienced both
relaxation and insights that assisted the realization of her goal.

The Pleasure Principle

Venus rules the pleasures of the body. And this sphere invites you to pamper yourself. Chocolate cakes, fancy restaurants, pretty trinkets and jewels all spring from the voluptuousness of the feminine goddess. Venus infuses life with pleasure. And pleasure is one of the greatest boons we know. Without this sensual creative force, our entire journey, all of life, would likely devolve into a dry, artless bore. Imagine the world without sensuality, partnership, caresses, music, dance, fashion, or big wide grins. Who'd want to?

The planet Venus itself sports a stunningly colorful atmosphere that drapes her like a beautiful dress. Venus often reigns as the brightest object in the sky at dawn and dusk. Known as the morning and evening star, she rises before all the other planets and sets long after the others have disappeared. For centuries in myriad cultures and tough times, the sparkling jewel of the heavens symbolized light and hope in the black loneliness of the night. Sailors at sea routinely reclined on deck to watch Venus rise and set, imagining her as their long-deprived paramour awaiting them onshore.

Pleasure, however we define or find it, nudges us forward. It yanks us out of the stagnation of routine. It propagates the species. It makes life go on. It makes it fun to go on. From Earth we are able to observe Venus approximately 263 days out of every year. The average human pregnancy lasts 265 days. No wonder this goddess has forever been associated with *Mother* Nature. A vital force in just about every culture, Venus over the ages has assumed many names: Ishtar in Chaldea, Benu in Sumeria, Nabu in Babylonia, Anahita in Persia, and Hoku-loa in Hawaii.

For all her wonders, Venus does wield a dark side: vanity, affectation, and profligacy. One day on Venus (243 Earth days) outlasts a year (225 days). In other words, it takes Venus more time to rotate once around her own axis than it does for the vain planet to travel millions of miles around the Sun. It's as if Venus won't turn. She's stuck staring at herself in the mirror. If you get trapped in this sphere of repetition, one slice of chocolate cake turns into two, into four, into an entire bakery. The pleasure of one lover repeats into infidelities or stifling possessiveness. And one beautiful new dress becomes yet another, becomes six closets full, becomes an obsession with material goods.

A Reason to Get Out of Bed

The hungry old man had not eaten in a week. Each sunrise, he rose from the mat on the dirt floor of his hut and walked to the nearby village in search of a job. Most days he returned home after dark with nothing in his pockets, chewing on a twig to quell the grumbling in his stomach.

One morning he finally found work constructing a new animal pen for the town's wealthiest family. He sweated all day under the hot sky, carting timber behind the great mansion and spiking the posts into the Sun-baked earth. At the end of the day, his rich employer dipped into his jacket and extracted a fat handful of coins. He picked the equivalent of two dimes from the pile and flipped them toward the scrawny laborer.

Aching with fatigue, the hungry old man shuffled into the village. He limped up to the baker and with the first coin he bought a small loaf of bread. He bit off a piece of the crusty nub and ambled across the plaza to the flower cart. With the second coin, the hungry old man purchased an exquisite lily. Even the flower vender, though grateful for the business, thought he'd gone mad. "But you're starving," the florist said. "Why don't you save your money for something better? For something to eat tomorrow?"

The hungry old man gnawed off another mouthful of bread

and grinned. "The first half of my labor is so I can live," he said. His grin broadened into an exultant smile. "The second half is so I have a reason to live." The hungry old man pressed the flower to his nose. He inhaled with gusto and hiked home rededicated to the proposition that without pleasure there can be no Victory; without pleasure there can be no life.

WISH MAKER: Live a little. Cultivate the energy of Eternity by indulging your senses and all of your favorite things. Take baths with oils and flowers. Buy a massage. Work in the garden. Listen to music. Wear beautiful clothes. In the preceding sphere, you attempted to see the beauty in others. Now exploit that fond feeling to connect one-on-one. Spend time with your partner and friends. Touch them. Dance with them. Tell jokes and laugh. Squander money on yourself. Dine at a lavish restaurant. This journey on the Tree is not all privation and sacrifice. For one week you are safe to enjoy your sensual desires.

Lucky Seven

Nothing demonstrates the irrepressibility of this energy like its number. Seven is ubiquitous. Repeated and repeated and repeated to infinity. "Nature delights in the number seven," declared Philo Judaeus, the illustrious Alexandrian theologian from the time of Christ.

- Seven days of the week.
- Seven chakras.
- The Israelites circumnavigated the walls of Jericho seven times to induce them to fall down. In Jewish wed-

dings, the bride circles the groom seven times—in a sense, to knock down the defensive walls girding his seven chakras, opening him up for a propitious union.

- Seven heads on the dragons of China, India, and the Celts.
- Seven days that Buddha sat for enlightenment.
- Seven sacraments of Christianity.
- Seven circumambulations of Islam's Ka'aba in Mecca.
- Seven dwarfs and seven samurai.
- James Bond, 007, the most repeated character in movie history.
- Seven deadly sins, and the irresistible allure of the mechanical altars to Lucky Seven in Las Vegas.

Many traditions espouse that God's work is revealed in the number seven—in the seven seas and seven continents of planet Earth, the seven heavenly bodies that can be observed with the naked eye, the seven colors of the rainbow, the seven chakras of the human body, and the seven horizontal rungs of the Tree of Life. The relentless mythology erected around seven intimates that whenever you spot a 7, it reverberates as a sign that reads: GOD WAS HERE.

 WISH MAKER: To ensure that you indulge the energy of Eternity to the utmost, give yourself seven presents this week. Even if the gifts are small, allot yourself one treat each day. Buy something you want, go out for ice cream, get a manicure, fritter away an hour alone with your favorite book, etc.

Bathsheba and David
(aka Venus and Mars on Another Date)

David, the warrior-king who unified the twelve tribes of Israel and established Jerusalem as their capital, climbed to his palace roof one night and gazed out at his city. Across the way, he observed a gorgeous woman taking a bath. In an instant he was smitten. He dispatched his messengers who discovered that her name was Bathsheba, which means "the daughter of seven." The daughter of the sphere Eternity. David had fallen for the Venus of Jerusalem.

It didn't matter that she was married. "Bring her to me," he commanded.

She came to David. They made love again and again. They were soulmates, the warrior-king and the daughter of seven. And in this saga too, the "Venus" of Jerusalem conceived.

King David, the composer of psalms, the beloved and favorite son of God, received the news and fretted. He still possessed some morals, though they were certainly questionable on the whole. And fathering a baby with another man's wife would do little to ennoble him in the eyes of his people or his God. To make matters stickier, Bathsheba's husband, Uriah—which translates as the Light of God—was one of the king's most loyal soldiers. When granted a holiday from duty, he chose to sleep in the street in sympathy with his comrades left behind at the front. Uriah said, "The servants of my lord are encamped in an open field, shall I then go into my house to eat and to drink and to lie with my wife. I will not do this thing" (Second Samuel 11:11).

Such virtue humiliated David. And he reacted with still greater dishonor. He ordered his generals to position Uriah at the front. In those days, the front portended something simple: assured and immediate doom.

Back in Jerusalem, Bathsheba mourned her slain husband,

and after a suitable term of grieving, she married the king and bore their son. "But the thing David had done displeased the Lord" (Second Samuel 11:27).

The prophet Nathan dropped in on the king. He told David a story. Two men lived in one city, the prophet recounted. One was rich and the other dirt poor. The wealthy man owned hundreds of sheep and cows, oxen and horses. The poor man possessed nothing except for one small lamb that he treated as a daughter. The lamb slept in a bed with the poor man's children and drank from the man's own cup. One day, an esteemed traveler visited the affluent man, but the stingy host balked at expending one of his own animals to entertain his guest. Instead, he co-opted the poor man's lamb and butchered it for his banquet.

The hot-tempered David went berserk. "The man who has done this pitiless thing deserves to die," he decreed. "Where is he? I will kill him myself."

Nathan paused. "My lord, you are that man," he said.

David fell silent in recognition and shame. And his son by Bathsheba fell ill and died. Repentant, David comforted his wife and she soon gave birth to another boy, whom they named Solomon. "And the lord loved him" (Second Samuel 12:12).

Solomon derives from the Hebrew root meaning "whole" or "complete"—the masculine version of Harmony, the offspring of Venus and Mars. He succeeded David to the throne of Israel, and this archetype of the wise and ultimate king matured into the glory of the sphere of Beauty. Solomon erected the legendary Temple of Jerusalem. Impeccably attuned with nature, he was able to communicate with animals. And blessed with Beauty, suffused with the loving sensual energy of his mother, the daughter of Eternity, he peaceably courted a thousand wives.

Biblical lore prophesizes that the messiah will descend from this family tree. From David's unspeakable sin, perfection is born. It ought to be a great comfort to us all. Out of the worst, the savior will come. Out of the refuse, a jewel appears, just as the oysters of Mercy fashion pearls from the trash of the sea. This saga imparts the essential reminder that whenever something dreadful occurs in your life, even as a consequence of your woeful mistakes, at some point somewhere the absolute best will arise.

The Apple Tree

In all kinds of myths, this lovely tree confers immortality (Eternity). The Garden of Hesperides, the Greek version of paradise that was governed by Aphrodite—this culture's name for Venus—contained a sacred apple tree that delivered eternal life to anyone who ate its fruit. In northern European legend, a paradisiacal apple tree flourished on the Isles of the Blessed. It was guarded by a serpent named Cerridwen, the custodian of the knowledge of the seasons (Mother Nature). The biblical Garden of Eden adopted this snake and apple tree, though the Hebrew text never identifies the type of tree that provided the infamous fruit. Eve, the temptress with knowledge of sexual passion, evokes the qualities of Venus, the goddess of relationships and pleasure.

The apple itself, deliciously dense with sugar, reminds us of the sensual inclinations of Mother Nature and Venus. The Druids included the intoxicating juice of the apple in their sacraments. Irish legend recounts a magical bough cut from an apple tree that hummed with irresistible music—also Venus's domain—which lulled listeners into a revelatory trance. Norse mythology contends that the gods awarded apples to humans to perpetuate youth and vitality. Jealous of her own daughter's youth, the mother of Snow White fed the girl a poisonous apple as a counterspell to her fresh-faced beauty. This woman was also notorious for conversing with her looking glass. "Mirror, mirror, on the wall, who's the fairest of them of them all?" Vanity and beauty pageants both fall under the slightly dark province of Venus and Eternity.

Apples have been employed to combat a host of physical maladies, from constipation to hypertension and coughs. Healers prescribe grated raw apples to ward off morning sickness (sometimes a side effect of relationship and sensual pleasure). Some believe that apple pulp and juice rejuvenate the skin. Apples have also played a prominent role in the fabrication of love potions. Sharing bites of the same apple with a friend is said to ensure amity and eternal companionship. Many European cultures deemed apple trees so beloved by the gods that they were immune to lightning strikes. Countless families planted apple trees adjacent to their houses to guarantee protection and to stimulate love within.

WISH MAKER: Identify someone whom you consider your teacher and present this person with an apple. Relish the fellowship that this gift inspires, and listen carefully for a lesson that will burnish your wish.

Name of God

Yod Hey Vav Hey Tzevaot, the mantra of Eternity, combines the name of God for Wisdom with a word that translates as "armies" or "hosts." This name (pronounced Yod Hey Vahv Hey Tzeh-vah-oat) invokes the armies of the energy of Wisdom. Down on the practical plane, we don't mess around with the elusive and flickering Yod Hey Vav Hey. We don't even call on El, the name of God for Mercy and the high god of many cultures. Here we summon the armies of God. We need action, and we need it now. We demand the general, the cooks, the infantry, the whole shebang.

In the Bible, the disconsolate Hannah could not conceive. She kneeled inside the temple and chanted the name of God for Eternity, pleading for a son. In return, she promised to give the boy "unto the Lord all the days of his life" (First Samuel 1:11). She mouthed this mantra again and again, working herself into a frenzied trance. Eli, the high priest, entered the sanctuary and accused the mad, intoxicated woman of defiling his altar. But Hannah wasn't drunk. She told him that she was praying to Yod Hey Vav Hey Tzevaot for a son. When he heard this name out of all the other names of God, Eli intuited that her prayer would be answered. She was pleading with Mother Nature for motherhood. How could Mother Nature refuse?

The miracle took root. Hannah became pregnant and Samuel was born. When he turned four, Hannah bequeathed the boy to the high priest to be educated as a servant of the Lord. Samuel ripened into a most illustrious prophet. He anointed and advised both Saul and David, the first kings of Israel. He set the stage for the messiah. He was Hannah's wish. And this mantra transported him into the material world.

 WISH MAKER: Employ this mantra any time you wish to attract material resources, money, or possessions of any sort. Chant this name of God for practical assistance with art, love relationships, fertility, or any social situation that you find troubling.

Meditation

Sit in a comfortable position. Breathe deeply and try to decelerate your breath and heartbeat. Imagine yourself sitting in a giant green meadow. You see nothing but sprawling pastures of lush green grass. You have the urge to sprint through this infinite space of sylvan serenity. In the distance, you spot a huge apple tree. Run toward it. As you approach, you notice that the tree is more beautiful than you had imagined. It is loaded with ripe green apples. Pick one and take a bite. The sweetness of the fruit reminds you of the simple pleasures of life; how natural they are, and how healing.

Now envision the green sphere growing denser and more verdant. Amplify this green energy by recalling a moment of pure pleasure from your past. Resurrect that blissful feeling as intensely as you can. Now project your wish into the iridescent green sphere. Picture it clearly in front of you. Imagine how much happier you will be once you attain your wish. Picture yourself announcing your success to friends and loved ones. Take your right hand and touch the ground. You are summoning Mother Earth as witness to the fact that you are entitled to your wish. As you touch the ground, you hear a voice emanating from the earth. It chants: *Yod Hey Vav Hey Tzevaot.* Join in. Intone this name of God for as long as you like.

When you are finished, take three deep breaths and hold the air each time as long as you can. Then allow a few moments of silence as your body absorbs the green forces reverberating around you. Now watch as the green sphere begins to shrink, contracting smaller and smaller until it disappears. Tender a thank-you to the apple tree. And return to the here and now, to your body and your room.

Wish List—Eternity

☞ 1. Choose one behavior that will further your wish and repeat it over and over again.

☞ 2. Seek pleasure. For one week, transform this entire process into one big party of fun, games, and indulgence.

☞ 3. Find your trance—your active meditation.

☞ 4. Use your Abralog to analyze and interpret the messages hidden in your interactions with the ambassadors of Eternity: green, nature, soil, seven, artwork, music, food, apples, money, sensuality, Venus, and your right hip and leg.

☞ 5. Wish progress: Since the third week of this process, you have outlined and implemented a plan designed to achieve your goal. Here on the action plane, you must plunge forward with consistent and practical effort to drive your wish ahead. Last week you glimpsed a reflection of your wish fulfilled. This week's repetitive behaviors should be directed toward bringing forth the details of that image.

Exercise Zone

☞ 1. **The Mars and Venus in You:** Try to recollect your childhood hero and heroine, your personal version of Mars and Venus. Remember back to the age of seven to fourteen. Whom did you admire? Who was on the posters you tacked up on the walls of your bedroom? Identify your hero and your heroine—fictional characters or actual people. They could be Mary Poppins, your favorite pop or sports idol, or a close relative. Write down their names in your journal. This exercise exposes your attitude toward your inner god and goddess, the divine male and female forces within you. They inhabit your inner mythology, which guides you to this day. Your hero represents you as the ultimate action figure—your premier conception of a provider. Your heroine symbolizes your image of the ideal nurturer. Collectively, this couple epitomizes the personality traits you might want to emulate to spur the Tree to fulfill your wish.

Since Eternity governs the energy of relationships, attempt to marry your hero and heroine. Imagine how they would thrive as a couple. Do they complement each other? Would such a union last? Award this pairing a grade from 1 to 100. It is likely that subconsciously you will seek a partner who resembles the hero or heroine of your childhood. And this measure of the caliber of their coupling probably reflects the quality of your relationships.

Now, most crucially, pinpoint the hero or heroine of your wish. It might be a person who has achieved enormous success in his or her field. Name the hero of your wish, and, no matter how farfetched it sounds, try to contact this person. If you dream of riches, perhaps Bill Gates stands as your hero. Write him an e-mail explaining your goal. If you aim to make films, send a note to someone like Steven Spielberg. If you want a relationship, talk to the person you know who enjoys the most enduring and commendable marriage. One man, who wished to publish a book on the practical applications of spirituality, chose the Dalai Lama as the hero of his wish. In one of the most foolhardy things he ever attempted, he tracked down the e-mail address of the Dalai Lama's office in India and sent him his work. A few months later, he received a reply that included an endorsement of the book signed in the hand of his hero himself.

☞ 2. **A Prophet of Your Own:** In Hebrew, *Nathan*, the name of King David's soothsayer, means "to give." Approach your dearest friend and ask him or her to give you a candid assessment of your best and worst traits and tendencies. These appraisals just might be the preeminent gift of Eternity. Confronting how others perceive us often presents the prescription for the most dramatic transformations of our lives. We can work on and alter our defects only when we recognize their existence, and we can magnify our talents only when we are cognizant of the specific attributes that make us grand. One man discovered that his most propitious quality was his generosity. He always showed up on outings with his friends bearing gifts. Armed with this knowledge, he began to dispense presents everywhere, even at business meetings. Nurturing his foremost strength resulted in heightened acceptance in every situation and granted him an enlarged capacity to accomplish his dreams.

CHAPTER EIGHT

SPLENDOR:

The Energy of Communication, Magic, Mercury, and the Messenger

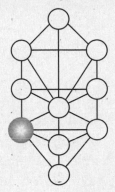

S P H E R E 8

KEYWORD: Communication

WISH IMPERATIVE: Converse with your wish and listen for answers that will thrust it forward fast. Rephrase and tweak your goal in more specific terms. Seek out messengers that will breathe life into your wish.

HEBREW NAME: Hod

MYTH AND PERSONALITIES: Hermes (Mercury); Thoth; the monkey god Hanuman; Mohammed; the mailman.

PLANET: Mercury

DARK SIDE: Lies and theft

COLOR: Orange

NUMBER: 8

TREES: Aspen and orange

BODY PART: Left hip, left leg

HEBREW NAME OF GOD (MANTRA): Elohim Tzevaot (the hosts of the energy of Understanding)

Neither snow nor rain nor heat nor gloom of night
stays these couriers from the swift completion of
their appointed rounds.

—Inscription on the General Post Office, Eighth Avenue,
New York, New York. (Note the synchronicity:
the motto of the eighth sphere engraved on a building
on Eighth Avenue)

I Communicate, Therefore I Am

E-mail, love letters, and Martin Luther King's "I have a dream";
satellites, cell phones, and telemarketing schemes; the *Cat in the
Hat* in a child's lap; "I never had sexual relations with that
woman"; police interrogations; therapy, peace talks, hieroglyphs,
and hip-hop; G4, G5, G6, gee-whiz; every word, every lightbulb,
every metaphor, and more.

Any and all communication originates in Splendor. It monop-
olizes the means and content of our lives most of all. The realm of
all the messenger gods, like Hermes of the Greeks and the
Romans' Mercury, Splendor translates to intense brightness or
luster. Good communication conveys brightness and clarity to
our lives. It funnels the infinite number of thoughts in the universe and the myriad interpretations of any situation into a sharp
clear picture that powers understanding and camaraderie. It
compensates for all kinds of discrepancies in beliefs, backgrounds, and offenses real or imagined. And it constructs bridges
to commerce, profit, and nobler pursuits like love and intimacy.
It's what humans do. It's how we spend the bulk of our days. And
more than our opposable thumbs and internal combustion four-
wheel drives, it distinguishes us from all other life on Earth. I
communicate, therefore I am. I speak, I write, I invent.

Relay Racing

It doesn't come easy. Boxloads of love doctors dispense the one-word panacea—communication—to patch all teetering relationships. Yet, millions of us flock to these Mars-Venus mavens because we fail to nurture Mercury. Instead of communicating, we too often miscommunicate, misconstrue, dissemble, delude, lie, and cry.

Here's why. Splendor reigns at the bottom of the restrictive pillar. Communication, therefore, is inherently restrictive. How can that be? Communication merges and connects. It opens and expands. It blesses. It praises. It whispers, "I love you."

But not always. Communication rarely operates like a pristine pipe that guarantees the untainted flow of water or words. Most often, communication exacts concessions and translations. And the meaning of the message often gets lost along the way. Consider the number of potential modifications each of your thoughts must navigate before it embeds itself in the cerebral tissue of another person. First, you generate the thought, and then you must communicate with yourself to select the most felicitous words out of all the millions of words to best express that idea. Second, the words fly—hopefully, smoothly—from your brain to your tongue. Third, the person you're speaking to registers whatever impressions his ears happen to pick up. And finally, he construes those words into his own reading of your original intention. Translation number four. Consider how many chasms of lost words, misapprehensions, and mutations that simple thought must traverse before it alights at its destination. And that's without any compensation for vocal inflections, accents, body language, a police siren screaming in the street, or whether you've had your morning coffee.

Splendor is the sphere of mutation—the force that terminates the endless cloning perpetuated by Eternity. Sometimes this energy generates mischief and mishap. But the mutative power unleashed by even the simplest verbal exchange is also an essential and tantalizing treasure. It unbolts the door to the creation of all things new.

> WISH MAKER: The first rule of Splendor is that the trickster will trick you. It's part of the process, integral to his job description. Don't allow yourself to be misled. This mischief will often guide you directly to your wish. Hunt for the good luck hidden within broken appointments, bad traffic, misplaced objects, wrong numbers, computer foul-ups, and any other incident that on the surface appears unbearably annoying. In the week of Splendor especially, these could well be signposts and treasure maps that point you toward fulfillment.

This true story, published in the *Los Angeles Times* on June 3, 2002, unmasks the guile of the trickster at his finest. A Palestinian man in the Gaza Strip misdialed a number on his cell phone. A woman answered. She scolded him for bothering her. He liked her voice. The following day, he purposely redialed her number—conveniently stored in the memory mechanism of the high-tech gadget. The man struggled to charm and draw her out and eventually he discovered that they both worked as accountants. He continued to phone with questions related to his job. In time, he eroded her defenses and she agreed to meet him for a date. A few months later, she agreed to marry him.

Mind Over Matter

The lower we descend on the Tree, the denser and more practical the energy becomes. Splendor, the architect of outward action, forges, molds, and consolidates thoughts and feelings from on high into actual physical stuff. It is the sphere of magic and prophecy—the engine of mind over matter.

In Genesis, God created the universe not with an idea, a thought, a notion, or a business plan. God created the world with the word. "Let there be light" and bang, there it was. The Torah starts with the letter *Bet*, the second letter of the Hebrew alphabet and the Kabbalistic symbol for the planet Mercury—the celestial body associated with this sphere. Creation does not begin with *Aleph*, the first letter, which symbolizes pure thought. It begins with *Bet*. It starts with the word. In Hebrew, *Bet* translates as "house"—Kabbalistic code for the dwelling place of the thought. The word confers a physical presence to any notion. With words we house or manifest our thoughts.

The Zohar, one of the most vital books in the canon of Kabbalistic literature, is called the "Book of Splendor." Many Kabbalists believe that Rabbi Shimon Bar Yohai channeled it about two thousand years ago directly from Moses and the prophet Elijah. Other scholars have traced the authorship of the text to a thirteenth-century Spanish sage named Moshe de Leon. This multivolume classic, written in Aramaic, contains mystical commentary on the Torah, keys to the secrets of the universe, and innumerable magic spells. The raison d'être of the Book of Splendor was to disseminate formulas to rid the world of chaos and magically transmit more light, brightness, and splendor to the lives of every human being. It translated the secrets of God into words in a quest to fabricate a divine luster right here on Earth.

Muslims honor their own herald of the word in the ubiquitous testimonial, "There is no God but One God and Mohammed is his messenger." The primogenial narrative of Islam recounts that the prophet Mohammed received the word of God when the angel Gabriel approached him in his cave and handed him a piece of paper. The angel commanded, "Read in the name of your Lord, the Creator, Who created man of a clot of blood. Read! Your Lord is most gracious. It is He who taught man by the pen that which he does not know" (Koran, 96:1–5). Mohammed then circulated the mandates of God throughout the world—and in the process created one of the predominant religions on the planet—via a book of words called the Koran.

WISH MAKER: The actual physical creation of anything starts with communication. That goes for your wish too. Anything you say about it, pro or con, exerts a profound influence. Be careful not to badmouth your wish. If you've struggled or bumped into impediments along the way, this is the week not to complain, but to overcome. If you assert, "It's too hard," "It will never work," "I can't," then the sphere of Mercury will build a physical structure to shelter those negative words and transport them into reality. Self-actualizing proverbs assert: "First you fake it, then you make it." "I will get a job that pays $200,000 a year." "I am going to find my true love this year." Faking it via affirmations about yourself and your wish might sound like a lie. But that's when the energy of Splendor kicks in. That's how you become your own prophet. If you speak the words often enough, eventually you will believe them, and the mind-over-matter magic of the sphere will make it so.

Divide and Conjure

The bottommost sphere on the restrictive pillar of the Tree, Splendor constrains the availability of any commodity by communicating the outrageous price. This sphere works the hype: "Diamonds Are Forever"; "Diamonds Are a Girl's Best Friend." It writes the glittery slogans that kindle desire and jack up the cost. Splendor powers the energy of business and negotiation. It animates the person or sales pitch that translates one little engagement ring into fifty thousand dollars.

Even when we're alone, the messenger refuses to rest. Our nervous system functions as our own personal Mercury, doggedly delivering communiqués from our brain to every part of the body. But what we generally regard as meaningful discourse requires two people; two points that yearn to trade information back and forth. Mercury operates by first splitting these two people apart to manufacture the space needed for the transmission of data. Then he attempts to bring them back together via his message. Splendor separates to unite. That's the deft trick of this magician. "Hey," the messenger, the peacemaker, says, lunging between two combatants. "She really didn't mean it. Don't be mad. Let's work it out." Thanks to Splendor prying them apart, the adversaries retreat, air their grievances, apologize, and shake hands.

But every mediator confronts a sticky paradox. If he spans the distance between two people without a glitch, his services won't be required any longer. He'll unite himself right out of business. In the Hindu epic the *Ramayana*, the ingenious monkey Hanuman toils supernaturally to reunify Rama and Sita, the masculine and feminine archetypes. But once he brings them together, his job is done. The high Hanuman, an authentic messenger, disappears. All he expects is that he live as long as the story is retold throughout the ages. The recognition is remuneration enough—his finder's fee is the reward of eternal life.

The position of the innermost planet, Mercury, mirrors the nimble two-step executed by every messenger. It orbits as near to the Sun as possible because the Sun—the source of light in our solar system—holds the message. Mercury hovers close to catch everything the distinguished star has to say. But Mercury must also maintain just enough distance to avoid being sucked into the mammoth ball of fire; to forestall losing his identity entirely. The adroit mediator labors to strike a slippery balance, situating him- or herself near enough to listen but remote enough to convey the information without assimilating the biases or desires of one side or the other. The skillful communicator comprehends that the messenger owes loyalty only to the message.

WISH MAKER: Take advantage of Splendor's push to create space in order to build unity. Detach yourself from the pursuit of your wish. Step back and view it from a neutral perspective. What would a savvy counselor advise to facilitate your success? Serve as your own messenger who aims to erect a bridge between you and the attainment of your goal. This job might exact a reality check and some rephrasing, refining, or tweaking of your wish. Just two spheres from the end, you might have to scale back your ambition. Remember, you can always wish again at the end of the process to complete whatever you have yet to accomplish. Mine the energy of Splendor to identify the obstacles in your way and act to surmount them. Be quiet and listen as the messenger discloses initiatives you can implement right now to drive your wish toward fruition.

One woman, for example, wished to attract investors for a new business venture. The energy of Splendor exhorted her to stand aside and reexamine her definition of success. Initially, her criteria for fulfillment had been $1 million in new investments. But by uncoupling herself from a fixation on that amount, she acknowledged that in the aftermath of a market downturn such a lofty goal had become unfeasible in the short term. The common sense of an impartial messenger prodded her to reduce her target to $300,000. Armed with this smart new evaluation, she then was able to wed herself to the fresh goal and forge ahead to achieve it.

Hermes' Tree

Zeus was a lonely god. He made love to anything that moved. He was the king of Olympus. Who could say no to the king? Zeus— the Romans called him Jupiter—transformed himself into a swan to ravish a woman down on Earth; he shape-shifted into a bull to copulate with another; he morphed into an eagle to force himself on the gorgeous boy Ganymede. He was addicted to sex; to quelling his loneliness with the comfort of flesh on flesh.

His wife, Hera, was a jealous goddess. Everywhere she turned she collided with yet another reminder of her husband's Olympian lust—Apollo, Artemis, Dionysus, Aphrodite, the Muses, Hercules, Perseus, Minos, Helen of Troy. It rankled her. How much could a poor wife stomach? Hera retaliated by tormenting his offspring and his lovers. And, most effective of all, she spied on her husband, crimping the pleasures of his wandering loins.

But in this battle of libido, Zeus wielded one insuperable weapon: Hermes, the messenger of the gods. The messenger, alone among all Zeus's illegitimate children, Hera loved. Everyone did. They had no choice. Hermes, known as Mercury to the Romans, controlled information. All of it. Everyone depended on him. No one dared antagonize him. Hermes could transmit Zeus's words of woo, and Hera could do nothing to thwart him.

Zeus beckoned his messenger. "Listen, son, take this staff."

He handed Hermes a thick slab of wood. "And deliver it to her down there. You see?"

"Take your wood to that earthling. Cool." Hermes flapped the wings on his feet.

"Wait!" Zeus screamed. He extracted a snake from his pants and coiled it around the staff. Hermes smirked and dashed off through the streets of Olympus.

"What's the word on the Phoenicians?" the god of war entreated.

"Hi, Hermes. Tell us a story," all nine Muses cooed at once.

More popular than e-mail, Hermes was mobbed wherever he roamed. "Hey, you!" Hera scampered into the street, delaying his flight. "It's been so long. Come have coffee with me. I just baked cookies."

"Cool," said Hermes. He trailed her into the palace and they settled in to chat.

"So, sweetie," Hera said, eyeing the seething contraption. "What do you have there?"

"This? It's your husband's, you know, and a snake, and I'm about to convey it to some pretty nymph down on . . ."

Hera pounded her fist on the table as death shot from her eyes. She whirled her gaze away fast, vaporizing a couple of houseplants on the windowsill. This was Hermes. She couldn't touch him. She couldn't interfere.

Hermes stuffed eight cookies into his mouth and flitted toward the door.

"Hold on," Hera said. She darted from the room and returned with a she-snake of her own. "Take this then too, please, honey." Her serpent wound itself around Zeus's and the rod in between.

"Cool," said Hermes. He zipped down to the world below. The fiery sexuality of the father god was mitigated by the watery emotions of the goddess of marriage and motherhood. The masculine and feminine snakes intertwined along the staff seven times, fashioning the seven chakras, the seven energy hubs of the human body. Hermes the messenger, the icon of words, the champion of the wind, happily transported this magic wand to Earth. Melding all four elements in harmonious wedlock—fire from Zeus, water from Hera, the air of Hermes, and earth, his destination—this scepter adorns ambulances, hospitals, and pharmacies around the globe to this day. It's called the caduceus. It is the symbol of healing; Hermes' message of health and balance for all.

But what it really is, is our Tree.

Zeus's snake represents the right pillar; the feminine snake is emblematic of the left pillar; and the rod in the middle exemplifies the central column. Even today, the Olympic games honor the faithful courier of the gods with relay races. Four athletes, each personifying one of the four elements, pass on a wooden stick. Enjoined with a double mission, they toil first to avoid dropping the staff, which symbolizes their fidelity to the message, and then sprint like mad to deliver it home as fast as possible. In symphony halls across the globe, the conductor waves his baton, which conveys the message of music to each musician. Enchanters of all kinds brandish this same magic wand, the Tree of Life in miniature. And with this wooden staff, the Lord of Exodus instructed, Moses was able to create God's wonders.

WISH MAKER: You carry God's wand of wonders with you every day wherever you go. It's called the spinal cord; and the two serpents of the caduceus symbolize the two branches of every spinal nerve (the dorsal, which transmits information from the muscles to the cord, and the ventral, which conducts instructions from the cord to the muscles). Nurture your spine this week. Mind your posture, stretch out your back and sit up straight. You don't want any kinks in your magic wand.

Echo Systems

Hod, this sphere's Hebrew name, also means "reverberation." This alternate translation reveals another important Mercurial trait. Just as an echo bounces less noisily off the muffling walls of a canyon, the edges of this sphere absorb a bit of the message for itself. The messenger always knows more than he transmits. Somewhere along the way, a fragment of the original communiqué plummets into the chasm. Only the messenger is privy to the nuances lost in translation. And that intelligence enabled magicians to initiate kings. Merlin didn't have to govern England himself; he enthroned Arthur and ruled with the magic of the messenger through him. Samuel, the prophetic virtuoso of the Bible, reigned via his reputation as the all-knowing link to a higher authority, even though Saul and David wore the crown as kings of Israel.

The splendid dominion of the messenger is unassailable. With the right words in the appropriate ears, he wields the ability to bankrupt McDonald's in a day. In the Watergate scandal, two unknown reporters at *The Washington Post* toppled the president of the United States, the most powerful man on the planet, with just a few news reports. Everyone understands that we need Mercury to prosper—to cut deals with people, even to love them. But this indomitable clout also marks the little rascal as a threat to those who presume that they have something to lose.

Can't Shoot the Messenger

We live in the Information Age. The era of CNN, the Internet, and instant contact with any nook of the globe. It's the hour of Mercury. It wasn't always so. For much of the past two millennia, prodigious forces conspired to snuff out his brilliance. The magnificent library in Alexandria, Egypt once housed more than eight hundred thousand scrolls before the Romans, Christians, and Muslims took turns torching it, thereby incinerating the bulk of the recorded wisdom of the ancient world. The Christian orthodoxy of the Dark Ages banned books and education. Though Alexandrine scholars had calculated the circumference of the Earth with pinpoint accuracy, the Church decreed that the world was flat. Even Galileo, the father of the experimental method and the inventor of the telescope, was sentenced to house arrest for defying church doctrine with his scientific truths. The Holy Inquisition targeted all free thinkers, alchemists, and doctors. It indicted the ladies of the forest, who crafted homeopathic remedies from flowers and twigs, as "witches" and drowned them in the river.

Some religious fanatics even killed cats. They incinerated millions of cats because of the animal's alleged association with magic, the forest "witches," and untamed spirituality. Two years later, half the population of Catholic Europe, including two popes, was dead from the black plague, spread by an explosion in the rat population after the cats were killed. Islamic powers similarly tyrannized the mystical Sufis. And Jewish leaders of Eastern Europe burned the esoteric texts of the Hasidic sect and prohibited these fellow Jews from marrying or setting foot in traditional synagogues. Influential rabbis vilified the Kabbalah itself and outlawed the study of its ageless wisdom for centuries.

But, as always, the trickster laughed last. Mercury eluded his enemies by virtue of this wily conundrum: They tried to excommunicate communication. Of course, that's impossible, because *communicate* makes up nearly all of the word *excommunicate*. Even the mighty suppressors of the word were forced to call on Mercury to communicate the names of those they aimed to condemn.

Secrets and Lies

After that Houdiniesque escape, it's no wonder that Mercury doesn't always shoot straight. Lying, stealing, and duplicity all emanate from Splendor, too. The word creates: "Let there be Light." But the opposite adage, "Talk is cheap"—"Read my lips, no new taxes"—rings true as well.

Mercury's propensity for treachery and untruths has always been an issue both in heaven and on Earth. Sometimes it proved quite handy. His little dark spot—his cheating and stealing— granted Mercury a free ticket to the underworld. He was the only god welcome in heaven, hell, and Earth, which enabled him to relay messages between these otherwise disjointed kingdoms. Yoruba mythology similarly considered Oshu-Elegba—the mischievous messenger spirit—the only entity qualified to negotiate between the forces of light and dark, living and dead.

Mercury chatters in riddles because puzzles force us to think for ourselves and evolve to new heights. Straight answers and pedantry, on the other hand, generally suppress the sort of original thinking that spawns invention. Mercury also swindles and deceives to confound the unyielding grip of our egos. He messes with our brains to debilitate them, to exhaust us into submission to the truth: We are One. All this nonsense of me talking to you talking to Republicans and Democrats talking to Muslim and Jew, capitalist and king, simply mocks us. "If you think you are different, special, chosen, richer, poorer, more tolerant, more generous, more anything," Mercury says, "then I will forever drive you crazy with the need for this converter to hook up your new PC to your old printer and operating systems that crash streaming video players and technical support that never answers the phone."

Mercury empties his bag of tricks to disrupt the fanatical clinging to our precious system of differentiation. He dupes us to illuminate the illusion of the mind. He flings paradoxes and illogical dramas like pigeon droppings to compel us to apprehend that the mind is merely a tool—not the goal—and as a tool it can be stolen. As long as ego and separation retain their hold on us, there will always be room for translators and adapters and new chances for bugs, shams, hanging chads, botched elections, and all manner of calamity. The bewildering 2000 presidential election in the United States obtrudes as a glaring example. The voting occurred on the last day of Mercury retrograde—the moment the messenger peppers us most zealously with his pranks. Mercury rules paper, ballots, choices, counting, fraud, and mendacity, and the snafus and controversy that ensued seemed tailored as a message to all that even the world's preeminent democracy probably would do well to rethink its priorities.

WISH MAKER: Exploit this sphere of lies to scrutinize your own. Where are you lying? Whom are you lying to? Stop and come clean. Remember that duplicities divide. Use the dishonesty as evidence of how and where in your life you separate yourself from others. Watch out for self-deception too. We fib to ourselves only to boost the power of our egos and hide from the Light. Prevaricating to yourself shows disloyalty to your best friend—to the messenger within. Jettison the lie and listen for the messenger's solutions.

Thoth and the Monkey Business

No one has authenticated whether Thoth, the ultimate Mercury on Earth, incarnated as an actual human being before he evolved into one of the most illustrious gods of ancient Egypt. He lived approximately ten thousand years ago, and he invented writing, language, the first hieroglyphs, numbers, math, medicine, government, religion, and all modes of communication. Legend relates that he authored 36,525 scrolls, one for each day in one hundred years. Ancient inscriptions from dynastic Egypt describe Thoth as "the self created, to whom none hath given birth. God, One, the measurer of the earth." A mural in the temple of the Egyptian ruler Seti I (1300 B.C.) portrays Thoth flourishing a staff with two snakes twined around it (Hermes' caduceus). In the Papyrus of Hen-taui, a priestess supplicates herself before the Horus eye, or Sun disk, while Thoth, in the form of a baboon, crouches at her side, interceding as the broker between humans and God.

Throughout myriad traditions, monkeys have personified the messenger archetype. Hindus, for example, celebrate the magical acumen of our monkey friend Hanuman. In the creation myth of Tibet, the monkey functioned as the mouthpiece of Avalokiteshvara, the Buddha of Compassion. Charged with promulgating the doctrine of loving-kindness among the selfish inhabitants of the Land of Snow, the monkey elected to mate with the depraved ogres of Earth, endowing his offspring—which eventually evolved into human beings—with the advantage of his genetic gifts of intelligence, eloquence, and compassion. This ancient tale chronicling the genealogical link between humans and apes predates Darwin by some two thousand years.

According to The Egyptian Book of the Dead, the peacemaker Thoth always turns up on the battlefield, preventing any one army from attaining a decisive victory. Ancient Egyptians revered him as the heart and tongue of Ra—the force that gave this god the words used to create the world. Man of letters, diplomat, and matchless magician, Thoth ensured the balance between good and bad, light and darkness. "The character of Thoth is a lofty and a beautiful conception, and is, perhaps, the highest idea of deity ever fashioned in the Egyptian mind," wrote renowned

Egyptologist E. A. Wallis Budge in *The Gods of the Egyptians*. "Thoth [is] the personification of the mind of God."

> WISH MAKER: Find your own messenger or magician this week. He might materialize in the form of another person or a word overheard on the radio or TV. The message might arrive in a book, a phone call, or a fax. Open your eyes. Open your ears. Anyone and anything can be your own personal Hermes.

During the week of Splendor, a man was sitting in a café with a friend. He spoke animatedly about some critical business decisions he faced that week, but he hardly expected his friend, who rarely intruded in the affairs of others, to offer any opinion. Mostly, he chattered to sort through his options, while his friend sat silently and stared at a bird pecking at some crumbs on the street. Suddenly, the friend pulled a baseball cap from his pocket and plunked it on his head to shield his eyes from the Sun. Then the friend began to talk. The man noticed that the hat was emblazoned with a picture of an eight ball. He remembered that eight is the number of the sphere of Splendor. "Maybe my normally laconic friend is my messenger," he thought. He tuned in. The friend explained some intricate strategies about how to structure a financial partnership so as to retain maximum ownership of the enterprise. The man was surprised that his friend knew anything about such matters. But later that week, he implemented much of his friend's advice in negotiating a contract with a new business manager. And that counsel translated into the preservation of untold thousands of dollars.

The Planet Mercury

The smallest, swiftest planet, Mercury is often difficult to discern because it orbits so close to the blinding brilliance of the Sun. This makes Mercury the ideal spy. Mercury also experiences only three days for every two complete revolutions around the star. Scientists hypothesize that if you stood on the surface of this planet, the Sun would appear to rise, stop, go back, and set where it rose, and then rise again and continue across the sky. Yet more chicanery from the planet of mischief.

Under the influence of the Sun's redoubtable gravitational pull, Mercury's eccentric orbit defies the laws of Newton and Kepler. It's as if this planet, this energy in charge of calculation and invention, cautions the scientist: "No matter how smart you are, I, the trickster, am always a huge step ahead." Many doubted Einstein's theoretical tack at first. But an analysis of Mercury's antics in the sky assisted in the verification of Einstein's general theory of relativity. In other words, the messenger planet served quite literally as the consummate PR agent for the principal genius of the twentieth century.

Eight Is Enough

Mercury circumnavigates the Sun every eighty-eight days. Splendor is the eighth sphere. The double eights signify the two coiling snakes of the caduceus. In math, eight symbolizes infinity—it is the only number that you can write again and again without lifting the pencil from the page to start anew. Eight's connection to infinity suggests that this number is pure magic. It signals that there are no limits. Anything is possible for anyone anywhere anytime. In the tarot deck, the Magician—the ambassador of Mercury—sports a figure 8 above his head, infusing him with the power of miracles, infinity, and Splendor. The Egyptians called Thoth the master of the "City of Eight," who, writes historian John Anthony West, "gives man access to the mysteries of the manifested world, which is symbolized by eight."

The piano, the communicator of music, features eighty-eight keys. In feng shui, eighty-eight, or double eights, means double happiness. But the ugly side of communication emerges in the cliché "talking in circles"—in other words, round and round just one of Mercury's two figure 8s to nowhere, without bridging the gap, without effecting harmony.

WISH MAKER: Every morning this week, imagine a figure 8 floating above your head. Then deliberately contemplate exactly what you need at that moment to fulfill your wish. The 8 will help you to conjure it. As you go about your business, seek out the number eight and examine the situation for signs of magic and infinite possibilities.

The Color Orange

Orange radiates eccentricity and youth, just as Mercury's bizarre orbit evokes the playful riddling of the messenger. For decades, designers have found orange apparel impossible to sell. But many in the fashion business report that orange is becoming increasingly popular, more and more hip, as the power of Mercury and information escalates. Style-savvy editors at *Vogue* magazine have advised that "orange is the new black."

Orange emerges from a mixture of yellow (the Sun, Light, the mane of the king) and red (blood, earth, and all that is common in us all). Orange facilitates communication between the yellow, kingly, godly world and the red-flesh realm of Earth. In Kabbalistic literature, the orange grove functioned as a chariot to the upper realms—a device to harvest messages directly from God. Color therapists employ orange to heal many ailments associated with breathing, such as asthma (Splendor governs the element of air), and the nervous system (the communication infrastructure of the body). An orange transparency overlayed a page of text sometimes helps those who suffer from dyslexia (a communications breakdown) to better decipher the words.

WISH MAKER: Locate the orange in your life. Do you have an orange shirt? Do you wear it? Is there orange in your home? Orange soap? Orange flowers? Do you lack candid, satisfying communication with your partner? Perhaps your bedroom suffers from an orange deficiency. Light an orange candle. Throw an orange pillow on the bed. Peel an orange and feed it to your mate. Immerse yourself in the buzz of orange and scrutinize the information it attracts your way.

The Aspen Tree

The smallest member of the poplar family, the aspen is known as "the quaking tree" because its dainty leaves rarely hold still. Its thin branches tremble in the slightest breeze. The rustling of the leaves prompted ancient cultures to call it "the whispering tree," the conveyor of the messages of the universe on the wind. Many pagan cultures viewed the shuddering aspens as portals to the world of magic and fairies. Meditations with the aspen are thought to transport us closer to the Light.

Crowns made from the golden leaves of this tree have been

found in burial plots dating back to 3000 B.C. in Mesopotamia. Though heroes on Earth often wore crowns of aspen to signal their conquests, these garlands also granted the hero the Hermes-esque capacity to venture to the underworld and then safely return home again. Many cultures instructed that contact with the aspen engenders a sense of endurance that enables humans to withstand the hardships of life. They manufactured shields from the tree because they believed that the aspen safeguards us from pain and darkness. It absorbs our fears and then infuses us with a brighter outlook and a revitalizing energy.

Name of God

Elohim Tzevaot, the mantra of Splendor, translates as the armies or hosts of Elohim. Elohim, the name of God for Understanding, governs the left hemisphere, logic, language, and the materialization of matter in time and space. This mantra invokes the armies of Elohim to foster the creation of material goods by way of language and communication.

 WISH MAKER: Chant this name of God whenever you hunger to improve communication, writing, public speaking, negotiations, or any kind of business.

Meditation

Sit in a comfortable position. Breathe deeply and completely relax. Bring yourself the stillness and tranquility you need to tap in to the higher realms. Let all the sounds and stimuli melt into your breath. Breathe in and out. Imagine a dimensionless point of orange light. Picture it hanging before you—the absolute potential: your connection, your hook to the One. As you breathe, this tiny dot grows larger and larger. Watch it inflate. Soon it envelops you, your room, your building, your entire block. Sit in the middle of that sphere, that splendid space of orange fog. And, like the fog, watch as it gently evanesces to nothing.

You find yourself now in an orange grove, relaxing under a gorgeous tree. The pungent aroma of the fruit surrounds you as you breathe in and out. Focus on your wish. Express it to yourself in two or three sentences. Phrase your wish as completely and persuasively as possible. Imagine that God has given you three sentences to tell Him your wish. Strive for precision. Tell God exactly what you want.

Now, up above, you espy the messenger. The messenger of the gods. Visualize this courier in any form that is meaningful to you. Picture him approaching in all his beauty and speed. The messenger has a delivery for you. It is a scroll. Accept it, open it, and envision yourself writing down your wish. All those thoughts and precise sentences you just conceived, jot them down in gold letters on this clean white scroll.

Now chant the name of God for this sphere: *Elohim Tzevaot* (pronounced El-lo-heem Tze-vah-oat). Chant it several times. Feel the mantra reverberating inside your body. Keep chanting as the messenger extends his left hand. He invites you to pass him your wish. Place the scroll in your right hand and reach toward the left palm of the messenger. Give him the message. Entrust him with your wish—signed by you and addressed to God. Chant Elohim Tzevaot again and again until you see that the scroll has been deposited into the hand of the messenger. Picture the messenger accepting your wish and watch as he elevates and flies back to the One.

As the messenger departs, rocketing upward with your wish,

you will find that the orange sphere has returned to envelop you. Watch as it begins to contract until it dissipates back into the dimensionless point. Breathe and hold the air inside. Then exhale. Breathe in again and hold it. Exhale, and when you are ready, move your head and hands and gently return to the here and now. Open your eyes and light an orange candle. Eat an orange to amplify the energy of this sphere and continue with your day.

Wish List—Splendor

1. Connect to your messenger. Locate a key to fulfilling your wish in the voices of others, a fax, a letter, anywhere.

2. Communicate with your wish. Figure out what you need to do right now to bring it to life (see exercise 2, below).

3. Rephrase your wish based on all that has occurred on your journey so far. Tweak and adjust your goal to award it a fighting chance to come true.

4. Find the magic of Splendor in the envoys of the sphere. These include orange; all forms of communication, including computers, phones, mail, newspapers, fortune cookies, TV, and radio; eight; Mercury; monkeys; and your left hip and left leg.

5. Wish progress: As you approach the end of the process, you must act to advance your wish. Last week you repeated a behavior designed to further your aim. This week, assertively seek to communicate with anyone who might be able to help you. Capitalize on any information that comes as a result of your previous efforts. Mercury is the speediest planet and time is short. Work fast. If necessary,

downsize your ambition. Identify any snags holding you back and strive now to untangle them.

Exercise Zone

1. **Talk Less:** Most of us speak far too much, yammering on about the weather, our new shoes, real estate prices, and which Hollywood starlet had her eyes done. But true messages, all the things we really need to hear, are conveyed through silence. So, for one week, talk less. In every conversation, speak only 30 percent of the time. Just three sentences for every seven your partner utters. Some of you probably will bristle at this directive. "I know exactly what this person is going to say. It's the same blah, blah, boring every minute." Still, do it. The words he or she says—the words you know are coming because you've heard them a million times before—don't matter. You don't have to listen to the words at all. But do pay attention to how this person says them. So much depends on the tone of the voice, the inflections, the music or lack of it. Great actors understand this crucial verity of communication. A simple switch in phrasing or modulation of the voice can alter the entire meaning of a scene. Check out the way Diane Keaton articulates the nonsense line "lah di dah, lah di dah, la la" in *Annie Hall*. The language itself transmits nothing, but the way her voice stops, starts, and sings these inane syllables divulges more about her character than a five-hundred-page biography crammed with every event of her life. Few of us heed these seemingly meaningless clues, and consequently we overlook the crux of

many matters. This week, eavesdrop on the message that hums between the lines.

☞ **2. If These Wishes Could Talk:** Conduct a dialogue with your wish. Converse with your wish as if it were another person. Ask it questions and wait for the responses. Record the discourse as if you were writing a two-character play. Don't censor yourself. This treatment is not for publication. It is designed to help you identify and surmount any obstructions to the fulfillment of your wish. You might want to begin with some of the sample questions below, but carry on far beyond these suggestions. Imagine that you are conducting a conversation with your dearest love, striving to resolve a crucial problem. You will entertain no thought of ever giving up. Listen attentively to your intuition and gut. They will supply the message of your wish.

☞ What do you (my wish) need from me to be born fulfilled?

☞ Where do I need to act?

☞ Why haven't you yet come true?

☞ What behavior should I modify to help make you a reality?

☞ Do I repeatedly slander or gossip about anyone? (If so, stop now, because talking behind another's back creates a boomerang effect that stymies your wish.)

☞ What thoughts about my wish bolster it? Which thoughts do it harm?

☞ Do I believe my wish will come true or do I sabotage it with negative expectations?

☞ What successes on the road to my wish have I achieved thus far?

☞ How will my life change when my wish is fulfilled?

☞ Am I in any way afraid of this change? Am I afraid of fulfilling my wish?

CHAPTER NINE

FOUNDATION:

The Energy of Sex, Death, Transformation, Joseph, Osiris and Isis

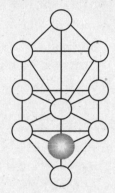

SPHERE 9

KEYWORDS: Sex; Death; Transformation

WISH IMPERATIVE: Blend all of your experiences to date into a revisualization of your wish come true. Let the old you die and witness yourself reborn as a wish-fulfilled human being.

HEBREW NAME: Yesod

MYTH AND PERSONALITIES: Osiris; Joseph (. . . and the Technicolor Dreamcoat)

PLANET: Moon

DARK SIDE: Fear of change; jealousy; lust

COLOR: Purple

NUMBER: 9

TREE: Willow

HEBREW NAME OF GOD (MANTRA): Shaddai El Hai (God is Alive)

Mixing the Cake

All the energies of the preceding eight spheres funnel down to Foundation, the purple sphere, which serves to shuffle them together. Foundation stands as the confluence of all three pillars of the Tree of Life—the great mixing bowl of the universe. When you bake a cake, you dump all the ingredients—flour, eggs, sugar, water, chocolate—into a container and stir them together. Is it then a cake? All the components of the final product have been set in place. You can lick the spoon and taste it. But it's not the cake. It doesn't even look like a cake. You must deposit all the blended elements into the oven, the deep, dark cave—the under-world. Only after they incubate in this shadowy womb will all the disparate ingredients be pushed out into Kingdom as the fin-ished cake. Only then is your wish fulfilled in the physical world.

This week, all the Tree's energies commingle. All the bright col-ors shed their singular identities within the purple womb of Foundation. In this underworld, the discrete energies die so that they might be reborn as something altogether new. Some elements of death encapsulated in the mythologies of the underworld are undoubtedly scary. But mythology reminds us again and again that mortality itself is not to be feared. For example, Pluto, the Roman god of the underworld, comes from the same word that means "riches." Almost everything valuable emerges from deep within the Earth. Gold, silver, diamonds, oil, the plants we eat, and the trees themselves all originate beneath the surface. The underworld—code for our subconscious—is the font of riches, the source of regeneration. While mortifying memories and emotions might gush from this murky reservoir, most spiritual and psychological models expound that demystifying these ghouls often diminishes their hold on us. Much of the world's sublime art derives from the shadowy subconscious as well. Artists often tap the mother lode of this furtive world to ignite their marvelous creations.

On the Tree, the Foundation of life is death and transformation. "The Kabbalists believed in a doctrine of transmigration of souls through various bodies and forms of existence," wrote Gershom Scholem, the renowned Kabbalistic scholar, in *On the Mystical Shape of the Godhead*. *The Bahir*, first published in France in the year 1176, delineated the concept of *gilgul* (reincarnation) in intricate detail. This book transcribed an oral tradition that stretched back thousands of years and ascribes much of its wisdom, including its authoritative views on reincarnation, to Rabbi Akiva (50–135 A.D.), one of the most revered sages in Jewish history. The doctrine of transmigration promises that when we suffer a loss in the family, a birth will soon ensue in the same clan. When a person dies, she will reincarnate as a new baby. Death is fundamentally a joyous event. Transformation makes all things possible. We yearn for it. Our inner, higher self deplores stagnation no matter how comfortable. Change keeps us going. It bequeaths hope. It supplies the reason to be. It doesn't matter if we began as a clump of cells or as foolish little children. The energy of death and resurrection, the power of Foundation, affords us the capacity to renovate ourselves into saints and Bodhisattvas. It awards us the chance to be better than we were the day before.

A Matter of Death and Life

Expect a death this week because every transformation, no matter how small, requires a demise followed by regeneration. Christ was sacrificed in Beauty only to be revivified after three days as a being of Light in the physical world called Kingdom. Osiris, the great Egyptian god, perished in order to father Horus, the god of the Sun. In other words, death and Foundation give birth to the Sun, to the manifestation of Beauty on Earth, to life.

Your wish itself must die so that it may be born. Foundation kills the state of wanting and engenders the final accomplishment. If you wished for a house, then the you who has a safety net of cash in the bank, few responsibilities, and little concern with insurance and drainage pipes must die to be resurrected as the new you, home owner. A man who longs for a mate must experience the expiration of bachelorhood and all its freedoms before finding himself reborn in a committed relationship. Labeling these mundane transformations "deaths" sounds somewhat absurd. But most change—even a modification as ordinary as laying out a down payment on a house or cohabiting with a spouse—arrives heaving with trepidation. Humans fear nothing as much as death. We exclaim, "I was scared to death," not, "I was scared to life" (or to sleep or to work). Shedding our skin to dawn anew petrifies just about everyone because every change—large or small—transpires from this same energetic cistern called Foundation.

WISH MAKER: Determine what sort of death you need to undergo in order to clear space for your wish. It's like pushing aside the furniture in a room or throwing out old clothes from your closet, creating a place for the new to blossom. What will you relinquish forever to facilitate the nativity of your wish? Ask yourself who you are without your wish. Single, unemployed, dissatisfied with your mate? Now kill that you—the you that perceives yourself as lacking.

Buyer's Remorse

In any creative process, this intense energy can be, well, deadly. Often, wishes or projects terminate early when suffused with the fear generated in Understanding and the leap of faith. But more

often, enterprises of all sorts collapse here on the threshold of fulfillment. The fear of change roars in Foundation and annihilates all the
hard work that came before. In real estate, brokers have dubbed this
phenomenon "buyer's remorse." The house is in escrow; the pur-
chasers have laid out a nonrefundable deposit as a sacrifice. But once
they witness the big chunk of money evaporating from their
account, they panic. "Stop, stop," they cry. "It's too much. It's crazy."
Foundation functions as a crucible of our fearlessness. It assesses
whether we are prepared to relinquish anything—including our
hypercosseted self-image—that impedes our spiritual progress.

WISH MAKER: Fear of success, fear of failure, fear of every
sort often bedevils us in Foundation. Beware of any self-destruc-
tive or wish-destructive tendencies as you approach the end of
your trek. Don't let your mind sabotage the process. Give your
wish a chance.

One man, for example, had implemented a brilliant new business plan and was knocking on the gate to his wish. But in the
week of Foundation he began to squabble with his partner about
everything, including such trivia as who would speak first at
their presentations. His uncharacteristic obstinacy toward his
ally nearly sank their enterprise. Fortunately, he continued to
meditate every morning, and midway through the week he realized that standing aside and allowing the process he had initiated to run its course would save him. Another sojourner had lost
quite a bit of weight by the time she arrived in Foundation.
Friends and co-workers noticed and complimented her newly
svelte figure. But the unfamiliar spotlight unnerved her. Deep
down, she was afraid to be seen. The anonymity of her heavier self

had suppressed this subconscious dread for years. Foundation unleashed it. But rather than acknowledge this fear and let it die, the woman winced and lapsed from her regimen. The disappointment she suffered a couple of weeks later when she climbed back on the scale inspired her to journey again on the Tree. This time she wished to understand and then surmount the feelings of unworthiness that prevented her from attaining the slim and confident appearance she'd always craved.

The Myth of Love and Death

Osiris and Isis, the exalted gods of the ancient Egyptians, adored each other. Their union sprinkled joy on all the world. They were the perfect couple—two pillars that nourished and inspired every living thing. But one powerful being bristled under their benevolence. Set, the lord of enmity and the younger brother of Osiris, coveted the adulation lavished upon his faultless relatives, and he plotted to usurp his brother's throne. He constructed an ornate casket and presented it to Osiris as a joke. When the playful Osiris hopped into the chest, Set pounced, sealing the coffin and submerging it in the Nile. The pretender then assumed rule over the Earth, and darkness, famine, and despair hung like a wet cloak from the spirit of every human being.

The sarcophagus meanwhile drifted out to sea and ran aground on the shores of Phoenicia. It nestled near the roots of a tamarisk tree, which extracted vitality from the magical box and grew double the norm in size and fragrance. The wonders of this tamarisk traveled on the lips of merchants. And when the story landed in Egypt, Isis recognized her lover's wondrous touch. She retrieved the casket and vowed to restore him to life. But before she completed the tricky task of revivifying her husband, Set's spies betrayed her. On the full moon, he absconded with the coffin, butchered his brother's body into fourteen pieces, and strewed them all over Egypt.

Isis's ardent devotion drove her on. She tracked down the body parts in every nook of the kingdom. Eventually, she rescued thirteen pieces—everything except Osiris's phallus. But Anubis— the kindly, jackal-faced guide of the dead and the son of Osiris by Nephthys—consented to loan his own sex organ to his father for one day. Isis assembled the fragments and resuscitated her husband. They made love with the borrowed phallus and conceived a son. They christened him Horus, the Lord of Light and progenitor of all the Pharaohs, the kings of the material world.

Osiris ceded rule over the living to Horus, the god of the Sun, and chose instead to preside over the land of the dead so as to infuse the spectral blackness of the underworld with a benign and regenerative power. This ageless myth affirms that Foundation operates to transmute our wishes from just wants or hopes into actualities. Osiris died, but through Isis's zeal and tenacity, he was resurrected (or transformed) into the couple's fondest dream: the brilliant light called Horus, the ruler of the Kingdom, the sphere of wishes fulfilled, just below.

WISH MAKER: The broken fragments of Osiris represent your previous eight weeks on the Tree. In Foundation, you collect the pieces and put them together. Any exercise that you overlooked along the way, any assignment that you let slip into the busy river of your life, pick it up now. If you neglected to forgive someone in Mercy, absolve him or her this week. If you failed to communicate with your wish in Splendor, have that conversation today. Foundation presents the last opportunity to weave all of the Tree's teachings into your own resplendent tapestry.

The Egyptian Book of the Dead

The ancient Egyptian mythology elucidates the trial of death—the test of letting go—enforced by Foundation. This more than thirty-five-hundred-year-old funerary text chronicles the voyage of the soul into the underworld. When a person dies, the soul, or Ba, meanders to the portal of the underworld at the western end of a ravine. Just as the Sun disappears in the west at the end of the day, the human soul vanishes in the west at the end of life. The Kabbalistic text *Kehilat Ya'acov* similarly contends that the west corresponds to the sphere of Foundation and the realm of the shadowy subconscious.

The funerary inscriptions of ancient Egypt relate that the soul undertakes this daunting jaunt through the gloomy mystery of the afterworld in order to locate and then blissfully merge with Osiris, who reigned as the god of the underworld as well as the god of fertility. The god of death and the god of life are one. First the Ba passes a few hours eluding fiery and fiendish ghouls, which lurk as nothing more than metaphors for all the old fears and bogeymen we failed to reconcile with during our life on Earth. Then the Ba arrives in the Hall of Judgment to learn its destiny: immortality with Osiris or reincarnation on Earth; eternal life or plain old regular life. The soul approaches a balance scale—the two sides symbolizing the right and left pillars of the Tree. Below the scale, champing his crocodile maw, reclines a monstrous brute called Ammut (the ambassador of Kingdom). In Hebrew, *Ammut* translates as "I shall die." But the word *Emet*, which derives from the same Hebrew root, means "truth." This creature kills whatever is not true.

Then Ma'at, the goddess of justice and divine order, enters brandishing a feather. She sets the feather on one side of the scale and the heart of the newly dead on the other. She weighs the symbol of Beauty on the scales of Foundation. If the mechanism balances, if the heart is as light as a feather, the soul ascends to join Osiris in idyllic immortality. If the heart—burdened with regret or sorrow—proves heftier than the feather, that side of the scale dips like a seesaw into the hungry jaws of Ammut, and the soul reincarnates again for a new go at living, unencumbered by a heavy heart.

Sex and Death of Ego

It sounds like a preposterous enigma: arguably the most pleasurable human experience and the episode most of us recognize as the absolute worst intertwine in this sphere. The energy of sex and death both lie—pun intended—in Foundation.

The sex act powers the mechanics of reincarnation. The Tibetan Book of the Dead, an instruction manual for the dying and the Bible of transmigration, pivots on the eternal yoke between sex and death. When the body expires, the soul embarks on a journey that offers several openings to circumvent an encore in samsara (our painful and illusory world of daily life). The newly departed soul begins in the crown chakra, but as it fails to prevail over the binds of the ego and fears of death, it tumbles to the third-eye chakra for another trial. If it falters there, the soul slides farther down the body. Most souls plummet to the sixth chakra—the sex chakra or the sphere of Foundation. Here, the soul awakens to an orgy—thousands of men and women from every nation making love. The Buddhist priest attending the death is directed to caution the soul to shun these amorous couples. "Whatever you do," the lama warns, "do not come between these people." One of these couples is the soul's next set of parents. Most of us, yet unfit for enlightenment, succumb to the sexual force field of Foundation. And the next thing you know, you're a baby delivered into Kingdom.

Beyond the logistics of reincarnation, sex and death interlink in a second vital way. The act of sexual union, the moment of orgasm, imparts one of the only opportunities we ever get to escape completely the shackles of ourselves. Sex wields the magical ability to obliterate the ego, if only for a few seconds—to shoot us beyond our mask, our persona, and our quotidian routine. The French recognized this connection by naming orgasm *petit morte*, or "little death." The American Buddhist teacher Jack Kornfield preaches that beyond the carnal pleasure and the biological urge to procreate, the supreme appeal of sex rests in this chance to kill, however fleetingly, our self and become a part of something glorious and new. In that peak of ecstasy, both partners die as individuals, only to be reborn as a unified couple. In that moment, we experience all of the energies of Foundation—sexuality, intimacy, death, and transformation—in a single intense annihilation of self. The melancholy that nags at us following so-called meaningless sex stems from the failure to fulfill our innate yearning for intimacy. We suffer the down because we feel cheated.

It is true that the sphere of Foundation blew up in the original breaking of the vessels, burdening us with all sorts of quandaries regarding the sexual energy. Fear of sex, sexual addictions, exploiting sex for power and ego gratification, jealousy, and possessiveness—all this ugliness finds its genesis in the glum shattered pieces of the sphere. But when we avert the abuse of this energy, the intimacy of sex induces the demise of who we are and the dawning of an unsullied connection with our partner. It strips away clothes and boundaries, exposing the deepest of secrets. This type of intimacy isn't reserved for sexual partners alone. This energy of death and regeneration pervades any relationship that unveils the self behind the mask.

WISH MAKER: Intimacy arouses your relationship with the energy of Foundation. If possible, make this a sexy week. At the least, wield the tools you mastered in Splendor to communicate your secrets to someone dear to you (see exercise 1, at the end of this chapter).

The Drive

Cars and all other vehicles of transportation fall under the jurisdiction of Foundation. We "drive" our cars and they transport (or transform) us to another place. The snide joke that a sleek sports car doubles as an extension of a man's penis rings true Kabbalistically because both our cars and our sexual organs emanate from this same vessel. On the Tree of Life, all of the spheres are *driven* into Foundation. It stands as the only repository in which the two outer pillars—the Abba and the Ema, the father and mother, the masculine and feminine—conjoin with the full force of their energies. In Foundation, they make love, obliterating all distinctions in favor of intimacy amid the central column of balance. But the keyword is *balance*. Just as the Moon reflects the Sun, the drive born of Foundation functions optimally only when it reflects the heartfelt purpose of the sphere of Beauty. The drive for intimacy should serve the heart. Sex should serve the heart. And when they do, Foundation promises to issue new life—any wish—into the material world.

Kabbalistic literature associates Foundation with the phallus, while Kingdom generally represents the receptacle or the female sex organs. Foundation pioneers the energy of the arrogant and erect penis, yearning to show off its power to the outside world.

Many mythologies employ the Tower as the symbol of the erect phallus (the masculine ego) striving to affirm its unrivaled potency. Often a princess peers out of a window at the top of the tower—which corresponds to the small opening for the urethra—awaiting rescue from a knight. She personifies the human soul languishing deserted inside the ego, while the knight signifies the positive masculine attributes of gallantry and courage without regard for himself. In the Bible, the Babylonians erected the doomed Tower of Babel in a chimerical effort to broadcast their grandeur to every corner of the world. And all modern cities that vie for encomiums for their own bigger, taller skyscrapers mimic the archetypal hubris generated by this formidable sphere.

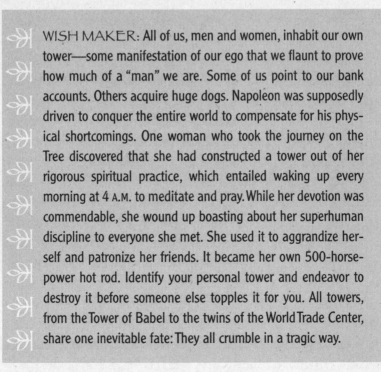

WISH MAKER: All of us, men and women, inhabit our own tower—some manifestation of our ego that we flaunt to prove how much of a "man" we are. Some of us point to our bank accounts. Others acquire huge dogs. Napoleon was supposedly driven to conquer the entire world to compensate for his physical shortcomings. One woman who took the journey on the Tree discovered that she had constructed a tower out of her rigorous spiritual practice, which entailed waking up every morning at 4 A.M. to meditate and pray. While her devotion was commendable, she wound up boasting about her superhuman discipline to everyone she met. She used it to aggrandize herself and patronize her friends. It became her own 500-horse-power hot rod. Identify your personal tower and endeavor to destroy it before someone else topples it for you. All towers, from the Tower of Babel to the twins of the World Trade Center, share one inevitable fate: They all crumble in a tragic way.

Joseph: Man of the Sphere

The biblical story of Joseph incorporates all of the qualities of Foundation. His famed coat of many colors unified the hues of the other spheres in one garment just as Foundation blends all the other energies into one vibrant quilt. His story also features one of the first documented cases of sexual harassment in the history of humankind. The saga hinges on the practical understanding of subconscious dreams. And Joseph plunged several times into the black pit of near death—deep into the underworld—only to resurrect time and again as a grander new hero.

Joseph was the favored son of Jacob. While his brothers toiled in their fields, he grew up pampered inside his father's tent, studying the secrets of the Tree of Life. One day, inflamed by his superior airs, Joseph's jealous brothers dumped him into a giant hole—symbolic of the underworld and death. They shredded the coat of many colors and told their inconsolable father that the boy had been slain by a wild animal.

Slave traders retrieved Joseph from the pit and sold him to a wealthy Egyptian minister named Potiphar. With his alchemical ingenuity, Joseph expanded his master's business empire manyfold. He earned a place of honor in the opulent household, and he and Potiphar became close friends. But the sex energy of the purple sphere ruined him. Potiphar's wife lusted for Joseph. One day she cornered him in her room. "Lie with me," she demanded. Loyal to his boss, Joseph demurred. Incensed and humiliated, the woman tore her dress and screamed, "Rape!" And once again Joseph was pitched into the dungeon—his second descent into the underworld.

Eventually, two of Pharaoh's servants joined Joseph in jail. One morning these men—who signify the right and left pillars of the Tree—turned to Joseph to decipher a pair of evocative dreams. Pharaoh's butler dreamed that he was walking to the palace with three branches pregnant with grapes, from which he squeezed a delectable cask of wine. The three fertile branches, Joseph understood, correspond to the three spheres in the expansive column of the Tree (Wisdom, Mercy, and Eternity). "That's easy," Joseph said. "In three days, Pharaoh will call for you and reinstate you as his steward."

Pharaoh's baker then recounted that he was rushing to the palace with three baskets of baked delicacies when a flock of birds besieged him and ate up every crumb. The three empty baskets match the three spheres on the restrictive column (Understanding, Severity, and Splendor). "I'm very sorry but that's easy too," Joseph said. "In three days, Pharaoh will call for you and chop off your head." Three days passed—symbolizing the logic of Understanding, the third sphere, which Joseph mined to solve the riddle of the dreams—and the transformations took root. Pharaoh liberated the butler and beheaded the baker.

Joseph continued to rot in the pit until Pharaoh himself awoke from a baffling nightmare. Seven fat and hearty cows emerged from the Nile, only to be devoured by seven emaciated skeleton cows. None of Pharaoh's magicians could elucidate his dream. But the butler remembered Joseph, and Pharaoh beckoned the prisoner to his throne.

"That's easy," Joseph said. "Your kingdom will enjoy seven years of plenteous harvest [the expansive column of the Tree], which will then be followed by seven years of unbearable famine [the restrictive pillar of the Tree]." But there was a way out, Joseph added, offering the solution of the middle pillar. If the kingdom's farmers banked a certain portion of the initial largesse, there would be enough on hand to sustain everyone in the years of deprivation. Pharaoh installed Joseph as the director of the entire enterprise. His enormous acumen for business—for life, really—rapidly multiplied the treasure of the realm. And he rose to become the most influential man next to Pharaoh in all the land, completing a remarkable roller-coaster transformation from adored heir of Israel to the pit of oblivion to the chief executive of the most magnificent kingdom on the planet.

Joseph managed to blend the two pillars evoked in Pharaoh's dream. He balanced the seven expansive years with the seven years of restriction through the power of Foundation. By deciphering the messages of the subconscious, Joseph seamlessly merged both pillars of the Tree and transformed Egypt's fate of death into a destiny of prosperity. He personified a true saint—a person blessed with the capacity to dig into the collective subconscious and initiate regenerative action prescribed by the symbols buried there.

WISH MAKER: This week, pretend you're Joseph, the incomparable dream reader. Write down and then analyze your dreams. Utilize the bank of symbols you have gleaned from the Tree—colors, numbers, keywords of the spheres—to locate your dream in a specific energy and take action accordingly. If, for example, you dream of traveling in a green car with a pile of work at your side, it might suggest that you would prosper from an infusion of the green sphere of Eternity. You might want to repeat a particular behavior pertaining to your work again and again so as to drive it to your preferred destination.

Many books have been published on dream interpretation. But only you know what your dreams mean. Each of us perceives symbols in his or her own way. A computer in a dream will resonate differently to a software programmer than to someone who barely knows how to find the power switch. You must apply your own connotations to the colors, numbers, objects, and events in your dreams. Jot down in your journal as many details as possible right after you wake up. Then free-associate on every image you have reconstructed. Let's say you dreamed about a spider. Deliberate on the topic of spiders—what they mean to you, how you feel about them—and record anything that comes to mind. Don't hold back. Your correlations might include silly stuff from a TV commercial, a childhood memory, or a line from a pop song. And don't hesitate to milk the symbolism of the Tree. For example, water equals emotions. Orange denotes Splendor and communication. Six is the number of sacrifice, balance, and the heart.

Now read through your dream, inserting your associations as you go. Hopefully, something will click. If not, stash it away for a while. Mull over your dream later in the day. Share it with friends and see if their comments trigger a fresh perspective. Some dreams, like those Joseph decoded, are prophetic. And some are pointless debris, our brains sifting through the mundane events of our lives. Acquiring the knack to unravel the symbols of dreams will immerse you in the regenerative energy of Foundation. And it just might transform you into the most popular guest at any cocktail party.

The Moon

Foundation functions as a screen, reflecting images of the upper spheres into the consciousness of the material plane. Joseph, for example, translated the images of his comrades' dreams into practical action. The Moon rules this sphere because our satellite reflects the light of the Sun back to Earth. The Moon hovers close just as Foundation looms above Kingdom. It is our constant companion, on hand always to bounce light into the gloomiest moments of our lives. It reminds us that the Sun, the Beauty, shines constantly, even when we cannot observe it directly at night.

But the Moon also mystifies and perturbs. We apply the word *lunatic*—from *Luna*, Latin for "moon"—to describe abnormal or crazy behavior. One side reflects the Sun, while the other forever remains black and unknown. Foundation vivifies this dark side too, the subconscious silo of unresolved emotions, doubts and fears. These denizens of the shadowy depths of the brain can alarm us if we fail to remember that dark and light and life and death are fragments of the same whole. The Moon reminds us of the inexorability of change as it fluctuates in the sky. It swells bigger and brighter and then shrinks to nothing, only to be resurrected afresh every month. It endures as a symbol of relentless renewal and rebirth. The Moon's phases also mirror the cycle of menstruation—again an overt echo of Foundation's ties to the sex organs, death, and transformation.

It seems illogical that in numerous ancient cultures, the Moon goddess also reigned as the goddess of the hunt, when in fact it was the men of the tribe who did all the hunting. Diana, for example, served as the Greek goddess of both the hunt and the Moon. Kali, the Hindu goddess associated with the Moon, galloped in on a tiger, while Egyptian mythology chronicles a female huntress called Sekhmet. Why this peculiar linkage between hunting and the feminine Moon? For most of our existence over hundreds of thousands of years, humanity has been easy prey for wild animals. (Children living in big cities today, though free of the threat posed by wild predators, harbor a genetically programmed fear of nocturnal beasts. They call it the bogeyman.) Menstruation exacerbated this problem for our defenseless ancestors. Back then, women living close to the Earth tended to cycle together in sync with the Moon. All the menstrual blood at the full Moon lured the wild animals into camp. And so the goddess of the Moon, the entity responsible for all this blood and peril in the first place, was looked upon to ride in on her beast to embolden and protect the tribe. Similarly, the legends of Dracula and the Werewolf, stories redolent of sex, death, and transformation, always invoke blood and the Moon.

> WISH MAKER: Foundation offers the chance to employ the movie screen of the Moon (and the subconscious) to reflect images of what you would like to see in your actual life. Devise a vision of your wish fulfilled exactly as you want it. In your mediations, envision these images flickering on the surface of the Moon. Or simply conjure them in as much detail as possible inside your mind. The energy of Foundation absorbs these mental pictures; it incubates them and then forces them out into the material world like a baby through the birth canal. Try it. Imagine. Repeatedly flood your subconscious with happy images and let Foundation make them real.

Nine

Nine always signifies completion, the final number before we start repeating the numerals that came before. Nine signals that your Tree is about to end, about to give birth to the tenth sphere, which is really the first $(1 + 0 = 1)$ sphere of another Tree. In many cultures, nine denotes the "foundation" of everything. One Egyptian myth recounts the birth of nine primordial gods that then created and ruled over the material world (the tenth sphere, called Kingdom). The Greeks dubbed them the ennead, meaning "the great nine," the foundation of the universe. Nine judges sit on the Supreme Court, the foundation of justice in a free society. G. I. Gurdjieff, the noted twentieth-century Greek-Armenian spiritualist, says that the enneagram—a nine-pointed star—contains all knowledge within its boundaries, just as Foundation embodies the energies of all the other spheres. Odin, the king of the Norse, hung himself upside down for nine days to achieve his ultimate transformation. It also takes nine months—nine moons—for a baby to gestate in the womb before it surfaces as a fresh member of Kingdom.

Since Foundation steeps the creation in the energy of sex, what happens if the Sun and the Moon—astrological code for the ultimate father and mother—make love? The Sun springs from Beauty, sphere 6, and the Moon from sphere 9. Stick them together and you get 69. Even the Kama Sutra resides within the Tree of Life. The 69—the union of the Sun and Moon, Beauty and Foundation—resembles the symbol of yin and yang; the perfect balance; the flawless integration of all the energies of the cosmos.

WISH MAKER: Nine evokes the concept of blending all the archetypes (all nine gods) into one commingled unit that serves and governs the creation (your wish fulfilled). This week, you might want to seek out the power of nine in organizations, clubs, or any combined force that can facilitate the manifestation of your goal. One man suppressed his usual resistance to joining groups and attended a network meeting of businesspeople. Trusting synchronicity, he approached a woman wearing a purple (the color of Foundation) amethyst bracelet. She informed him that she was about to retire and was looking for someone to take on her clients.

The Willow Tree

Orpheus, the paragon of art, music, and poetry, toted willow branches along with his lyre on his trek through the underworld. These sticks furnished him with the power of magic and emotional eloquence that moved Hades to unshackle Eurydice. Ancient cultures worshiped the willow tree fairy named Heliconian as the poet's muse, while the Greeks treasured the talents of the *nine* muses. The reverberation of the wind through a willow was said to instill the ingenuity necessary to mine the dark subconscious for truth, feeling, and beauty. Artists, musicians, and prophets all made pilgrimage to the willow for magic and revelation.

Many cultures employed the willow in funeral rites. Mourners laid branches of the willow inside the coffin and planted willow saplings atop the grave. The Celts believed that the spirit of the departed migrated into the tree, which then retained the essence of that person for as long as the willow thrived. British tribes installed willows around the borders of cemeteries to protect the souls interred within.

Pagans revered the willow as a symbol of the Moon goddess and witchery. Many chilling legends recount the willow uprooting itself in the night to chase after hapless travelers—a resonance of the demons that loiter in our subconscious. Healers employed the willow as a painkiller; the bark and leaves of the tree contain salicylic acid, the source of aspirin. The Chinese considered the willow an herb of immortality because new leaves will sprout from even the smallest branch stuck haphazardly into the ground.

Willow Magic

Dan Morrell was heading home from a night of clubbing when his car skidded on an icy English road and slammed into a telephone pole, splintering his skull. He disappeared into a coma for three days, drifting back and forth between the world of the living and the realm of the dead. When he awoke, he'd lost his ability to write, speak, and socialize. The Foundation of his world had been shattered. But from the moment he regained consciousness, even before he could speak again, he knew that he had been trans-

formed. He resolved to ditch his previous life as a hedonistic entre-
preneur who ran in the company of rock stars and supermodels.
The old Dan Morrell died. And a new man with a new purpose
sprang into being. "I need to plant trees," his inner voice sang.

He rehabilitated in the English countryside. Day after day, he
roosted under the branches of a gorgeous willow tree, thumbing
through an ancient Kabbalistic text, nursing his wounds, and
plotting his future. After several years cocooning within the
nooks of his favorite willow, he had resurrected his voice and
fashioned his wish into a palpable plan. He headed back to
London and founded Future Forests—an organization dedicated
to counteracting global warming and the ecological damage
wrought by the poisonous stream of carbon dioxide emitted
from cars, airplanes, and power plants. In the last two years,
Morrell's foundation has planted about three million carbon-
dioxide–neutralizing trees worldwide.

Purple/Violet

The color purple vibrates on the highest frequency discernible to
the human eye. Ultraviolet—the next oscillation in the spectrum—is invisible. Here on the doorstep of the wish fulfilled, we
require a boost up to elude the demons of the underworld. This
royal color, often woven into the robes of kings, helps us to avoid
fixating on the fears and attachments aroused by this sphere.
"The power of meditation can be ten times greater under violet
light falling through the stained glass window of a quiet church,"
wrote Leonardo da Vinci, the glory of the Renaissance (rebirth).

Name of God

The mantra of Foundation, Shaddai El Hai (pronounced Shah-die El Hi), translates as "My Shader, God is Alive." (In Hebrew, *Shaddai* also refers to demons or the repressed issues of the subconscious, aka our "dark side"). This name of God operates as a protective spell. Though Foundation implants the energy of death and apprehension (your personal demons), we chant repeatedly, "God is Alive." It reminds us that it doesn't matter how much we fear death because in the structure of creation, death is life, life is death, then again is life. Death happens, but God and your eternal soul are alive in these deaths and they guarantee a new birth. In Foundation, we submit to the push to transform. Shaddai El Hai inoculates us against the poisons of doubt and negativity, against looking back fretfully, as we do.

WISH MAKER: Chant this mantra for help with letting go of stubborn attachments such as ties to old, entangled relationships. Use this name of God to enhance intimacy and sexuality and to stimulate major changes in your life.

Meditation

Sit in a comfortable position. If possible, practice this meditation in a spot from which you can see the Moon. Breathe slowly and deeply. Imagine that you have journeyed to a high plateau overlooking a magical lake. It is midnight, and the full Moon floats high in the sky. You hear wolves howling at the Moon, but their cries resonate like prayers. Notice that the surface of the lake reflects the light of the Moon. A trail of white light skips all the way across the placid water. Stare up at the full Moon; drink its light and breathe its energy.

Focus on your sexual organs and cover them with your personal purple sphere of Foundation. Chant the mantra *Shaddai El Hai*. Chant it several times. Breathe in deeply and vibrate the name of God for the purple sphere. *Shaddai El Hai*. After you have chanted for several minutes, stare up at the sky and project your wish fulfilled onto the face of the lunar surface. Use the Moon as a movie screen. Envision your wish accomplished in as much detail as possible. Imprint this image on the huge bright Moon.

Now picture a shimmering bundle of light emanating from the Moon. As it descends from the sky, the figure within the light becomes bigger and bigger. You recognize it as a gorgeous masculine angel with strong white wings and a sparkling white aura. The angel lands just to your right as another ball of light slides toward you from the Moon. It contains a beautiful female angel. She drops closer and closer, gleaming in the night sky, and settles on your left.

Imagine that a gigantic purple sphere envelops the mountain, the cliff, and the lake. The entire vista is tinted a rich violet hue. Relax in the center of this purple mist as the two angels begin to touch you—first on the right and left sides of your head, then on your shoulders, then on your hips. They have activated the right and left pillars of your Tree. Watch now as the angels join each other in an erotic dance. Observe their motions, their expressions, their grace and power. They represent your feminine and masculine sides, balancing each other before you, making passionate love. At the end of their dance, they embrace and project themselves into your personal purple sphere hovering about your sexual organs. United, they have come into you. Sit quietly for a moment and enjoy this sensation of intimacy. Breathe it in. And when you are ready, gently move your head and hands and come back to your room, back to the here and now.

Wish List—Foundation

☞ 1. Experience the death of your state of wanting in order to encourage the prospect of your renascence as a wish-fulfilled human being. Let go of all expectations of both failure and success.

☞ 2. Seek intimacy with other people (see exercise 1, below).

☞ 3. Repeatedly suffuse your subconscious with visualizations of your wish exactly as you want it.

☞ 4. Decipher the import of your synchronicities. Hunt for the number nine, purple, the Moon, shadows, dreams, sex and sexual organs, towers, fast cars, and any symbols of change, intimacy, or death.

☞ 5. Wish progress: Even if you don't recognize it immediately, this week you will experience a transformation that marks a crucial step toward the realization of your goal. Allow all the other energies to coalesce and incubate in the womb of Foundation as you focus inside and prepare for your rebirth. Within this rich amalgamation, you should also glimpse fragments of all the other spheres in action. You will find a moment of compassion, an insight, a telling bit of communication, etc. Watch for all of these multicolored strands and see if you can use them to animate your wish.

Exercise Zone

☞ 1. Intimate Lives: Cultivate intimacy with someone in your life. You can entrust this person with one of your deep dark secrets, or you can visit with a friend and vow to discuss only personal matters from your past rather than all the trivialities you accomplished that day. Before you meet your companion, dredge up some of your most intimate memories. Venture back to your childhood and recall the first time you learned about death. Perhaps it was the passing of a relative or a family pet. This moment signifies the dawning of your mortality; the first time you recog-nized that you are human. Then resurrect the memory of your first sexual experience. This event represents the death of your innocence and the initi-ation of your ability to create new life. Now, if possi-ble, disclose these intimacies that helped forge the Foundation of you. One woman treated her husband to a romantic dinner on the condition that neither of them would speak about work. Instead, she shared intimate details and feelings about the death of her grandmother and the day she lost her virginity. Her husband was so moved by her tales that he in turn divulged confidences about his youthful encounters with sex and death that he had never confided to anyone.

2. **The Best Goodbye:** Monitor the way you say good-bye when you leave the house or the office. These everyday incidents symbolize our little deaths. Often, the way we bid farewell to people, places, and situ-ations molds the quality of our future interactions with them. The Tibetans believe that the manner in which we die sculpts our psychological state in our next incarnation. If you perish traumatically in a car accident, for example, they espouse that your next life will be inundated with anxiety over separation.

Try to modify the way you say goodbye. Perhaps you could add a hug, a kind word, or a blessing. Notice too how you end phone conversations. Each of these routine partings pries open a tiny space in your relationships that you can imbue with intimacy and transformation. The way you say goodbye to people and situations reveals how open you are to transforming yourself and your life. By repairing these commonplace behaviors, we can prepare ourselves for more critical changes. One man realized that before every business trip, he instigated an argument with his wife before storming off to the airport. On the plane, he often found himself delighted to be apart from her. Fighting made it easy to say goodbye. This exercise urged him to let go of the acrimony the next time he had to travel. He hugged and kissed his wife farewell instead. It was much more difficult to leave her. On the plane, he felt sad. But he also realized that he often departed from his partners and clients with a similar iciness. He'd wished for the successful expansion of his business, and consciously altering the way he said goodbye smoothed out a few wrinkles standing in his way.

CHAPTER TEN

KINGDOM:

The Energy of the Material World and Your Wish Come True

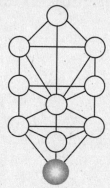

S P H E R E   1 0

KEYWORDS: Experience; Live!

WISH IMPERATIVE: Thank yourself and the universe for a wish come true. Pick a new wish and voyage on the Tree again.

HEBREW NAME: Malkhut

MYTH AND PERSONALITIES: Your life story from birth to this moment

PLANET: Earth

DARK SIDE: Materialism; greed

COLOR: Olive green, red, black, and blue

NUMBER: 10 = 1

TREE: The nearest tree to you right now

BODY PART: Feet and the root chakra (the sacrum, at the base of the spine)

HEBREW NAME OF GOD (MANTRA): Adonai Ha'aretz (Lord of the Earth)

For behold, the Kingdom of God is within you.

—Jesus Christ (Luke 17:21)

The Stuff of Life

In the end, we land in Kingdom—where there is no mythology except the stories of our lives. Kingdom holds our physical universe, our terrestrial body, our bed, our family, our aches and our gains, sandwiches, airplanes, tubas, and picnics under a munificent tree; what Pulitzer Prize–winning novelist Michael Cunningham dubbed "the city, the morning, our hope, more than anything, for more." It is the realm of your wish fulfilled and wishes wished anew.

Kingdom encompasses all material existence. If an alien space ship landed on your front lawn, the creatures inside—with their freaky physical anomalies and supertechnology—would still reside in the same sphere as humankind. Kingdom is so big that it includes the farthest galaxy in the sky. Its Hebrew name, *Malkhut*, translates as "sovereignty." It owns dominion over all potential that has been rendered tangible. It embodies the aggregate energy of all the previous spheres harnessed for practical use.

The Will to Receive

Kingdom is not a generator of a particular energy, but a receptacle for all the other archetypes. Just as the body functions as the vessel for the soul, Kingdom serves as a house for all the energies of the cosmos. It supplies the ability to receive. Kingdom grants us the capacity to receive gifts as well as challenges. Here we get the good stuff. In Kingdom, your wish has come true. And in Kingdom, you implement all the lessons and wisdom you have harvested over the course of this journey—not just today, but for the rest of your life.

Kingdom provides the reason why we are here. The Hebrew word *Kabbalah* means "to receive." This ancient spiritual system draws its name from the energy of reception, from Kingdom, from the lowest of the spheres. But the purpose of Kabbalah—the central tenet of this luminous theosophy—is to receive in order to share, to transform the selfish impulse into a selfless act of giving. This doctrine applies to money, love, energy, everything. We take it all in here in Kingdom and then like the trees we give it back to others. Your journey on the Tree of Life already has awarded you with this sublime talent. While you might delight in the fulfillment of your wish in a celebration tonight, your ingestion of the fundamental maxim of Kabbalah will remain forever the primary gift of your ten weeks on the Tree. You have augmented your understanding, your compassion and initiative, your relationships, your communication, and your ability to cultivate intimacy. You have enhanced your spiritual awareness and your peace of mind.

Without knowing it, you have planted seeds of transformation that will pay dividends today, tomorrow, and for generations to come. When you received these teachings, strapped them to your wish, and generated change in your life, you sparked a chain reaction. Your practice with the meditations and exercises undoubtedly has made you more accepting and agreeable—a windfall likely to rub off on your family and friends. The superior relationships that you have created with all of these people, especially with your children, in turn will result in fewer trials in their lives with loved ones and colleagues. Your grandchildren and everyone they touch subsequently will profit from the amplification of love, equanimity, and joy catalyzed by your growth. Together with the Tree, you have succeeded in altering the future. It is no small thing. It is, in fact, a miracle.

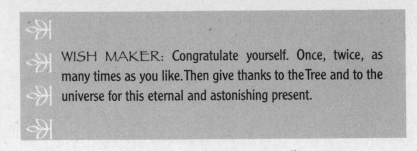

WISH MAKER: Congratulate yourself. Once, twice, as many times as you like. Then give thanks to the Tree and to the universe for this eternal and astonishing present.

Prison of Selfishness; School of the Soul

Kingdom sits at the bottom of the Tree of Life. It is the ultimate and densest container, yearning to fill itself up with palpable matter. Selfishness exists and persists so intractably because we were constructed with the instinct to receive and receive and receive still more. That proclivity allowed the Kingdom to hold the Light and to reveal the Creation. Without this appetite, there'd be nothing here, nothing corporeal, nothing to touch, nothing to eat. The nine previous energies would simply whoosh through invisibly into the nothing.

Some view Kingdom as a prison of the soul awaiting release someday to a finer place; and some recognize it as a school. Attitude determines everything. If you consider life a penitentiary, a vessel of misery, penance, and pain, then most likely the people you draw near will be prisoners and jailers. If you perceive it as a school—an academy of learning how to balance giving and receiving—then you will attract friends who are teachers and fellow students.

The ugly side of the impetus to receive explains why many theologians have slandered Kingdom with the nickname "evil." Such a facile label discounts the true point: Kingdom is the sphere where we can make things happen. Like a tiny seed that contains the DNA of an enormous forest, Kingdom teems with the potential of all the cosmic energies and the possibility of rapid growth. It is all up to us.

Exercise 1: Zen and the Art of Receiving

Since Kingdom embodies the world of concrete matter, logic dictates that our work in this sphere skew toward the practical as well. The exercises sprinkled throughout this chapter have been devised to magnify your awareness of how the Tree functions in your life; to provide a means to employ the energies and mechanics of the Tree in any situation, mundane or dramatic, that might arise in your world; and to permit you to evaluate the progress of your wish.

Start with this question: What is the state of your Kingdom? Examine your capacity to receive. How well do you accept the energies that come your way? This week the universe will present you with many gifts. Evaluate and then regulate your reactions to them. How do you respond when someone offers a compliment? Do you blush, change the subject, or offer a compliment in return? When you learn that you won a contest, a promotion, or a date with someone special, do you diminish your good fortune with self-deprecation or skepticism? Do you take it for granted? Or do you thank God and yourself for a job well done? Be mindful of the way you receive this week. Appreciating the awards that fall to you will open the door to additional bonanzas. The Zen of Receiving is simple: If you receive with enthusiasm, gratefulness, and the conviction that you deserve the endowment, then you automatically confer something special back to the person who handed you the present. We all know how sweet it is to give a gift to someone who really knows how to receive with gratitude.

> Researchers in the South American rain forest shot a
> pesticide straight up the trunk of a lush tree. In the
> giant cone designed to catch everything that
> tumbled out of the canopy, these scientists were
> stunned to discover more than two hundred thou-
> sand distinct species of life, all alive and flourishing
> in a single tree.
>
> —Source: ABC News

Your Tree, Everybody's Trees

For thousands and thousands of years, every culture, every
human civilization, has revered the Tree. Every single one. Except
one. Ours.

In the new Western culture, the industrial global economy
"clear-cuts" thousand-year-old groves to erect shopping malls and
newspaper empires. We eviscerate tropical forests to make room
for grazing cattle that will wind up on our barbecues. According
to scientific estimates, the human ax massacred nearly half of the
Earth's rain forest in the twentieth century. We surgically removed
one of our own lungs. How long would you last with only one
lung? How fast could you run after your dreams? Some experts
predict that if this suicidal behavior continues at the current rate,
the entire rain forest will be extinct by the year 2050. And it's not
only trees that will perish, but all the other plants, herbs, animals,
insects, and fungi that thrive there too. No big deal until you consider that many of our antibiotics have lost their efficacy against
mutating bacteria and killer diseases. The plants and fungi of the
rain forest likely will supply the cornerstones of many future med-
icines. If they disappear, with them fades our best hope to defeat
cancer, AIDS, and all the plagues of the future.

In the affluent community of Brentwood, California, city

leaders threatened the removal of dozens of sixty-year-old ficus trees because their unruly roots were breaking up the cement sidewalks in front of stores. Will they rechristen their city No More Wood? Across so much of the world, we are left with names where forests once ruled: Orange County, Hollywood, Oakland, Forest Hills, Cedar Rapids, Ann Arbor, Redwood City.

Books with titles like *The Trees Are Dying* line the shelves of our chain stores, detailing the deforestation of the planet as a result of greed, acid rain, and ultraviolet radiation intensified by chemicals that we pump into the sky every day. Meteorological data warns that over the past fifty years, peak summer-afternoon temperatures in Los Angeles have risen five degrees and continue to climb at a faster and faster rate. What fights global warming? Trees. According to a study conducted by the Lawrence Berkeley Laboratory, simply planting an additional ten million trees in Los Angeles County—approximately one per person—would cool the region's temperature by five degrees. This new urban arboretum would also filter out noxious exhaust and reduce by 75 percent a lethal form of pollution called particulates.

It appears that humankind prefers to ignore such evidence and the sweltering skies. Each year the average American consumes in paper goods the equivalent of a hundred-foot tree. Even as timber companies reforest small plots of land with immature saplings to replace the old, worldwide we slash more than five thousand square miles of timberland every month, an area larger than sprawling Los Angeles County. Every year, human beings slaughter groves, orchards, thickets, woods, copses, and jungles that once would have covered every inch of North Carolina.

We lost another fifteen acres in the time it took you to read this one unhappy sentence.

Hey, we're killing our teachers here! And it is this cavalier attitude, this conviction that everything is disposable, that trumpets our growing estrangement from the One. It screams to us loudly and urgently our dire need to reconnect to the magic of the Tree of Life as fast as we can.

WISH MAKER: Counteract your contribution to the pollution of our skies. Plant trees. Carbon dioxide–eating trees offset the pollutants emitted by each of us as we go to work, drive our cars, fly in planes, and flip on the lights, the computer, the heat, and the TV. According to analysis by environmental scientists, planting five trees neutralizes the carbon dioxide produced every year by the average car. Eight trees counterbalance the pollution generated by the electricity usage of the average home. Kingdom supplies the regulatory force of our planet. Use this week to regulate the advance of global warming. If you have yet to plant a tree or you feel the urge to plant more, capitalize on the practical energy of Kingdom to manifest this good deed. Turn back to the tree-planting exercise at the end of Chapter 1. Log on to AWishCanChangeYour Life.com, or to www.TreeofLifeGrove.com, or call 1-800-545-TREE and help to create the Tree of Life Grove. Join all of your fellow travelers on this voyage of wish fulfillment and spiritual enrichment in erecting this living communal shrine in the Tahoe National Forest. Thanks to everyone who has embarked on this journey through the spheres, the Tree of Life Grove has been infused with a spiritual consciousness—rich with dreams, imagination, and magic. This week, here in the material world that comprises your daily life, spread the word. Let the people you care about in on the creation of this magical forest. Give everyone you know the chance to reap the benefits of its enchanted potency.

Appraising Your Journey

In Foundation, we encountered the phallus of God. In Kingdom, we experience the *Shekinah*, Hebrew for "indwelling," or God's female essence. Proverbs calls it "the bride of God." In Genesis, the spirit of the *Shekinah* hovered over the Creation. It is the Holy Ghost, the Hindu *Shakti*, always with us, always within us, always binding us to the One. Gershom Scholem, the renowned Kabbalistic scholar, describes the *Shekinah* as God's visible or hidden presence in any given place. It embodies God's "immediacy."

Invigorated with nourishment from this divine spirit, we pause now to assess all that we have received along the way. In Kingdom we examine and appreciate the materialization of our wish (the will of Crown). It charges us to analyze and then regulate how well we have integrated the intermingled energies of the cosmos into our practical reality. Over the course of these ten weeks, you have planted a robust tree in the astral plane. Now you check out the condition of your earthly tree.

Exercise 2: Under the Tree of Life

Conduct an appraisal of the gifts you have received independent of whether your wish has come true. Go sphere by sphere and write down everything that this journey has awarded you over the course of these many weeks. Review the entries in your Abralog to jog your memory.

☞ Start with the **Crown** and record what you learned or achieved under the spell of the white energy. Have you grasped that the will of God is equal to the will of each of us? What did you do to unify yourself with the Oneness of the universe?

☞ Then move to the silver realm of **Wisdom**. What intuitions flashed? What did you learn without learning?

☞ Revisit **Understanding**: List all of the teachings you internalized over the course of your voyage. What benefits did you derive from your discipline?

☞ **Mercy**: Where did you practice compassion? How often? Has your generosity continued over the succeeding weeks? Did you discover how to step into the shoes of other people? Did you forgive?

☞ **Severity**: Did you master your anger? What actions did you initiate? Were you able to bring forth your inner warrior?

☞ **Beauty**: What sort of creativity did you instill in your life? Did you learn to see the beauty in others and the world? Did you balance your emotions? Did you express your love?

☞ **Eternity**: Were you able to bolster your relationships? Where did you find pleasure?

☞ **Splendor**: How well did you communicate? How well did you listen?

☞ **Foundation**: Examine your experiences with death, sex, and intimacy. Did you manage to say goodbye to the old you and transform yourself into something new?

No doubt, each archetype conveyed something new to your life. For example, one man recognized that in Mercy he had forgiven his mother for neglecting him at an early age. In Foundation, he'd become more proficient at interpreting the symbols of his dreams. He mustered the courage in Severity to ask his boss for a raise. Eternity spurred him to relish the joy of cooking a weekly dinner for his wife. During those dinners, he decided to speak only 30 percent of the time (Splendor) and found that his wife spontaneously stopped complaining that he didn't give enough. He also reported that practicing the meditations and chants had endowed him with strategies to cultivate relaxation and flow more contentedly with the ups and downs of his life.

Kingdom is situated at the bottom of the middle pillar of balance. It marks the most concrete manifestation of the energies of the central column. The logic of this configuration dictates that we enact this appraisal of the journey not simply to pat ourselves on the back or to score our spiritual growth but to find a place of equilibrium. A happy Kingdom necessitates balance. It is here in the most receptive and practical of the spheres that we actively balance our receiving with our giving. Try to share your magnificent harvest with others. Perhaps you have a friend who is having trouble letting go of an old love. Take the opportunity to disseminate the teachings of Foundation. Suggest some of the Wish Maker exercises. Recommend that your friend take this journey on the Tree herself. Be a Cable of light to the world. Be a Kabbalist!

Your Wish

In Kingdom, your wish comes true. It has materialized in some form even if you don't realize it yet. Your wish might not have been fulfilled as brilliantly or as precisely as you had hoped. But you have made progress. Much has changed. In nature, trees develop at varying rates depending on the type of tree, quality of the soil, climate, and sunlight. Some take years to grow a foot. Others shoot up dramatically in a few months. Some require decades to mature and bear fruit, while a few flower and reproduce right away.

Wishes materialize like trees in the forest. Some arrive spontaneously, while others blossom in protracted, methodical phases. Fulfillment also depends on the type and size of the wish and the amount of water and nutrients—the degree of dedication to the mantras and mechanics of the Tree of Life—the wisher has invested. If you have yet to realize your goal as you envisioned it, don't despair. Perhaps after these first ten weeks, the seed of your wish has been planted deep within the earth. It rests there, germinating, dispatching a few tender roots farther into the soil to forage for additional nourishment. From the surface, from your perspective, nothing has happened. But of course that's untrue. The seed simply needs more time, more fertilizer, and more persistence to reveal itself. It would be folly to destroy the seed or to cease watering and nurturing it.

If you can't see your wish quite yet, try spending several weeks in Kingdom, repeating the exercises and meditations of the sphere, cementing within yourself the higher teachings of the Tree of Life. You might also consider commencing the entire process afresh with the same wish or a small piece of it. "As above, so below" promises that the Kingdom of your original Tree is also the Crown of your next. If you hopscotch through all the spheres again, additional transformations will occur. You will surely reap new insights about yourself and your life.

One woman, who asked the Tree for a boyfriend, landed in Kingdom as single as ever. But along the way, the Tree managed to educate her on how to have a relationship with herself. Before she embarked on this journey, she perpetually avoided her own company, seeking fulfillment, self-respect, and diversion only through others. She failed to value her talents and capacity to amuse and comfort herself. She'd been deaf and blind even to that possibility. After ten weeks with the Tree, she arrived at an appreciation of her gifts for the first time in her life. When she settled in Kingdom, she felt content to sit home calmly, without berating herself that she must be an unlovable loser. She did not fulfill her wish as she requested. But what she obtained outshone that entreaty by a dozen stars. After a few weeks of savoring her new relationship with herself and repeating the exercises and meditations of the final sphere, she boarded the Tree anew. She again wished for a love relationship. And with the bonanza of self-assuredness and serenity as her base, she began to attract many men.

Many people discover that their wishes transmogrify along the way. Another person who traveled on the Tree longed to attain a more consequential commitment with his girlfriend. After ten weeks, the Tree had established the injudiciousness of that wish. It had substantiated that he and his lover were not equipped for a more enduring relationship. The life changes that the Tree pressed on this man were heartbreaking. The couple split up after more than a few tears and rancorous accusations. He became angry, certain that the Tree had obliterated a perfectly good alliance. But, in truth, the Tree had granted his wish—or at least the first step on the road to his real aspiration. This man had wished for intimacy. He lacked it with his girlfriend, and as long as he persevered in his entanglement with her, he remained inaccessible to anyone else. The Tree liberated him to pursue his true ambition. It necessitated some licking of wounds, but eventually he apprehended what a precious present the Tree had dropped in his lap. Several months later, he met and began to date a woman as desirous of intimacy as he was.

Another man wished to locate a buyer for his business because he longed to dedicate more time to his family. During his journey on the Tree, he instead discovered the depth of his devotion to the operation. His work made him happy. It imparted strength, pride, and purpose. Without it, even leisure time with his family left him grumpy. This insight prompted him to hire two managers to oversee vast segments of the business, permitting him to maintain his ties to his career while freeing him up to travel with his wife and children at the same time.

Like any new tool, the Tree of Life requires practice. You cannot purchase a guitar and expect to play like Segovia the minute you remove it from the case. Few prodigies assemble dazzling successes the first time they pick up a new instrument, tennis racket, or hammer. It takes repetition and persistence to become proficient. Only then do we create a song, a wicked forehand, or a tree house for the kids. On your debut voyage through the sequence of the spheres, you likely roused your spiritual muscles from a stubborn slumber. You simply got the hang of it. Don't cry uncle after just one round. Don't quit now that you are primed to accomplish your dreams. This is not the end but the beginning.

Exercise 3: Finding Your Wish Come True

☞ 1. Copy your wish into a new page of your Abralog. Then rewrite all of the details of the best-case-scenario results that you listed and imagined along the way. You can find a snapshot of the myriad specifics, outcomes, and rewards of your wish in exercise 1 of Understanding, in which you devised a plan and budget for your wish.

☞ 2. Now catalog all the ways in which your wish has come true. If the entire wish hasn't appeared fully formed as you imagined it, list any pieces that have materialized in your world. Scrutinize your life for details that reveal partial progress. Maybe you have delivered samples of your artwork to a number of gallery owners but have yet to receive replies from them all. Maybe you've lost ten pounds instead of twenty-five. Perhaps these developments simply require more time to blossom fully. One man wished for his ideal job as a talent scout and producer in the record business. After diligent adherence to this ten-week program, he still hadn't realized his goal. He had flirted with a few possibilities, but none of them suited his dream precisely.

He decided to step back without judgment or expectation. He set aside his wish, trusting that it would bloom at its own pace. Two months later, he was offered a position with a budget and creative freedom that exceeded his most optimistic hopes. "I couldn't have designed a job this perfect," he reported.

🖎 3. Other options include using the partially realized pieces of your wish as building blocks for your next wish. After spending a couple of weeks continuing the pursuit of your goal in Kingdom, start over and wish again. With every journey on the Tree, you will advance closer to the life you want.

🖎 4. The Tree always works. But sometimes, like in the real-life cases outlined above, it supplies us with auspicious surprises. Identify all the unanticipated gifts you gleaned from the Tree—a better relationship with yourself, freedom to pursue real intimacy, a new plan to integrate your business and family time. Log all of the presents you amassed along the way that you didn't know you wanted or needed when you first set out. Write a new wish based on these unexpected windfalls, and travel the Tree again.

🖎 5. Celebrate your Kingdom. Take a loved one to dinner or throw a party to rejoice in your accomplishment. Share your successes and insights with your partners and friends. Revel in their congratulatory grins. And spread the secrets of the Tree to others.

Permutations of Ten

The Sefer Yitzerah writes of the spheres: "Their end is imbedded in their beginning and their beginning in their end." Other Kabbalists reiterate: "In Crown is Kingdom and in Kingdom is Crown." As above, so below—there is no difference between the high and the low. Numerology concurs. Kingdom is sphere 10, but 10 actually signifies $1 + 0 = 1$. Kabbalah purports that the cosmos is comprised of an endless arrangement of interlocking and interdependent Trees that resembles the configuration of molecules in the physical world. The Kingdom of one Tree doubles as the Crown of the Tree below. Crown marks the will to give the endless Light to all of the Creation. Kingdom embodies the will to receive. They appear to be polar opposites until we apprehend that Kingdom actually epitomizes the will to receive in order to give. It metamorphoses Kingdom back into Crown—the container of the will to bestow. The process of creation barely pauses, sprouting new branches to infinity.

The number ten signals the return to unity. Odysseus wandered for nine years and returned to his Kingdom in the tenth. Troy was besieged for nine years and then conquered in year ten. Moses imparted the Ten Commandments of the Decalogue, instructions on how we ought to behave in the tenth sphere. In Roman numerals, ten is represented by X—the cross, the point of the confluence of heaven and Earth. The symbol of the cross also stands for *Tav*, the last letter in the Hebrew alphabet, yet another sign of completion. And we all wiggle ten fingers and with them we build the stuff of the Kingdom.

Ten also equals the sum of the first four numbers: $1 + 2 + 3 + 4$. These four digits correspond to the four elements—fire, water, air, and earth—which constitute all matter in the Kingdom. "And a river went out of Eden to water the garden; and from there it was parted and became four heads" (Genesis 2:10). The Kingdom, the universe into which the biblical Adam and Eve tumbled, was divided into four parts—into the four elements. And it's probably no coincidence that exactly four amino acids construct all the genes that dictate our every physiological trait.

Fixing the Cracks

In the primordial breaking of the vessels, Kingdom escaped destruction. It hung together after the six preceding spheres exploded into shards. It survived to hold and manifest everything. But it did not weather the cataclysm unscathed. It fractured into the four rivers that flowed from Eden, into the four elements, into the four points of the cross—up, down, right, left; divine, mundane, masculine, feminine. Geologically, the fissures that divide the tectonic plates of the Earth's crust symbolically mirror these metaphysical rifts in the Kingdom. We reside in a gigantic cracked cistern; a flawed and broken vessel; a sphere that is far from whole.

And that's the good news.

It is much easier to repair a chipped ceramic bowl than a receptacle that has shattered into a thousand tiny bits. In a pinch, you might resort to a cracked bowl to serve food or water. Likewise, we all can subsist in the damaged Kingdom. But it certainly would be more pleasant, less chaotic, and far lovelier if we smoothed out the chinks.

We have been hired to do that. We were born to do that.

How? Alchemy. The four elements represent the four fractured pieces of Kingdom. We mend these cracks by eliminating the separations between them; by rectifying and balancing fire (action), water (emotions), air (intellect), and earth (practicality) inside ourselves and in everything we do.

Only within the opaque world of matter and material is such a feat possible. Only Kingdom affords us the chance to perfect the flaws in ourselves and in the Creation. The density of the Kingdom, then, is not evil, but wonderful. It allows us to participate in the grand design. It is what the Creator intended. God passed us the paintbrush—or the glue gun—and said, "Here, you finish up. See if you can fix this work of art." It's a stunning and generous gesture of trust and love to endow us with such a remarkable reason for being. Think about it. If you were painting the Sistine Chapel, would you hand your little child a bucket of paint, point to your masterpiece, and say, "Do something here?" Only if you loved that child more than you loved the work of art or your own legacy. Only if you wanted that child to know what it's like to be you. Only if you intuitively understood that the child and you are the exact same thing.

Mergers and Acquisitions

Webster's New Collegiate Dictionary defines alchemy as "a power or process of transforming something common into something precious." Alchemy aims to fill the fissures between the four elements, blending the discrete components of matter into a seamless whole. It endeavors to merge fire, water, air, and earth into gold; into perfection. This is our job. And Kingdom, the fractured universe of physical substances, endures as our laboratory.

Alchemy divides the elements into masculine (fire and air) and feminine (water and earth). The masculine elements operate on the principle of elevation. Fire and air tend to rise. The feminine elements adhere to the laws of gravity. Both water and earth sink to the lowest spot. As a result, the masculine elements mingle easily with each other. Fire requires air to sustain itself and air springs into existence when heat from the fire transforms water into vapor. Likewise, the feminine elements intermix rather effortlessly. In a garden, the amalgamation of earth and water creates plants, flowers, food—life itself.

But genuine alchemy asks us to effect balance between these

two dissimilar teams. And that's why you so rarely find a listing for alchemists in the Yellow Pages. When we attempt to wed these two couples, chaos and failure most often ensue. Both water and earth act to extinguish fire, while fire wrestles hard to destroy water and earth. Meanwhile, earth suffocates air, and unless you're manufacturing soft drinks, nothing much comes of the union of air and water. The feminine and masculine do not cohabit without major adjustments. The prevailing ruptures in the Kingdom stubbornly resist the ultimate renewal.

But Kingdom awards us the tools to do the job. We have our bodies, which enable us to harmonize the attributes these elements represent within ourselves. The authentic spiritual person constantly strives to balance the amount of action, feeling, intellect, and practicality present in his or her personality and behavior. And we have our wishes, which grant us the opportunity to repair the rifts in ourselves and our Kingdom every single day of our lives.

Exercise 4: Fixing the Cracks in Your Wish

Alchemy asks us to blend all of the elements to create perfection. You must therefore infuse your wish with a sufficient dose of each of them. Strive to ascertain which of the four elements is missing from your efforts to achieve your goal. Perhaps you lacked excitement or the "go get it" vibe. Maybe you needed to *do* more. These attributes relate to the element of fire. Return to Severity and try to augment the warrior energy in your life. Connecting to Beauty and the passion of spiritual love might also infuse your efforts with extra fire. Water represents feeling. If you didn't invest enough emotion in this process, if you performed the tasks robotically or out of a sense of duty rather than because you really wanted to do them, your wish probably could benefit from an extra splash of Mercy and Foundation. Revisit the meditations and exercises from these spheres and douse your wish with water. If your journey suffered from a dearth of the air ele-ment, if you didn't communicate enough with other people, if you lacked sources of information or contacts that could advance your wish or found it difficult to locate synchronicities and interpreta-tions of these messages, reconnect to Splendor and Wisdom. And finally, if your wish requires more earth, more money, more time or physical exertion, if you could not muster the discipline or com-mitment to diligently engage in this process, devote additional attention to Eternity and Understanding.

Exercise 5: The Tree of the Moment

This assignment aims to etch the principles of each sphere into your life forever. Tap the ten archetypes to analyze any meeting, conversation, movie, book, or place—any activity at all. Use this technique to evaluate an entire day. Write the names of the ten spheres on a sheet of paper and deliberate on how the energies performed in any situation.

Crown: What was your will or intention when you entered the meeting? What was the will of the other person?

Wisdom: What sort of insight did you gain about yourself, the other person, or the issue that you discussed?

Understanding: Did you understand what the other person was trying to say? Did he understand you? Even if the encounter terminated in disaster, what was the lesson you reaped from it? Why did it happen? Can you discern any parallels to previous meetings or conversations that resulted in frustration?

Mercy: What kind of emotional exchange did you experience in this encounter?

Severity: What conflicts or judgments flared? Did any re-strictions arise that hampered the connection between you and the other person? For example, your counterpart repeat-edly answered his cell phone in the middle of your sentence.

Beauty: Did anything occur that you deemed beautiful, inspiring, or creative? Was any sacrifice required?

Victory: What sort of repetitive behavior transpired? What about the five senses? Did you eat or drink? Did you notice a pleasurable fragrance in the garden?

Splendor: What sort of information did you transmit and receive? Were you able to deliver all of your intended messages without a hitch?

Foundation: What sort of integration occurred in the meeting? How much intimacy developed? Were you in any way transformed? Will anything new result from this interaction? Or, just as fruitful sometimes, did you realize that something you had hoped for is not going to materialize?

Kingdom: Award yourself a score from one to ten based on how fervently the archetypal energies of the Tree functioned in the meeting. In Kingdom, you should be able to determine if there ought to be another interaction with this person.

Apply this same evaluation to anything. If you attend a movie, appraise it using the spheres. In Kingdom, you will discern whether you would like to watch another film by the same director. Try it when you go to a new restaurant, a store, a park, or a party. Check out your last romantic date, or your last year at the office.

The more you measure your daily encounters, duties, and habitats for the presence of the energies of the Tree, the more you will invite these magnificent forces to influence and transform your life. This exercise will also magnify your ability to locate and identify the synchronicities and magic the Tree arouses whenever you work a wish from Crown to Kingdom. (AWishCanChangeYourLife.com, the Internet partner of this book, supplies additional variations of these exercises that are designed to intensify your work with the Tree. For example, the web site features an inventive technique that mines the secrets of alchemy to repair, augment, and maximize any of your personal relationships. It also showcases a Tree of

Life–inspired analysis of the blockbuster movie *The Matrix* as an example of how you can apply the ten archetypal energies of the cosmos to any experience, event, or circumstance.)

Exercise 6: Tarot Tree

Count out ten index cards or slips of sturdy paper. Leave one side blank and write the name of the spheres—one per card—on the other. Now use these ten cards as your personal system of tarot. Whenever you have a question or dilemma about a relationship, job, or upcoming event—or if you merely crave a hint about the rest of your day—shuffle and then spread the cards out face down. Then select one with your left hand.

Let's imagine that you aspire to improve your relationship with your mate, and you draw the card of Beauty. This sphere counsels you to focus on all that is beautiful and childlike in your partner. Express your appreciation for these attributes. Perhaps you should spend some time watching the sunset together or engaging in a joint creative project. Maybe you need to make a sacrifice—to relinquish some expectation or some personal hobby that limits your time together for long stretches of the weekend—in order to reinforce the amity between you.

Pick a card in the morning before a crucial business lunch with your boss. If you choose Severity, for example, you probably ought to assert yourself at the meeting and advocate adamantly for your position. You also might profit from wearing something red.

Name of God

Adonai Ha'aretz, the mantra for Kingdom, means "My Lord of the Land." It is the most practical, down-to-earth of all the names of God. It galvanizes the divinity that rules the physical elements.

> **WISH MAKER:** Chant this mantra whenever you yearn to ground yourself or your fanciful ideas in reality. Use this name of God to relieve anxiety attacks and whenever you experience nightmares or the need for physical security. In general—whenever you want to get things done.

Meditation

Sit in a comfortable position. Make sure that your spine is straight. Imagine that you have traveled to a castle located in the most beautiful place on Earth. It rests on a mountain overlooking a fertile valley. You spot a massive Tree of Life flourishing in the courtyard. Stroll beneath the canopy of this Tree and enter the palace.

Picture yourself sitting in the middle of a great hall. A golden ray illuminates you like a spotlight. Face the east and convene the ten spheres of the Tree. Begin with the transparent Crown, just above the top of your head. Chant *Eheyeh*. Then invoke the gray sphere of Wisdom on the right side of your brain and whisper *Yod Hey Vav Hey*. Place the dark sphere of Understanding at the left side of your skull. Intone *Elohim*. Summon the blue of Mercy to your right shoulder by calling *El* and then the red sphere of Severity to your left shoulder with *Elohim Gibor*. Beckon the energy of Beauty with *Yod Hey Vav Hey Eloha Vada'at* and watch the golden sphere appear at your heart. Raise the green sphere of Eternity to your right hip by singing *Yod Hey Vav Hey Tzevaot* and then the orange sphere of Splendor to your left hip with *Elohim Tzevaot*. Invite the purple energy of Foundation to your sexual organs using the mantra *Shaddai El Hai*.

And finally, imagine the Earth itself as a sphere beneath your feet. Slowly intone *Adonai Ha'aretz* several times. *Ah-doe-nai Ha-ah-retz*. As you chant the name of God, imagine a root extending from the base of your spine into the floor beneath you. Let it dig its way, forcing itself deeper and deeper into the ground. Picture branches emerging from the central root and watch as they absorb water from the soil. Feel this nourishment surging through your body. Watch as the roots tunnel into the fiery magma at the Earth's core. Feel the warmth of the fire traveling up your spine. Envision additional roots sucking up rich minerals from the ground to sustain you. And then a few others shooting from your spine to absorb oxygen from the air. Now imagine branches growing from your body. Merge yourself with the Tree of Life. Become the Tree of Life. And imagine the ten spheres arrayed about your body as the fruit that you share with the world.

Chant the mantra, *Adonai Ha'aretz*, again and again. Allow the light from the Crown to descend throughout the entire Tree. Notice how the roots conduct the four elements of the Earth into your Kingdom. After you finish chanting, sit in silence for a few moments, contemplating all that you have experienced during your voyage on the Tree. And slowly return to the here and now.

Wish List—Kingdom

☞ 1. Congratulations!

☞ 2. Appraise your journey and appreciate everything that you have accomplished.

☞ 3. Engage in the great art of alchemy. Incorporate the teachings of the Tree into your life from this moment until the day you depart this world. Practice the meditation and the exercises of this chapter for several weeks. Some people have found that four weeks in Kingdom—one for each of the four elements—produces optimal results.

☞ 4. The world is your Kingdom. Open yourself to the magic of the synchronicities generated by each and every sphere. Witness the fabric of life complete. Allow all of the archetypal energies to guide you toward your goals.

☞ 5. Make a new wish. And travel the Tree again.

EPILOGUE

Your True Treasure Found: You Have Become a Warrior of Light

The Last Big Secret

No matter what happened, whether you fulfilled your wish entirely, or in part, you have succeeded in making your real wish come true. Indisputably, you have attained your goal.

By embarking on this journey, you have certified to the universe that your genuine wish was not for a boyfriend or more money or a house on the shore. Your true wish was to undertake the journey, to engage in the universal process of creation, to experience the Tree of Life. The mundane wish for a material thing functioned merely as an excuse to force you to travel the Tree. That wish personified a mythical hero whom you cared about and identified with as he caromed through the ten spheres. If the hero triumphed in his quest, if she captured the Holy Grail, if the story had a happy ending, then hallelujah. But what you truly relished was the story, the twists and novelties of the plot, the resiliency of your protagonist. Movies that don't wind up tidily perfect often gratify us most. We derive just as much pleasure, understanding, and wisdom from witnessing a hero discern something crucial about himself as we do from watching him get the girl or slay Darth Vader.

This process has elevated your relationship with the energies of each sphere. It has magnified your ability to apply these qualities—will, wisdom, understanding, compassion, initiative, love, relationship, communication, and transformation—in any and every situation of your life. By engaging the Tree, you have commenced the correction of your cracks and karma here in Kingdom.

But you have accomplished much more than that.

Through your courtship of these ten archetypal powers, you have achieved something spectacular. You have stimulated the collective force of rectification of all the spheres above. The more you chanted El, for example, the more you practiced the exercises of loving-kindness, the more you enlarged your capacity to dole out compassion to yourself and to others, the more you have helped to revitalize and mend the shattered vessel of Mercy in the astral plane. It's like a breeder reaction. Just as your acts of munificence most likely stirred others to spread compassion themselves, your personal activation of the energies of the Tree has begun to accelerate the rejuvenation of the wounded spheres of Mercy, Severity, Beauty, Eternity, Splendor, and Foundation up above. As the Buddha said, one seed contains the entire forest. And one graceful deed can mature into an entire forest of generosity.

Here's another secret. Your higher self guided you to the Tree of Life because it too harbors a wish: to repair all the shattered spheres of Creation. Your higher self, the higher self in us all, yearns to rectify the Tree. It is driven to restore and unify all the broken pieces into the seamless will of the One. By working the Tree, you have discharged your soul's ultimate purpose. You have become a Creator. You have become a hero. You are a warrior of Light.

The Tree beckons you to continue. Your soul has unveiled its calling. Go forth and rectify. It's time to put Humpty-Dumpty together again.

WEB RESOURCES

- www.AWishCanChangeYourLife.com: The Internet partner of this book provides additional exercises, stories, and information about the Tree of Life, answers to common questions about the wish-fulfilling journey, free music files for meditation, and a mechanism to connect with others engaged in this same spiritual process.

- www.GahlRadio.com: A live Internet radio talk show hosted by Gahl Sasson about Kabbalah, world mythology, astrology, and current metaphysical issues that includes phone calls from those who want to ask questions about the Tree of Life or their voyage of wish-fulfillment.

- www.TreeofLifeGrove.com: This web site offers a simple and immediate way to plant your trees in the magical Tree of Life Grove in the Tahoe National Forest.

SELECTED BIBLIOGRAPHY

Campbell, Joseph. *The Inner Reaches of Outer Space.* Novato, Calif.: New World Library, 2002.

———, with Bill Moyers. *The Power of Myth.* New York: Broadway Books, 1988. The revered scholar of myth managed to bestow scientific and anthropological credibility to the stories of spirituality. His work helped open the door to the import and vitality of the world's ancient myths and religious rites.

Capra, Fritjof. *The Tao of Physics.* Boston: Shambhala, 1975. Appealing to spiritualists and academics alike, this book illustrates that the intangible axioms of metaphysics jibe rather perfectly with the quantifiable laws of science.

Ehrenreich, Barbara. *Blood Rites.* New York: Metropolitan Books, 1997. A social anthropological study of the ceremonies and rituals of various cultures throughout history.

Graves, Robert. *The White Goddess.* New York: Farrar, Straus and Giroux, 1948. A masterpiece of Celtic studies and the explication of the feminine aspect of the divine.

Halevi, Z'ev ben Shimon. *Adam and the Kabbalistic Tree.* York Beach, Maine: Samuel Weiser, 1974.

———. *The Anointed.* York Beach, Maine: Weiser Books, 1987. This is a Kabbalistic novel that uses the archetypes of the Tree of Life to relate a powerful story. Halevi's nonfiction books provide additional study into the intricacies of Kabbalah.

❦ Hauck, W. Dennis. *The Emerald Tablet.* Harmondsworth, N.Y.: Arkana, 1999. A thorough and scholarly digest of the history of alchemy and its applications.

❦ His Holiness the Fourteenth Dalai Lama and Culter C. Howard, M.D. *The Art of Happiness.* New York: Riverhead Books, 1998. An authentic work of compassion that poses Western-thinking dilemmas of the contemporary world to the Dalai Lama. It demonstrates how the ancient wisdom of Tibetan Buddhism can enrich anyone's life today.

❦ Kaplan, Aryeh. *Sefer Yetzirah—The Book of Creation.* York Beach, Maine: Samuel Weiser, 1997. Probably the finest and most complex book on the Kabbalah available in English, it translates and interprets the oldest and most essential Kabbalistic text known to man.

❦ Kirsch, Jonathan. *Moses: A Life.* New York: Ballantine Publishing Group, 1998. Kirsch's books invigorate the old Bible stories by bringing a fascinating human shape to these sacred characters.

❦ Miles, Jack. *God, a Biography.* New York: Vintage Books, 1995. An overview of how humankind has perceived God throughout time and all traditions.

❦ Pakenham, Thomas. *Meeting With Remarkable Trees.* New York: Random House, 1998. This book of photography brings trees to life on the page.

❦ Paterson, Jacqueline Memory. *A Tree in Your Pocket.* London: Thorsons, 1998. A compact compendium of the myths and herbal healing properties of numerous types of trees.

❦ Scholem, Gershom. *On the Mystical Shape of the Godhead.* New York, N.Y.: Schocken Books, 1976. Scholem invented the modern academic field of rigorous research into the Kabbalah.

❦ Sogyal, Rinpoche. *The Tibetan Book of the Living and Dying.* San Francisco: Harper Collins, 1994. This highly readable interpretation of The Tibetan Book of the Dead examines the Buddhist vision of life after death and how to apply such theosophy to the way we live.

ABOUT
THE AUTHORS

GAHL SASSON teaches workshops in Kabbalah, mythology, throat singing, meditation, and astrology in the United States, Mexico, and Israel. He has served on the faculty of Deepak Chopra's multimedia project, MyPotential; contributes regularly to *Olam* magazine; and is on the Sputnik list of Progressive Cultural Thinkers along with Fritjof Capra, Kevin Kelly (founder/executive editor, *WIRED*), and Hans Moravec (principal research scientist, Carnegie Mellon University Robotics Institute). Gahl is also a professional musician and uses sound as a method for healing and telling stories. He currently teaches at the University of Judaism in Los Angeles.

STEVE WEINSTEIN is a screenwriter and a journalist who spent twelve years writing for the *Los Angeles Times*. Both authors live in Los Angeles, California.